Henry S. Edwards

**The Lyrical Drama**

Essays on subjects, composers, & executants of modern opera. Vol. 2

Henry S. Edwards

**The Lyrical Drama**
*Essays on subjects, composers, & executants of modern opera. Vol. 2*

ISBN/EAN: 9783744797030

Printed in Europe, USA, Canada, Australia, Japan

Cover: Foto ©Thomas Meinert / pixelio.de

More available books at **www.hansebooks.com**

# THE LYRICAL DRAMA.

# ESSAYS

ON

SUBJECTS, COMPOSERS, & EXECUTANTS
OF MODERN OPERA.

BY

H. SUTHERLAND EDWARDS.

VOL. II.

LONDON:
W. H. ALLEN & CO., 13, WATERLOO PLACE,
PALL MALL, S.W.

1881.

# CONTENTS.

|  | PAGE |
|---|---|
| CHAPTER XXVI.—Aïda and the Manzoni Requiem | 1 |
| CHAPTER XXVII.—Some of Rossini's Works | 14 |
| CHAPTER XXVIII.—Donizetti and Bellini | 31 |
| CHAPTER XXIX.—The Mignon and Hamlet of Ambroise Thomas | 44 |
| CHAPTER XXX.—Shakesperian Operas | 57 |
| CHAPTER XXXI.—Carmen | 64 |
| CHAPTER XXXII.—The ever-popular Martha | 71 |
| CHAPTER XXXIII.—An Operatic Centenary | 77 |
| CHAPTER XXXIV.—Decline and Fall of the Tenor | 86 |
| CHAPTER XXXV.—Extinction of the Ballet | 91 |
| CHAPTER XXXVI.—Operatic Management | 97 |
| CHAPTER XXXVII.—Musical Agents | 108 |

|   |   | PAGE |
|---|---|---|
| CHAPTER XXXVIII.—Libretti | | 116 |
| CHAPTER XXXIX.—Operatic and Theatrical Anomalies | | 127 |
| CHAPTER XL.—The Literary Maltreatment of Music | | 144 |
| CHAPTER XLI.—Dictionaries of Music | | 164 |
| CHAPTER XLII.—Grove's Musical Dictionary | | 199 |
| CHAPTER XLIII.—Quartett Concerts and the Classical in Music | | 230 |
| CHAPTER XLIV.—Reasonableness of Opera | | 243 |
| CHAPTER XLV.—Tatra Füred, and the Music of the Hungarian Gipsies | | 253 |
| CHAPTER XLVI.—The Byeways of Bookmaking | | 271 |
| **INDEX** | | 293 |

# THE LYRICAL DRAMA.

## CHAPTER XXVI.

### AÏDA AND THE MANZONI REQUIEM.

*Aïda*, Verdi's latest opera and, with the exception of the *Requiem for Manzoni*, his latest work, was produced at the Royal Italian Opera in 1876, with Mdme. Adelina Patti in the principal part. Composed for the Khedive of Egypt and brought out at Cairo in 1872, it crossed the Atlantic and was represented at New York; travelled to St. Petersburg and Moscow, and was performed in both the Russian capitals; was played at all the principal theatres of Italy and Spain; was heard at the Théâtre des Italiens of Paris; but, until the season of 1876, seemed to be prevented by some fatality from reaching London. The particular form taken by "fatality" in the case of *Aïda* was, it is said, an unusually large demand made by the composer or his representatives for the right of representation. However that may have been, the long-looked-for work was at last given.

The subject of *Aïda*, which is tragic in the extreme, and which but for the bright and often splendid musical surroundings given to it by Signor Verdi would be gloomy, is said to have been suggested by the Khedive himself. To the musician who first made his mark by an opera on the subject of Nebuchadnezzar, a drama of which the scene is laid at Memphis and at Thebes, of which the action takes place in the time of the Pharaohs, and which numbers among its chief personages a triumphant King of Egypt, a captive King of Ethiopia, with an indefinite number of mysterious priests and priestesses, gorgeously attired soldiers and many coloured slaves, could scarcely fail to prove attractive; and the composer of the so-called *Nabuco* seems to have revelled in the pageant music, dance music, religious choruses and military hymns which together make up a very considerable portion of his Egyptian work. *Aïda* is as full of show and glitter as *L'Africaine*, and some of the themes presented in the characteristically Egyptian scenes are alleged to be of Egyptian origin. Indeed, one would not be surprised to hear that the really curious subject of the chorus in praise of "the immense Phtah" had, like the subject of the libretto, been furnished by the Khedive himself.

Egypt is at war with Ethiopia. Aïda, daughter of

the Ethiopian king, is a prisoner in Egypt, where Radamès, an Egyptian officer, has fallen in love with her. But Radamès is beloved not only by Aïda, but also by Amneris, daughter of the King of Ethiopia. Tempted by Aïda,—who is forced thereto by her father,—Radamès, commanding the Egyptian armies, tells a secret which has the effect of revealing the plan of campaign. He is condemned to be buried alive. Amneris would procure his pardon if he would renounce Aïda. But he remains constant to his love, and Aïda joins him in the tomb.

The final act is "dramatic" in more than one sense of the word. It is full of emotion, and it abounds in contrasts. Two scenes in this act impress themselves particularly upon the memory. In the first Amneris, after a passionate but unavailing interview with Ramfis, deports herself, musically and dramatically, somewhat after the fashion of Leonora in *Il Trovatore*—giving vehement expression to her feelings in the front of the stage, while at the back the tribunal of priests, in tones of Egyptian darkness, pronounce the doom of the man she still loves, and whom she yet might save. In the second the action takes place simultaneously in the brilliantly illuminated "Temple of Vulcan," where, in glittering attire and surrounded by the golden symbols of their faith, the priestesses sing the sacred chorus and dance the sacred dance with which we had already made acquaintance in the opening scenes of the opera; and in a vault immediately beneath, where Radamès has been thrown to die, and where he is soon found by Aïda, resolved to perish with him. Amneris, after a time, appears in the temple, and, kneeling on the stone which closes the vault, prays. Aïda gets weaker and weaker, Radamès is in despair, the priestesses continue to move their feet to the quaintly solemn strains of the chorus and dance-tune in praise of the "immense Phtah," Amneris utters a few despondent monotones, and the curtain falls.

The last scene of all is not, and ought not to be, so terrible as one would imagine it to be from the mere mention of the fact that it shows us the two most interesting characters buried alive. There are various modes of interment; and it seems that in Egypt, as in the country where Sinbad the Sailor was cast living into a vault from which there was apparently no means of exit, the interment of live criminals or live survivors of defunct spouses, does not involve their being placed in immediate contact with the earth. When the story of Aïda was first made known there was something really alarming in the notion of a soprano and tenor singing admirably throughout the evening, and then being suddenly hurled into a grave and having their mouths stopped with clay. But the final home of the ill-fated Radamès and Aïda is sufficiently spacious, and they are able to sing with vigour to the very last. Never, until *Aïda* was brought out, had a scene in two stories been exhibited on the Italian operatic stage. In the case of *Aïda*, the scene below is really the complement of the scene above. The priestesses in the Temple are celebrating the punishment of the very offence which is being expiated in the vault beneath. Thus the scene in two compartments forms but one picture. Nor does the music in the one compartment interfere with the music in the other, as speaking would interfere with speaking in the case of ordinary dialogue. The contrast between the mystical, half-voluptuous, half-religious chants of the priestesses and the passionate sobs and heart-broken sighs of the victims is intensely dramatic; and the brilliant ritualistic music of the Temple, the prayers of Amneris, and the despair of the dying lovers combine to produce a mixed but not a confusing effect.

*Aïda* has often been described as an opera composed by Verdi in the style of Wagner. *Aïda* presents reminiscences of Wagner, as of other composers. But it contains too much tune for the sake of tune to resemble a Wagnerian opera. Poets who spurn imagery, composers who despise melody, do so, no doubt, in both cases because what they contemn does not readily occur to them, and is, in fact, beyond their reach. Whether writing for the church or for the theatre, Verdi will be melodious as long as he preserves his faculties. But *Aïda* contains fewer formally constructed pieces and pieces complete in themselves than any of the composer's previous works; and this may or may not be attributable to the influence of Herr Wagner. The libretto of *Aïda*, instead of being chopped up into the usual airs, duets, trios, &c., with repetitions of exclamatory phrases in the concerted pieces, first by one character, then by another, is a continuous poem; which, indeed, suggests that Verdi may have intended to make it the basis of what Herr Wagner calls "continuous melody." But in the so-called "continuous melody" of Herr Wagner the melody is sometimes difficult to discover; whereas the music of *Aïda* is strikingly melodious. The writer of a memoir of Verdi prefixed to the pianoforte edition of *Aïda* sets forth that "the Italian opera under Verdi's pen is no longer a collection of pretty cavatinas, arias, duets, and more or less concerted pieces, but a living lyric drama, in which the music, as far as theatrical exigencies permit, closely follows the action, the whole being more tersely connected than in the productions of most of his predecessors. But notwithstanding his adoption of the new idea of reform, all his works," continues the writer, "are full of fascinating, free, and original melody, while the absence of this, the charm of operatic music, is conspicuous in the works of most other composers of the new school." There is some truth in this, though the biographer's next assertion that in *Aïda* Verdi seems "to have realised more than the Wagnerian idea of the modern lyric drama" may well be questioned. An aim, indeed, is here attributed to Verdi which he, in all probability, never entertained.

The representatives of Aïda and Amneris at Milan were the two admirable artists whom the London public heard at the Albert Hall in the soprano and mezzo-soprano parts of the *Manzoni Requiem*.

Italy's modern operatic composers have not shown themselves entirely forgetful of the fact that their country was once renowned, among all others, for church music. Rossini produced two sacred works, a *Stabat Mater* and a *Missa Solemnis*; Donizetti one—a *Miserere*, which has never, to this day, been heard in England; and Verdi wrote, for the first anniversary of Manzoni's death, a funeral mass, or requiem, which was soon afterwards performed in London.

Bellini seems never to have turned his attention, even for a brief interval, to the ecclesiastical style; and in the absence of any church composition from his pen, the beautiful melody introduced by the tenor in the finale to the third act of *I Puritani* was made part of the musical service at his funeral, where no one, assuredly, could have found it out of place. No composer, in fact, whose melodies are of a simple and elevated character can be looked upon, merely because he may have written habitually for the theatre or for the concert-room, as incapable of rising to the sacred heights where the professional composers of church music are supposed to dwell.

People are inclined, all the same, in England to be very hard upon foreign operatic composers who venture to write for the Church; which is the more remarkable inasmuch as the Church they write for is not ours. In this country, on the other hand, every composer is thought, as a matter of course, to be capable of producing an oratorio; and, provided he exercises a certain amount of self-restraint and never allows himself to give way to the promptings of the melodic spirit possibly within him, he may produce a sufficiently dry work to content the severest judges. One could mention a good many English oratorios, successful enough in or rather on their day, which no one would find fault with on the ground of their being too dramatic or too full of melody such as the heathen delight in. A Rossini, however, a Gounod, or a Verdi who risks himself within the precincts of a church, is sure to be told, with more or less politeness, that he is not in his proper place; that he has mistaken the house of the Lord for a theatre; that the language of the opera is not that of prayer, and so on. It is very difficult to dispose of such objections by argument. But, as regards Rossini's *Stabat Mater*, practical proof of its being suited to the end for which it was designed seems to be afforded by the fact that it is frequently performed in the Catholic churches of all countries. Whether the highly dramatic piece for soprano solo and chorus, "Inflammatus et accensus," the impressive solo for the bass, "Pro peccatis," or the beautiful passages for the chorus of female voices in the "Eia Mater" are wanting in religious feeling must be left for each individual listener to decide for himself. The point cannot be settled by reference to any universally accepted standard; though judgment in the matter has often been given against Rossini on the plea, consciously or unconsciously entertained, that his "Stabat" does not resemble other and earlier Italian "Stabats," composed in a stricter style; and that it has scarcely anything in common with the church music of the German composers.

As a matter of fact, Rossini's *Stabat Mater* is the only Italian church music known to our public; and probably if the religious compositions of his predecessors, Pergolese and Paisiello, were now performed, they would make no better impression than was produced by the operas of those composers when, as if by way of experiment, the *Serva Padrona* of the one was given in London, and the *Barbiere di Siviglia* of the other at Paris. It would, doubtless, too, be found that resemblances existed between the opera music and the church music of these ancient masters, as things with a common origin must of necessity resemble one another on some points. Haydn's sacred music and secular music were very much alike, the *Creation* belongs to the former, the *Seasons* to the latter category. Handel's sacred music is often secular music in disguise. Thus he transferred airs from his operas to his oratorios, and developed his pianoforte fugues into fugues for sacred choruses. It is by no means easy to decide that such a piece of music possesses an absolutely religious, and such another piece an absolutely dramatic, character. Mrs. Hemans wrote a hymn called the "Hour of Prayer" to a melody which, under the title of "Rendez moi ma patrie," belongs to Hérold's *Pré aux Clercs*. A hymn known as "Jesus lead us with Thy power" is sung to the tune of the principal melody in Beethoven's "choral fantasia," in which there is no question of religion, but only of dancing. "Adeste fideles" has more than a general resemblance to "Voi che sapete" in the *Marriage of Figaro*. The "Agnus Dei" in Mozart's *First Mass* is substantially identical with "Dove sono" in the opera just named, and identical note for note as regards the first few bars. No one, however, says that the "Agnus Dei" in question is operatic in character because it presents a striking likeness to an air by the same composer which occurs in an opera; and it would be a great mistake to say that Signor Verdi's *Requiem* is operatic because, without containing any phrase or fragment of a phrase which suggests anything like it in any one of his operas, it reveals, throughout, the hand of the master to whom so many fine operas are due. Indeed, the remarkable thing in the *Requiem* is not that it is like, but that it is often so very unlike, the music Signor Verdi has composed for his operatic works. This may be accounted for in two ways; partly by Signor Verdi's having been on his guard against the objection which he might have felt sure would be made to his work as coming from the most famous operatic composer of the day; partly by the fact that the words of the *Requiem* have a dramatic character of their own, so that, impressed by their terrible significance, Signor Verdi could not, even in his character of dramatic composer, fail to produce music of a very different complexion from all he had given to the world before.

Verdi's *Requiem* having been blamed by some as too operatic, by others as not operatic enough, it may be interesting to turn to the letter written some thirty years ago by Heine on the subject—much discussed at the time—whether Rossini's *Stabat Mater* ought or ought not to be looked at as sacred music. "Rossini's *Stabat Mater*," wrote Heine to the *Allgemeine Zeitung*, "has been the leading event of the season. It is still the topic of general conversation, and the denunciations which, from the North German standpoint, are hurled at the master, prove forcibly the depth and originality of his genius. It is held that the treatment is too worldly, too sensuous and trivial for so sacred a subject; that the work is, moreover, too light and amusing. With musicians, just as with painters, there is quite a false notion with regard to the proper treatment of such subjects. The latter believe only in subtle delicate contours, and claim that the work should be as subdued and colourless as possible. In this respect the drawings of Overbeck furnish an ideal; but to refute this error by facts one need but look upon the sacred pictures of the Spanish school. In them there is fulness of contour and richness of colour; and yet no one will deny that they breathe an unfaltering Christian spirit and that their creators were as fully inspired as those celebrated masters at Rome who became converts to Catholicism in order that their works might receive a more direct inspiration. Christian Art does not manifest itself through dryness and pallor, but in a certain overflow of feeling which neither in music nor in painting can be the result of baptism or of study . . . . . Heaven forbid that I should be construed as finding fault with so great a master as the composer of *St Paul*. Least of all would the circumstance of Mendelssohn's being by birth a Jew, cause me to object to the oratorio as lacking in Christian feeling. Still, I cannot forego referring to the circumstance that at the age at which Mendelssohn embraced Christianity (he was baptised in his thirteenth year), Rossini had already dropped it and had entirely given himself up to secular-operatic music. When at a more advanced age Rossini abandoned the latter, and, as it were, dreamed himself back to the Catholic reminiscences of his youth—to the time when, as a choir boy, he sang in the Cathedral of Pesaro, or as an acolyte officiated at the service of the mass—when in his memory the old organ tones pealed afresh, and he seized his pen to write a *Stabat*, he surely had no need to construct the spirit of Christianity scientifically, nor slavishly to copy Handel or Sebastian Bach. All that he needed was to reawaken in his soul the sounds of earliest childhood. And strange to say, although these tones are both earnest and painful, although they forcibly express the most exalted emotions, they yet retain a childlike character and remind me of a Passion play that I once witnessed at Cette in which all the actors were little children. Exalted, awe-inspiring martyrdom was expressed in artless, childish accents. The agony and the lamentations of the Mater Dolorosa seemed to issue from the throats of little maidens; side by side with crape of deepest mourning there rustled the wings of all the cherubs of grace; the terrors of the crucifixion were tempered as if by tripping pastoral measures, and the sense of the infinite seemed to envelop the whole, like the blue skies that looked down upon the procession at Cette, or the blue sea on whose shores it marched, midst songs and ringing bells."

## CHAPTER XXVII.

### SOME OF ROSSINI'S WORKS.

When Madame Patti returns to us at the beginning of each season, "plus Patti que jamais,"—to quote the Russian critic, M. de Lenz,—and, as often happens, makes her reappearance as Rosina in the *Barber of Seville*, such a storm of applause bursts forth as the public reserves for only its very greatest favourites.

Rosina is a part which the composer may be said to have treated on what, in the language of commerce, is called "the double-entry system." It secures two first appearances for the prima donna; and though this very arrangement is said to have been one of the causes of the disfavour with which the masterpiece was received on its first production—when it was hissed by many and applauded by no one except the half-ironical, half-indignant composer, who stood up manfully for what he knew to be an achievement of some merit—it renders *Il Barbiere* a very suitable opera in which to re-introduce a thoroughly popular artist. Rosina appears first of all in the balcony, where she is received with the applause of recognition. This is renewed when she comes on in the second scene—which might well be considered a second act—to sing the long-delayed air out of which the Roman audience of the year 1813 fancied the original Rosina meant to defraud them. There is yet another opportunity for touching the heart of the public—ready, in the case of Mdme. Patti, to respond with the greatest warmth to the very slightest advances—when Dr. Bartolo's interesting ward takes her music lesson; and the culminating point is reached at the fall of the curtain, which cannot but be accepted as a sign for recalling the heroine of the evening, and offering her the homage which she has earned anew by one more fascinating performance.

The comic and the serious author in *Le Diable Boiteux*, after exchanging fulsome compliments, disputed as to which of their respective styles was the most difficult, and thereupon came to blows. Mdme. Adelina Patti, if any such question as this were to arise in connection with operatic performances, might take either side at will. Those who may have seen her only in great dramatic parts will not be likely to admit that comedy is her forte. Those who are, above all, familiar with her Rosina in *Il Barbiere*, or with her Norina in *Don Pasquale*, may well believe that she was born to represent the heroines of lyrical comedy. But the fact is, her dramatic genius has as extensive a range as her own beautiful voice, every accent of humour, of sentiment, and of passion being equally at her command. Without, however, attempting to decide which of the two great styles is the most difficult, it may safely be said that the comic style—or, to be precise, the style of comedy—is the most rare. We have several Aminas, many Marthas, a remarkably large number of Margheritas, but we have only one Rosina; and Mdme. Patti, rising constantly to new heights, and embellishing the music year after year with ornamentation of a more and more dazzling description, would seem to take a malicious pleasure in placing the part farther and farther beyond the reach of all other vocalists. But if any other artist were able to sing Rossini's brilliant music more or less as Mdme. Patti sings it, the difficulty of impersonating the character as we are accustomed to see it impersonated by the perfect Rosina of the Royal Italian Opera would still remain. "Qui dit Rosina pense Patti" has been well said by the author of "Beethoven et ses trois styles,"—already cited—who, after a long course of symphonies and sonatas, seems to have found true musical happiness in listening to Italian music as sung by the greatest operatic artist of our time.

When such singing as comes from the mouth of Mdme. Patti is heard, the most hardened Wagnerian must be led to reflect. For were the Wagnerian system established on the operatic stage, to the exclusion of all others, there would be no place for such vocalization as Mdme. Patti's. If Herr Wagner had not aimed at universal dominion he might not, it is true, have gained even such space as has been accorded to him at the great opera-houses of Europe. It is as well, all the same, to remember what the pilgrimage to Baireuth really meant; and one great object of the stern fanatics who led the way on that grave journey was the subjection of the vocalist. The prima donna—the flightiest, no doubt, of the whole flock of human singing-birds—is to be caught, clipped, and imprisoned within the iron cage of dramatic necessity. Without denying the poetic beauty of *Tannhäuser* and of *Lohengrin*, it is impossible not to see that the abandonment of the lyrical stage to such works would involve the sacrifice of singing as an art—of singing for the sake of singing such as the public applauds with enthusiasm whenever it has an opportunity of hearing Mdme. Patti in a thoroughly vocal part. Mdme. Patti can equally awaken the admiration of her audience when she undertakes characters in which a strict adherence to the musical text is required. But of the various kinds of excellence which together make up her incomparable talent, one is her perfection as a vocalist; and it is only in genuine Italian opera, and chiefly in the works of Rossini, that this excellence can be displayed.

There is something in Rosina's manner of making her first appearance—already spoken of—which, in the case of a new comer, is very tantalizing. She shows herself in a balcony, without singing, and, seen but for a moment, retires. Then she is heard behind the stage, echoing Almaviva's serenade, without being seen. Finally she comes forward and straightway begins her well-known air, in which, during the last sixty-five years, so many *débutantes* must have broken down, but in which at least a dozen have made a marked success. The first eight bars of "Una voce" form the only passage of expressive music which the part of Rosina contains. That, however, is enough to enable a singer to show that she is a mistress of the simple as of the florid style. The latter, in fact, includes the former, as power to run includes power to walk.

It has long been the fashion for Rosina to introduce in the scene of the music-lesson any piece in which she considers herself likely to produce a good effect. For the situation in which Rosina is now expected to present one or more airs after her own taste and of her own selection, Rossini had written a trio which somehow, as his biographers assure us, got lost. Probably no Rosina ever regretted the missing trio; while audiences willingly overlook, perhaps even do not perceive, the fact that unity of time, place, and colour are alike destroyed when side by side with Rossini's music of the year 1815 a popular English ballad, or a French romance, or an Italian waltz, or some outlandish "national air" is brought forward. All the good-natured public demands is to be pleased; and all that Rosina, equally amiable, cares for, is to please it.

A list of pieces sung by the most celebrated Rosinas since the year 1813 would be a curious document. Rode's air with variations seems at one time, and for a considerable period, to have been in favour with all Rosinas. Grisi, as Rosina, used to sing "Rode's air." Alboni also sang that historical violin tune, which at last was discovered to be old-fashioned—though every piece in the opera it was intended to adorn remained as fresh as when it was first written. Then Mdme. Bosio, in place of the discarded "Rode's air," introduced the air in polka time from Alary's *Tre Nozze*. Mdme. Gassier sang Venzano's waltz, which was adopted by every Rosina until, a few years afterwards, they all substituted for it the favourite "Il Bacio," by Signor Arditi. Mdme. Viardot used to put into the mouth of Rosina a popular Spanish air; which, as Rosina's musical language is that of Italy, was no more in keeping with the rest of the part than "Home, sweet home"—sung, as everyone knows, by Mdme. Adelina Patti in response to the encore which her execution of the bolero from the *Vêpres Siciliennes*, or Strakosch's waltz, or whatever her first air in the music-lesson scene may be, is sure to

2 \*

elicit. Prime donne of European fame belong to no country in particular; and it is, and should be, part of their business to make themselves at home, and to impress upon the public that they feel themselves at home, wherever they happen to be singing. Accordingly, when Mdme. Patti attacks the susceptible English public with "Home, sweet home," it accepts the compliment in the sense in which it is intended to be received. In Ireland she would probably substitute for "Home, sweet home," the "Last rose of summer"; in Scotland, "Robin Adair"—which plays in Boieldieu's *Dame Blanche* the part played by the "Last rose of summer" in Flotow's *Martha*. Similarly, in Russia, Mdme. Patti captivates the Russians and makes them feel how thoroughly Russian she is by singing a Russian air— the one known as "Solovei" or "The Nightingale," for instance. According to Professor Macfarren, who is not likely to make a mistake on that or any other musical subject, there are several Russian airs in the *Barber of Seville*. I forget whether he says three or four. But the statement is made in a review of a collection of songs by Glinka, contributed by Mr. Macfarren many years ago to the *Musical World*, and, as far as I remember, he says "four." It seems difficult in the long series of melodies contained in the *Barber of Seville* to recognise as Russian more than one—the dance tune arranged as an air for Bertha, which Rossini is supposed to have placed in his opera with the view of pleasing a Russian lady, residing at Rome, in whom he was particularly interested just then.

On the whole it may be fairly said and arithmetically proved that Mdme. Patti has nowhere obtained so much success as in London; for the simple reason that, successful everywhere, she has appeared in a greater number of characters in London than in any other city in Europe. And of all these characters there is none with which she has more completely identified herself than that of Rosina. Her representation of the part makes us forget her immediate predecessors as they in their time had caused the Rosinas of an earlier period to be forgotten. So Rossini's setting of the *Barber of Seville* eclipsed Paisiello's version, which in its day outshone Beaumarchais's comedy, which had itself been recognised as an improvement upon Molière's piece *Le Sicilien*—that dramatic sketch of which Beaumarchais's *Barber of Seville* is little more than a full development with variations and embellishments. The main idea of *Le Sicilien ou l'Amour Peintre* may yet be produced in other forms. The lover of a spoken drama disguising himself as a painter that he may obtain an interview with his mistress under pretence of taking her portrait, is in an appropriate character when in an opera he appears as a music master; and in a ballet on the same subject he would, with equal fitness, be introduced as a dancing master. But the *Barber of Seville* has doubtless found in Rossini's setting the mould in which it will finally remain; while as regards the heroine of this charming work, Mdme. Patti embodies the character so admirably that by the opera-goers of the present day she must always be remembered as the type of the perfect Rosina.

Rossini, who, like some other men of genius, was modest, used to say of his works that he believed the second act of *William Tell*, the third of *Otello*, and the whole of the *Barber of Seville* might live; and in *Otello* there are, indeed, scenes where the composer rises almost to Shakespearian heights. The opera is beautiful throughout in a musical, and especially in a melodious, point of view; in addition to which the second act contains some magnificent dramatic scenes; while the third, devoted entirely to the scene of the bed-chamber, is beautiful, dramatic, and seemingly, like a perfect poem, one continuous inspiration. There is nothing in all dramatic music more pathetic, and not much that is more terrible, than this final act of Rossini's *Otello*; and there is certainly nothing equal to it in regard to pure melody: melody both "absolute" and, inasmuch as the flow of ideas never ceases, "continuous."

Rossini's music, however, requires singing, and the part of Desdemona must, moreover, be acted; and those who have not seen the Desdemona of Mdme. Patti and have not heard Mdme. Patti sing Desdemona's appeal to her father, the willow song, and all the music of the bed-chamber scene, are not yet thoroughly acquainted with Rossini's *Otello*. This opera, the earliest of Rossini's really great works in the serious style, and the first in which he paid much attention to dramatic effect—or, without aiming at any such effect, attained it—has often been presented on the Anglo-Italian stage with a remarkably complete cast; Rubini and Mario (Otello and Roderigo) having been heard together as the two tenors, Tamburini and Lablache (Iago and Brabantio) as the two basses. Then Malibran and Grisi are remembered as two of the most celebrated Desdemonas; and there is not one part in the opera which, in the memory of experienced opera-goers, is not associated with some great artist. A good many years ago, at the Royal Italian Opera, Tamberlik and Ronconi were heard together as Otello and Iago. In those days, and with the particular cast of that time, the great scene, in a work full of great scenes, was that of the highly dramatic duet wherein Iago excites the jealousy of Otello to the point of madness—a climax which the tenor indicates (when his means permit it) by rising to a C sharp not contemplated by Rossini, and causing that exceptionally high note to resound if possible from the chest, but, as a rule, from the throat. In the whole repertory of Italian opera there is scarcely a work that admits, and, indeed, demands, so strong a cast as *Otello;* a circumstance to be accounted for by its having been composed for a sort of sensation company, got together by the illustrious Barbaja, which included about twice the ordinary number of leading artists.

*Otello* is the first serious work in Italian opera containing a prominent part for the baritone or bass; and —what is, however, merely accidental—the only one that comprises two effective tenor parts. It is known that Roderigo, in Rossini's *Otello*, is presented—or he would not be a tenor—as a personage capable of inspiring interest; and some may think that it would have been better after all for Desdemona to have lived quietly as the wife of this somewhat lackadaisical Venetian nobleman than to have been smothered by the heroic Moor. The one thing for which *Otello*, as played at the Royal Italian Opera, should be seen is Mdme. Patti's Desdemona; in which the celebrated prima donna shows herself once more the greatest lyric actress and the greatest dramatic vocalist on the stage. Remembering well her Rosina, Adina, and all her lighter parts, and fully impressed by the beauty of her "half-character" impersonations—such as Amina and Linda, one must yet say that Mdme. Patti has never displayed more varied natural resources nor higher artistic qualities than in the profoundly interesting and deeply tragic character of Desdemona. There is something for the painter, much for the actor, more still for the musician, to admire in each of her scenes; so that but for the thorough spontaneity of the representation, which excludes all idea of application in detail, one might say that she had studied with equal advantage Titian, Shakespear, and Rossini. In a purely vocal point of view Mdme. Patti's performance shows her to be as richly endowed with contralto as with genuine soprano tones. The notes of the violin and of the viola are combined in the same wonderful instrument, which the fortunate possessor exercises with the skill of a Paganini, and with an expression that is all her own.

In mentioning those of his works of which portions at least might, he thought, survive him, Rossini ought not to have forgotten *Semiramide*. Apart from the undying beauty of its melodies, which, until modern taste undergoes some radical change, must always make it a favourite work, *Semiramide* ought to be performed every season, if only to confound heathenish critics imagining vain things on the subject of the dramatic in music. Many very able men, remarkable for fine perception in literary and artistic matters, have written such strikingly contradictory things concerning *Semiramide* and the dramatic significance of its music, while other critics of equal authority have denied its dramatic significance altogether, that the opera, to anyone who seeks to reconcile the conflicting judgments of its admirers (leaving its ignoble detractors to themselves), assumes a mysterious, enigmatical character which is itself Babylonian. Stendhal declared this, the most thoroughly Italian of all Rossini's works, to be a German opera, and congratulated the composer on the skill with which, having quitted the Adriatic, he "navigated the Spree." But he so little quits the Adriatic that in the most tragic scene of all—in the duet of "Giorno d'Orrore"—Semiramide and Arsace warble reminiscences of the Carnival of Venice. Méry, a Rossinian of the year 1827, when the productions of the new Italian composer were extolled by one half of Paris and decried by the other, tells us, in the preface to his very clever adaptation of the *Semiramide* libretto, that the music, whether German or Italian by its composition, is in the result so perfectly Assyrian that when he hears it he sees "monsters from the Assyrian temples." That, however, only means that music always recalls what has been once associated with it. "Largo al fattotum," without being peculiarly Spanish, reminds everyone, not perhaps of Seville, but at least of Seville's celebrated "Barber"; and if the melodies of *Semiramide* had been put to the libretto of *La Donna del Lago*, Méry would, hearing them, have had imagination enough to see, not "monsters from the Assyrian temples," but Highlanders from the Scottish lochs. Méry's idea, however, was that the music possessed an appropriately strange, mysterious character; which can scarcely be maintained, except in regard to the magnificent chorus and march of the opening scene. It was possibly the abundant and at the time novel employment of wind instruments in this very march, together with the introduction of a military band on the stage, that made Stendhal say that the composer of *Semiramide* was getting Germanised. In any case, the music of this fundamentally Italian work seemed to Méry Assyrian, to Stendhal German, while Berlioz declared it to be absolutely without character. One thing quite certain is that it is full to overflowing of the most delightful melodies. Rossini was never more richly inspired than in composing this, the last of his long series of operas for the Italian stage.

With the exception, perhaps, of Spontini and Cherubini, no Italian master had ever attempted to write such thoroughly dramatic music as Rossini composed for *Guillaume Tell;* and no master, without exception, has produced more thoroughly beautiful music than that of which *Guillaume Tell* consists throughout. The introduction, the duet, or rather series of duets, for Arnold and William Tell, the duet for Arnold and Mathilde, the trio for the three men (which, in a dramatic point of view, may be regarded as one of the finest pages in all opera), the meeting of the cantons, and the scena for the disconsolate Arnold—"Asile héréditaire," with its sequel, "Suivez moi"—are all admirable. In citing the above pieces I have named almost everything of interest (apart from the ballet music) that the work contains—at least in the form given to it at the Royal Italian Opera, where it is played, not in five acts, but in three. A great deal of very fine music is of course cut out, and abridgments are made in some of the pieces retained. With all that, the opera lasts until past midnight; so that, much as it has been shortened, it is still considered somewhat long.

The French, often as they are reproached with levity, have certainly produced much that is heavy even to oppressiveness in every branch of art. A five-act opera is a kind of work which could only have been invented in France, and which, out of France, is in fact unknown. What German, what Italian, ever composed a five-act opera except for the French Académie; and out of the city of Paris which of these five-act operas is ever played in its original five acts? On the strength of a few opéras bouffes which are performed in every part of the world the French are thought to exhibit a light disposition in music as in other things. But their formidable five-act repertory exists to prove the contrary. In the days of Lulli and of Rameau, when music was in its infancy, dramatic composers were quite content—in fact, were only competent—to write a number of songs for solo voices, broken here and there by choruses of the simplest kind. Interesting or not, their five acts were certainly not spun out. When, however, the great operatic masters had developed the art of producing elaborate concerted pieces and finales half an hour long, the five-act arrangement became too much for the public. Often, too, it proved too much for the composer, as in the case of Donizetti with *Don Sebastien*, Balfe with *L'Etoile de Séville*, and Verdi with *Les Vêpres Siciliennes* and *Don Carlos*. Even Wagner, who is far from believing that the composer has no right to demand serious attention from the public, has never thought of asking his audience to listen to his music for five consecutive hours—which is what five acts usually mean. The *Flying Dutchman, Tannhäuser, Lohengrin, Tristan and Iseult,* are all three-act works; and when Wagner, elated but not confounded by his success, resolved to go beyond his usual three acts, he was considerate enough to divide his interminable operas into " days." Some such arrangement should be come to in the case of *Guillaume Tell*, with its five incomparable acts, forming one well-nigh intolerable, because interminable, whole. The first three acts might be played one night, the last three another. Thus the third or middle act would be played twice; an arrangement to which the admirers of Rossini's last manner and last work for the stage would certainly not object. Each of the two performances would be more interesting than *Guillaume Tell* as it is played now; and the crowds of musicians and amateurs who would attend both would for the first time (at least, in England) hear every piece and passage in Rossini's greatest opera precisely as Rossini wrote them.

But *Guillaume Tell*, however presented, can never be a great opera for the prima donna. No light soprano of the very highest pretensions would care to come out in the character of Mathilde. Yet in the whole range of opera there is no more beautiful scena for the prima donna than Mathilde's " Sombres forêts." The duet, too, for Mathilde and Arnold is charming, and full of emotion.

In fact, it is the great merit of Rossini throughout his admirable work that he has known how to reconcile truthfulness of dramatic expression with high musical beauty.

## CHAPTER XXVIII.

#### DONIZETTI AND BELLINI.

THE heroine of *Lucia di Lammermoor* has open to her at least two different ways of going mad. Lucia, as represented by Mdme. Patti, Mdme. Nilsson, and Mdme. Albani, does not rave, is not insanely eccentric, is scarcely ever flighty. She takes leave of her senses in a regretful, melancholy, moonstruck sort of manner, which has a poetry of its own not unlike that of certain *nocturnes* by Chopin and by Stephen Heller.

The Lucia of Mdlle. de Murska is an impersonation of quite another kind. Mdlle. de Murska is the most impulsive of Lucias ; and before her appearance among us the impulsive Lucia had never been made manifest at all. Quiet, gentle Lucias were familiar to us; Lucias who, after being tender in the first act and supplicatory in the second, became mildly deranged in the third. This conception, however, of Scott's, or, by adoption, Donizetti's heroine did not suit Mdlle. de Murska's peculiar and very original temperament. Not deliberately and for the sake of a "new reading," but by the force of her own natural disposition, she gave character and colour to the interesting, inoffensive personage, who in her hands ceases to be absolutely inoffensive and becomes more interesting than ever. Lucia, according to Mdlle. de Murska's presentation, is by no means the spiritless young person for which the public were at one time in the habit of taking her. In the struggle with Ashton she seems half inclined to stand up against him; and when she signs the fatal contract she is not merely feeble and helpless, she is already distracted and partially demented. She is at her best, however, when she is completely crazed, in the great scene of the third act. Here Mdlle. de Murska's Lucia, instead of suffering from depression, is agitated by excitement. Her brain is full of the wildest fancies, and she flies from one idea to another like a lunatic who, actually harmless, might at any moment become dangerous. Her singing in this scene is as wild and flighty as her appearance, gestures, and general demeanour. Method is, of course, not only desirable but indispensable in vocal madness; and Mdlle. de Murska's singing is admirably sane as regards delivery. It is only in the tones of the voice that madness seems to lurk.

In Rossini's time the principal female parts seem all, or nearly all, to have been written for the contralto voice; and such, no doubt, would be the case again if the supply of soprano voices, of late years so abundant, were to fail and a new Giorgi-Righetti or Colbran or Brambilla or Alboni were to appear and take for herself alone the place now occupied in public favour by our Pattis, our Nilssons, and our Albanis. The part of Leonora in *La Favorita* was written for the comparatively famous contralto, Mdme. Stolz, who happened to hold the post of prima donna at the Paris Opera House when Donizetti was composing or rearranging for that establishment the one serious opera with which he has permanently enriched the French repertory. It was from no notion, then, of dramatic fitness that the composer in this instance gave to the contralto voice a part which under ordinary circumstances he would have assigned, as in all his other operas, to the soprano. It is a good thing all the same that soprano voices should not have the absolute monopoly of leading parts. Singers with contralto voices should also from time to time have an opportunity of showing such dramatic qualities as belong to them; and for this reason *La Favorita* is an opera for which every first contralto ought to entertain, and doubtless does entertain, a high regard. According to an operatic legend which possesses some mythical features, but which, like other myths and legends, may be supposed to have its origin in a fact, Donizetti added the fourth and most dramatic act of the opera after he had completed the work, according to the original design, in three acts—terminating, we must suppose, with the finale to Act iii. as it now stands. But this finale ends nothing but the third act. The drama is far from being over when Fernando, indignant at the deception practised upon him, divests himself of his chain, the token of some military exploit, breaks his sword, and throws the "fragments of his blade" at the King's feet. It is quite impossible that either Scribe as a dramatist or Donizetti as a composer would have allowed the opera to finish with this animated scene of confusion—a dramatic knot which demands absolutely in some subsequent act to be untied or cut. The plan of the work evidently required that Fernando, after his stirring and most distressing adventures in the world for which, in spite of Father Baltazar's advice, he had rashly quitted the peaceful retirement of a monastery, should in due time return to this monastery, where alone he could find rest and satisfaction for his soul.

The fourth act of *La Favorita* could no more have been an after-thought than could the fourth act of *Otello*. Apart, too, from all question of dramatic propriety, it is to be observed that the libretto of *La Favorita* was not the work of Scribe alone but of Scribe and Alphonse Royer, who, it may be presumed, after the manner of

Scribe's collaborators, handed to the great master of dramatic construction a complete work, not a work which to be rendered complete needed the addition of another act. Alphonse Royer, moreover, was a careful student of the Spanish drama, to which, in the way of plots, the French drama owes so much; and since the production of *La Favorita*, nearly forty years ago, he has published a translation of Lope de Vega's and of Tirso de Molina's principal works. Nothing is more probable, then, than that M. Royer took the subject of *La Favorita* from some Spanish play. The fact that the action of the piece takes place in Spain need not count for much. The Spanish origin of the work is suggested far more forcibly by the nature of the affront offered to Fernando—who, like so many Spanish heroes, is wounded on a point of honour—and by the great moral or religious lesson of the piece: that happiness is not to be looked for in the world, and that—as the title runs of Calderon's most celebrated play—"Life is a dream." Fernando, when at the end of his adventures he retires once more to the monastery, must have looked upon it as a sort of nightmare.

*Don Pasquale* is an opera which, to produce its due effect, should be exceedingly well played. Composed for Grisi, Mario, Tamburini, and Lablache, it had the advantage, when first produced, of being performed by as perfect a vocal quartet as ever was written for. Numbers of people, on hearing *Don Pasquale*, must have fancied that they were delighted with Donizetti's music when they were in fact charmed by the singing of the artists entrusted with the principal characters. *Don Pasquale* contains an abundance of pretty if somewhat trivial melodies, much fluent dialogue-music, and an excessive amount of talk in the form of recitative. It is decidedly inferior to the graceful *Elixir of Love* by the same composer, and is not to be compared to Rossini's comic masterpiece, which it recalls here and there by the form and style of those conversational duets in which the characters half recite, half sing to the accompaniment of a flowing orchestral melody. Composed some thirty years later than the *Barber*, *Don Pasquale* has already a somewhat old-fashioned air, such as can never, one must think, belong to Rossini's ever-fresh, ever-youthful work.

The subject of *Don Pasquale* is about as simple a one as was ever set to music. It reminds one of t e theme of Méhul's *Irato*. As a matter of fact, it is borrowed from an old Italian piece called *Ser Marc Antonio;* and such intrigue as it possesses is probably, for a light comic opera, about sufficient. The plot is quite primitive in its simplicity. Consciously or unconsciously, the author of *Ser Marc Antonio* was an imitator of the old Italian pantomimes; and one can recognise in Norina Columbine, in Ernesto Harlequin, in Dr. Malatesta Clown, and in Don Pasquale Pantaloon. The author of all the fun is the clown Malatesta; the ludicrous victim is the pantaloon Pasquale. The resemblance between the pair of lovers in the pantomime and the pair of lovers in the opera need scarcely be pointed out. As for the music, it is full of gaiety and brilliancy, but its brilliancy requires bringing out. The serenade, however, is thoroughly melodious, and the quartet is one of the finest pieces of concerted music that Donizetti ever wrote. The baritone's graceful cavatina, too, "Bella siccome un Angelo," deserves a word of praise, not only for its own intrinsic merit, but by reason of the contrast it presents to the light, comic, conversational music, and to the decidedly comic airs of the bass.

*Don Pasquale* is now played as an eighteenth-century piece. Formerly the doctor, the lover, and the characters generally—with the exception only of Pasquale—wore modern dress; which in opera—so unreal is that entertainment—cannot fail to have a grotesque effect. It was rather absurd, moreover, to represent the old gentleman as of one century, his intimate friend the doctor, who is himself a middle-aged man, as of another. Finally, *Don Pasquale* is not very well suited to such a large theatre as the Royal Italian Opera; and Norina ought to be, in the words of Malatesta, "bella siccome un angelo," and to have an angelic voice, if we are to forget her many faults and not to regard her as the virago which in some of the scenes she shows herself to be.

Looked upon as a drama, *La Figlia del Reggimento*, to call it by its Italian name, is full of merit; though the merit of the original idea belongs not so much to M. de St Georges, librettist of *La Fille du Régiment*, as to Cervantes, author of the *Gipsy of Madrid*. Change gipsies into soldiers and name the gipsified heroine Maria, and the conversion of the Spanish into the French story is nearly complete. The young Spaniard who rather than lose his beloved joins the wandering gipsies, has his counterpart in the interesting Tonio; while the Marchioness di Birkenfeld (curious alliance of Italian with German) is the dramatic equivalent of the Spanish girl's mamma.

As for the music of *La Figlia*, it is almost the prettiest Donizetti ever wrote; not absolutely the prettiest when one remembers the charming *Elisir d' Amore*, nor the most brilliant, *Don Pasquale* being borne in mind, but very attractive all the same, and here and there very engaging. Maria's one sentimental air is full of expression; and Tonio has much allotted to him that is worth singing—though the part is not much in favour with tenors. It, indeed, contains nothing to be compared to the "Una furtiva" of *L' Elisir d' Amore*, or the "Com' e gentil" of *Don Pasquale*. Donizetti was in his happiest mood when he wrote those two perfect airs for the tenor voice; and the mood seems to have lasted him during the whole time that he was engaged in the operas which they adorn. *La Fille du Régiment*—composed to a libretto broken up, like all the libretti written for the Opéra Comique, by much intolerable dialogue for the speaking voice—is not "all of a piece," like the two other easy-flowing, thoroughly homogeneous works. It retains signs of its local origin, and, though the talking has of course been cut out and replaced in the Italian version by a small modicum of recitative, the pieces do not run smoothly and almost imperceptibly one into the other, as in the composer's thoroughly Italian comic operas. The necessary excisions have been made; but, as was said of one of Lord Russell's most notorious despatches mutilated by himself, "You can see the scars."

Donizetti, to judge by the number of his works represented every season at one or the other of our operahouses, would seem to be the most popular of all the Italian composers. Bellini is constantly represented at both establishments; above all, when a new prima donna undertakes to fascinate the public by that ever-fresh musical idyll *La Sonnambula*. A tragic prima donna at very rare intervals favours us with *Norma;* and attempts are now and then made to interest the public by means of *I Puritani:* which, full as it is of beautiful music, is not a very admirable work as a whole. It cannot be said to keep the stage with anything like a firm footing. *Beatrice di Tenda, Il Pirata,* &c. need not be mentioned; they are forgotten. Donizetti, however, though he has produced no one work flowing with melody as with milk and honey like *Semiramide,* no musical comedy to be compared to *Il Barbiere,* no musical drama to approach *Guillaume Tell,* is always before the public with one or more of the seven or eight operas from his pen which are still found valid and fit for representation. *Lucrezia, Linda, Lucia, Don Pasquale, La Figlia del Reggimento* are frequently presented at both houses; while *La Favorita* is one of the stock pieces of the Royal Italian Opera, where *L' Elisir d' Amore* may also be heard, though not so often as many would desire.

*La Sonnambula* is as good an opera as any other of the same class, and a great deal better than most. The time has already arrived for opera-goers, under the influence of Herr Wagner's intensely dramatic works, to smile at the alleged triviality of the beautiful melodies which Bellini introduces in the most serious and most critical moments of his charming pastoral. *La Somnambula* is, however, dramatic enough, if, setting aside the formal orchestral accompaniments and the conventional orchestral interludes between the principal movements of scenas and airs, attention be given exclusively to the parts for leading characters. Elvino's air is full of passion; and those over-acute critics are mistaken who point out that the brilliant solo with which the opera concludes is not the sort of air that a peasant-girl would sing. It is precisely the sort of air that an exceptionally sensitive being like the sympathetic and somnambulistic Amina might sing in a state of rapture bordering upon ecstacy. Besides belonging to a family of respectable peasants who probably farmed their own land, she is, moreover, a "thing of impulse and a child of song"; and she particularly requests the audience *not* (as the English version has it) to "mingle one human feeling" with the divine joy she is experiencing. The idea that Amina at such a moment ought to sing in the voice and style of an ordinary rustic is one that only a person of extraordinary rusticity of mind could entertain. The principle that everyone ought to sing gorgeously, brilliantly, simply or grotesquely, according to his or her social position, would require Amina, as well as Elvino, to sing like peasants, while Count Rodolfo should execute aristocratic roulades in the Almaviva style. But Bellini thought of Count Rodolfo, in the one air given him to sing, as a man returning, after many years' absence, to the place of his birth; and on such occasions Counts may be supposed to feel much the same as Barons, and the great mass of inferior beings left without recognition by that exclusive naturalist who held that *L'homme commence au Baron.*

Amina is, indeed, a part for which every prima donna who has ever appeared in it with success should feel deeply indebted to the composer, Bellini, to the librettist, Romani, and, finally, to the ingenious dramatist, Scribe, who first gave life and form to the interesting and touching story on which *La Sonnambula* is founded. But it is to Bellini that she owes the beautiful melodies which have made the opera of *La Sonnambula* live, and with no failing life, when both the ballet of *La Sonnambule*, and the original vaudeville or drama with couplets, of the same name, have long since disappeared from the stage; and in the admirable scena of the last act it is to Bellini alone that Amina, when she sinks on her knees, should offer thanks.

*I Puritani* was composed for that marvellous quartet, Grisi, Rubini, Tamburini, and Lablache; and for some years all who proposed to hear Grisi, Rubini, Tamburini, and Lablache, desired to hear them in the opera written expressly for them by Bellini. It has been asserted over and over again, by persons having authority, that *I Puritani* is Bellini's masterpiece. But neither is it a masterpiece in an absolute sense, nor is it by any means the masterpiece of Bellini, who was never so much in his element as when he was writing the idyllic music of *La Sonnambula*. In *Norma*, replete as that work is with melody of the purest kind, the composer does not always rise to the tragic height of his subject.

In *I Puritani* the subject was far too obscure for the simple, naïf genius of the young Sicilian composer, who, when in doubt, seems to have resolved all difficulties by setting whatever words he had before him to the most beautiful airs he could invent. This, of course, is a fault with which all Italian composers are charged, and which, for adequate reasons, is never likely to be attributed to certain modern German composers. But it is above all conspicuous in the works of Bellini, and in none more so than in the melodious, unmeaning opera of *I Puritani*.

It must be admitted, however, that the hymn-like concerted piece in the third act of this opera possesses a more elevated character than the rest of the music; and no one will deny the beauty and brilliancy of the charming polacca. If little else in the opera is dramatic " Son Vergin Vezzosa" is at least in character with the situation, and with the frame of mind of the young lady who has to sing it. The most popular piece in *I Puritani* used unquestionably to be the duet for the baritone and bass, in which Rossini—who, when the opera was first brought out in Paris, sent a description of it to a friend at Milan—seems to have been chiefly struck by the sonority of the accompaniments. "I will say nothing about the duet for the two basses," he briefly wrote, " for you must have heard it where you are."

## CHAPTER XXIX.

### THE MIGNON AND HAMLET OF AMBROISE THOMAS.

SOMEONE has said that in the presence of an undisputed masterpiece, as in that of a great personage, you should remain silent until it speaks to you. But suppose it says nothing? A man cannot remain silent beyond a certain time if it is his profession to make utterances; and M. Ambroise Thomas in presence of *Wilhelm Meister*, like Verdi in presence of *Macbeth*, and like Gounod in presence of *Romeo and Juliet*, has spoken first. That is all that need be said on the subject; and it is, perhaps, scarcely necessary to say as much as that. *Wilhelm Meister* is a novel for the serious, holding some such place among novels in general as among plays is enjoyed by those works which are said to be "better suited to the closet than to the stage." It is no treason against Goethe to suggest that *Wilhelm Meister* finds more favour with literary students than with the eager, superficial readers of the circulating library. One must doubt whether, in spite of Mr. Carlyle's admirable translation, it has ever been in much demand at Mudie's. It certainly wants the "happy ending" which is one of the first requisites of the perfect specimen of the circulating library novel; and it might be said of *Wilhelm Meister*, with much more truth than it was said of *Clarissa Harlowe* by Dr. Johnson, that if any one tried to read it for the sake of the story he would cut his throat before he had got through a dozen pages. For these and many more reasons, though it was quite open to the librettists and composer of *Mignon* to leave *Wilhelm Meister* alone, one does not see how, having once resolved to take it in hand, they could attempt to give us a musical *Wilhelm Meister*, as the same librettists, in conjunction with Gounod, did really attempt to give us a musical *Faust:* something, that is to say, which should be the analogue in music of what *Faust* is in poetry. Meyerbeer, who, better perhaps than any composer, could have put *Faust* and *Wilhelm Meister* into something like operatic form, took good care to do nothing of the kind. The death of Mignon and the whole of *Faust* were pressed upon him as suitable subjects by the assiduous M. Blaze de Bury; who, however, has told us himself ("Meyerbeer et ses Œuvres") that in regard to *Faust* Meyerbeer thought the legend had already found its appropriate and permanent artistic form, and for that excellent reason ought no more to be meddled with. All Meyerbeer would agree to do was to write a few incidental pieces for Goethe's drama, and to set to music in *Wilhelm Meister* just those portions which obviously invite musical treatment; for instance, Mignon's aspirations and regrets, and the dirge sung at Mignon's funeral.

The composer, however, of *Hamlet* may find in *Wilhelm Meister* itself his justification for the manner in which he has treated both the works just named. When Wilhelm Meister objects to the proposed curtailment of *Hamlet*, and remarks that *Hamlet* is a complete growth, with trunk, branches, leaves, blossoms, and fruit, one of his theatrical associates replies, " Yes, but you don't place an entire tree on the table." Profiting by this idea, the French librettists have contented themselves with presenting on the stage that flower of poetry, Mignon, with just as much to surround her as may serve to exhibit her to advantage. The part of Mignon, originally written for a mezzo-soprano, has apparently been rewritten for Mdme. Nilsson. Otherwise, let the heroine be a soprano or a mezzo-soprano, the four indispensable operatic characters are equally to be found in *Wilhelm Meister*, as in almost every effective libretto. The heroine would not be a heroine if she were without a lover, and her lover has naturally a tenor voice. Instead of suffering, as in some operas, from the opposition of a dark-minded contralto, she is, as in some other operas, made the victim of a light-minded soprano, who has the hardness and brilliancy of the diamond, while she herself, a sentimental sympathetic soprano, has the softness and charm of a flower. We have a ready-made baritone or bass in the grave Lothario (not to be confounded for one moment with the more notorious "gay Lothario"); and though there are other incidental personages in the piece, the veritable drama on which M. Ambroise Thomas has worked is made up of the various combinations in which Mignon, Philina, Wilhelm Meister, and Lothario take part.

Of the four principal characters two have been developed with especial care—the young girl Mignon and the old harper Lothario; and to each of these two personages the composer has succeeded in giving a certain musical physiognomy. The authors have done well to call their work by the familiar and fascinating name of *Mignon*, which Goethe took from France, and which the French have a perfect right to take back from Goethe; a name which, with questionable appropriateness, had already been made to do duty first as the title of a novel by Balzac and afterwards of a tale by M. de St. Germain. But the Mignon best known in France was the graceful, sentimental, dreamy Mignon imagined by Scheffer, which has often been mistaken for the Mignon of Goethe himself. We look in vain, or rather we do not look at all, for the wild vivacity of Goethe's Mignon in the charming and touching figures which it pleased Scheffer to draw;

and in the opera of *Mignon*, as indeed in that of *Faust*, the librettists have kept Scheffer's designs constantly in view. It was intended, no doubt, that the expression and the well-known poses of the always charming though always sorrowful Mignon imagined by the painter should at the proper moments be suggested by the looks, attitudes, and gestures of Mignon's stage representative; and it is quite right that the general make-up of Mignon, equally with that of the old harper, should be imitated, as closely as possible, from Ary Scheffer's pictures.

Mdme. Nilsson gives new beauty to the part by her wonderful singing, which was the one thing wanting in Mdme. Galli-Marié's very dramatic and picturesque performance at the Opéra Comique, where *Mignon* was originally produced; and whether instinctively, or as the result of study, she reproduces the gaiety and the passion, tinged by a certain appropriate savagery, as well as the grace and sentiment of Mignon. It may be said, then, of Mdme. Nilsson's Mignon, what was in a less degree true of the Mignon presented by Mdme. Galli-Marié, that it bears a far greater resemblance to the veritable Mignon of *Wilhelm Meister* than the exclusively sentimental figures offered as representations of Mignon by Ary Scheffer. Nevertheless, the Scheffer aspect of the character—which, it need not be said, is a true aspect, though only one of many belonging to it—is not neglected by Mdme. Nilsson in her really perfect embodiment; with which, could they witness it, the poet and the painter would be as delighted as the composer who has set *Mignon* to music is known to be. *Mignon* might fairly be called an opera in three pictures; so clearly have Scheffer's pictures suggested the three great scenes which are devoted to Mignon, and which form the most characteristic part of the work. First we have "Mignon thinking of her native country," in which the memorable "Kennst Du das Land?" ("Connais-tu le pays où fleurit l'oranger?" as it becomes in the French version) occurs. Then Mignon and the old harper are grouped together in a duet scene written evidently for the sake of the situation, which calls to mind the least celebrated picture of the Mignon series. Finally, Mignon comes on in a white robe, kneels down on the stage, and prays, in order that she may look as much as possible like the well-known "Mignon aspiring to Heaven."

The original version of the work, being produced at the Opéra Comique, contained much spoken dialogue for which recitative has in the Italian version been substituted. It is a great relief to miss the spoken dialogue, and the relief would be greater if the added recitatives were shorter. But the opera altogether has gained immeasurably in its transplantation from the French theatre to the Italian Opera. M. Ambroise Thomas has written some very brilliant ballet music for the new version, and his work meets with an execution such as he never could have dreamt of when he first composed it.

It has been well suggested that M. Ambroise Thomas's lyrical version of *Hamlet* should have been called *Ophelia*. The question would not then have been raised in too direct a manner, whether or not Shakespear's tragedy has received worthy treatment at the hands of its operatic adaptors. Moreover, Ophelia, who is not the chief character, who is scarcely even a character of the first degree of importance, in Shakespear's *Hamlet*, is the principal personage, both in a musical and in a dramatic point of view, in the *Hamlet* prepared for the composer by MM. Barbier and Carré. Finally, the longest, most elaborate, and altogether the best scene in the operatic *Hamlet*, does not exist in the *Hamlet* of Shakespear at all. Here the name of Shakespear cannot be used against M. Thomas; and if he had confined himself to this scene and entitled it *The Death of Ophelia*, one universal feeling of admiration would have been expressed for the work. The object, however, of M. Thomas was to produce not a poetical little cantata, but a grand opera containing a great part for Mdme. Nilsson; and accordingly the scene of Ophelia's death is followed by an act which is superfluous, and is preceded by three acts which are in a great measure irrelevant. The parent notion of the opera was certainly the idea that the fair-haired, soft-voiced, Swedish soprano would be in every way an admirable representative of Shakespear's Scandinavian heroine; and so indeed she has proved. Mdme. Nilsson has deeper qualifications for the part than purely external ones, which, nevertheless, may be said to suggest others. All the sentiment of the character seems to belong to her naturally, so that as an actress alone, if she had not a note to sing, she would still be an admirable Ophelia. Then the pure fresh quality of her voice is quite in harmony with the rest of the personage. If the Shakespearian heroines may be divided into two categories, like the heroines of modern opera, Ophelia is eminently a "light soprano" part, as Lady Macbeth is a part for a "dramatic soprano." The amount of Scandinavianism discoverable in the character of Shakespear's Ophelia, is, probably, very slight; but M. Thomas has given a tinge of national colour to the music sung by the Ophelia of his opera. This he has done, not by the vulgar expedient of dragging in one national air in complete form, but by reproducing the character of the Swedish melodies (for operatic purposes Sweden and Denmark are one) in both the heroine's grand scenas, and by employing here and there actual passages of Swedish origin.

In the power of characterisation belonging to music lies one of the strong points of opera as a form of art. A Scotchman sings something in the Scotch style, or a Russian something in the Russian style, and the nationality of the personage is at once painted beyond the possibility of mistake. This process, however, easy

4 *

enough in regard to solo music, ballet music, marches and choruses, cannot well be applied to concerted music, and not at all to finales. The Russians have a national opera called *Life of the Czar*, the Poles a national opera called *Halka*, the Hungarians a national opera called *Hunniades*. In these works, each of which is considered in its native land second only to *Don Giovanni*, all the dancing, marching, chorus-singing, and a certain amount of ballad-singing is done to quasi-national tunes. In the more ambitious portions, however, we are at once reminded, and by contrast very forcibly, that in the "national" opera of primitive nations no such modern cosmopolitan inventions as dramatic concerted pieces and finales can legitimately have a place. There is no such thing in a special national sense as a Russian, Polish, or Hungarian finale. Neither does M. Thomas make any endeavour in *Hamlet* to give us a Scandinavian finale, wisely contenting himself with such a finale as the Hebrew-Prussian Meyerbeer might have written. Ophelia's solos are interspersed with little Scandinavian snatches; and the villagers of the neighbourhood of Elsinore dance, in one place, to a quaint but very graceful melody which is apparently of Scandinavian origin. But another dance tune in the same scene is clearly derived from the Anglican, not to say cockneyfied, tune of "Billy Taylor." Others, again, might have been written for any ballroom of the present day. M. Ambroise Thomas may, indeed, be acquitted of all intention to give a Scandinavian character to his music elsewhere than in the strikingly-coloured part of Ophelia, and in the dance tunes of her young companions.

There are few characters, one would think, in all dramatic literature, less favourable for musical treatment than Hamlet. The address to the ghost, the interview between Hamlet and his mother are, to be sure, dramatic enough in the ordinary sense of the word, and furnish suitable groundwork for operatic scenes. But the character of Hamlet is chiefly known to us from the two great monologues; and the monologues, though a composer of the very highest genius might, doubtless, be able to find appropriate music for them, are not the sort of "words" that any ordinary composer would like to set, or could adequately deal with. M. Thomas, differing from all the Italian composers who have grappled with Shakespear, seems to have made an honourable endeavour to give to his principal personages their proper musical physiognomy. Verdi (to take a flagrant instance) makes Macbeth, in the most terrible moment of his career, when its tragic termination already stares him in the face, sing a sentimental air of the conventional pattern, which might just as well be sung by Renato in the *Ballo in Maschera*, and which— if it had not been written some years earlier—would be regarded as a very close imitation of Balfe's "Come into the garden, Maud." Signor Verdi would doubtless have treated "To be or not to be?" as he has treated the "words" which in the libretto of *Macbeth* replace "Canst thou not minister to a mind diseased?" &c. But though his intentions would not have been so meritorious as that of M. Thomas, the thing achieved would have been at least melodious. The air would have had no philosophical character, but it would have been singable and what is called "expressive." It would have been, so to say, in rhyme; whereas M. Thomas's Hamlet sings persistently in blank verse. The only notable case in which the operatic Hamlet breaks into evenly-balanced, sharply-defined rhythm is (if we except a few graceful passages in the finale to the second act) in the drinking song which he addresses to his friends the players in lieu of the well-known hints on acting. Here, again, we are reminded of the scene in *Macbeth* where the King "obliges the company with a song," to be interrupted in the midst of his effusion by Banquo's ghost. A drinking song is worth nothing in an opera if not relieved at intervals by some anti-jovial incident or reflection; and in M. Thomas's work the necessary contrast is supplied by a passing change in Hamlet's ever-changing humour.

After Ophelia and Hamlet, the only personage whom the composer seems to have thought it worth while to characterise is the ghost. Alas! poor ghost. At the thought of this dreadful, because preternaturally dull and dismal, apparition, we can only cry with Hamlet:

"Angels and ministers of grace defend us"—from ever meeting with such a ghost again. In the first place we deny his ghostliness. It is not the voice of a disembodied spirit that we hear, but of a dead man singing. The statue of Don Giovanni (of which it would be unfair to speak if M. Thomas did not in a certain way invite the comparison) repeats the same note to varied harmony, then repeats another note to another succession of chords; but the dead body of the King of Denmark emits the same sound—makes the same noise, that is to say—so unintermittently for so long a time, that instead of the divine sentiment of terror inspired by the figure on horseback, we feel the sort of awe and about the same admiration that would be excited in us by the unlooked-for appearance of an undertaker's mute. However, in these operatic presentations of great dramatic masterpieces (*Faust, Mignon, Romeo and Juliet,* and now *Hamlet*) "realism" is the great principle cultivated; and it was, perhaps, intended that the music given to the ghost of Hamlet's father should be directly suggestive of the grave-yard.

Much has been said about M. Thomas's knowledge of orchestral effect, but it must be possible to abuse such knowledge. "If God had given me, instead of the faculty for creating, capacity for judging, I do not know," said the late Alexandre Dumas in one of his most amusing prefaces, "whether I should have had wings powerful enough to raise me to the level of the poet;

but I think I should have had sufficiently robust legs to be able to walk round him." Without presuming to criticise M. Thomas's orchestral work, one may say, judging only by its effect, that it is laborious and pretentious writing. It is in many cases "full of sound and fury," whatever it may signify. A melody, or fragment of melody, is often begun on one instrument, continued on a second, and finished—or left unfinished—on a third. In some of the most agitated portions of the opera the accompaniments suggest not merely agitation, but epilepsy. In others they recall the view taken of modern instrumentation by a certain satirist, who declares that its great secret consists in treating trombones as clarinets, and assigning violin passages to the bassoon. In many places, on the other hand, especially in the quieter scenes, the combinations of instruments are charming.

The composer of so many agreeable operas in the light style and of so much pretty ballet music, seems in *Hamlet* to have forced his talent. Yet a decided exception must be made in favour of his truly poetical Ophelia ; and opera-goers must at least thank M. Thomas for having furnished one of the most graceful and accomplished artists on the lyric stage with a part which suits her as if she had been born for it.

## CHARTER XXX.

### SHAKESPEARIAN OPERAS.

HAMLET, except in the pretty ballet music and the really poetical scene of Ophelia's death, is the work of a man who is perpetually urging himself to be solemn and sad when nature created him light and cheerful. Our opera-going public, for the most part, knows nothing of Shakespear, and consequently is not shocked by the terrible absurdities of which the operatic *Hamlet* is full. But in itself, apart from what it suggests, M. Thomas's music is very depressing. The *Romeo and Juliet* of M. Gounod, who first taught M. Thomas the art of marrying feeble music to immortal verse, is far preferable to *Hamlet*, inasmuch as M. Gounod, deeming himself a sort of Shakespear in music, does not think it necessary to make unnatural exertions with the view of raising himself to the level of his poet. All he feels called upon to do is to write as his nature prompts him; and the result is that, though M. Gounod's music is no more Shakespearian than that of M. Thomas, it is at least spontaneous, and possesses even some *naïveté*—a quality in which M. Thomas's high-pressure strains are wholly wanting.

As a rule, indeed, but little success has been achieved by operas founded on Shakespearian subjects. *Julius Cæsar* and *Hamlet* were turned into lyric dramas more than a century and a half ago. *Giulio Cesare* and *Ambleto* were both performed at the King's Theatre, under Handel's management, when the part of the world-conqueror was, with strange inappropriateness, given to the "sopranist," Signor Nicolini, the hero of the celebrated vocal and gladiatorial combat with an operatic lion, so humorously described in the *Spectator*. *Ambleto*, the composition of Gasparini,—libretto by Apostolo Zeno,—was brought out at Venice, and afterwards performed at the King's Theatre, standing on the site now occupied by Her Majesty's. Dr. Burney gives some account of it in his "History of Music," and tells us in particular that the overture had four movements, the last of which was a jig. One must infer from this description of the overture that the instrumental prelude to *Ambleto* was but little in correspondence with the subject of *Hamlet*. It would not, then, have suited the present day, when it is generally admitted that the music of a drama should above all be dramatic—should possess, that is to say, what is called "dramatic significance."

It is now twenty-five long years, as the man in the melodrama would say, since it occurred to Verdi to compose an opera on the subject of *Macbeth*. Everyone in England who heard of the Italian master's intentions declared without hesitation that there was something too daring in the choice of such a theme. Nevertheless, the apparition of the murdered Banquo at the feast, Lady Macbeth's sleep-walking scene, the choruses of witches, and Macbeth's despair in the later scenes of the tragedy, together with the supernatural agencies with which the whole work is surrounded, might well have inspired a composer of true genius— such a composer as Verdi has shown himself to be in *Rigoletto*, in *Un Ballo in Maschera*, and especially in *Aïda*.

Meanwhile, the *Midsummer Night's Dream* had suggested to Mendelssohn incidental music of the most graceful, most fantastic kind; and some years afterwards this drama was made the basis of a species of half-burlesque opera by Ambroise Thomas, who, in conjunction with his librettist—for the blame of the transaction may be fairly divided between them—introduced Shakespear as the lover and tenor of the work, and represented him as engaged now in stealing deer, now in making amorous advances to Queen Elizabeth. Charming incidental music has been written for *The Tempest* by Mr. Arthur

Sullivan; who has similarly illustrated the *Merchant of Venice*. Both the *Merchant of Venice* and *The Tempest*, moreover, have been treated in formal operatic style.

When Jenny Lind was singing at Her Majesty's Theatre, Mr. Lumley invited M. Halévy to compose for his establishment *La Tempestà*; and *La Tempestà* was actually brought out, though with no great success, the only remarkable " numbers " in the work being a scena for Caliban (impersonated by Lablache), and a piece of ballet music in which the melody—much praised by the foreign critics who heard it—was borrowed from Dr. Arne's " Where the bee sucks."

The *Merchant of Venice* has been treated operatically by Signor Petrella, a contemporary composer, whose *Mercante di Venezia* is one of the few modern Italian operas which have made a decided mark.

*Romeo and Juliet* has attracted the attention of composers more than any other Shakespearian play; it would, indeed, be strange if a tragedy which abounds in love passages and in which whole scenes are devoted to love had not been deemed a fit work for musical setting. Besides love-making, however, there is in Shakespear's *Romeo and Juliet* a great display of wit, as in the character of Mercutio; of courage, as in the duels between Mercutio and Tybalt, and between Tybalt and Romeo; of wise philosophy, as in the speeches of the Friar; and of philosophy of the bitterest kind, as in the speeches of the Apothecary. French and Italian composers, however, who have undertaken to turn Shakespear's *Romeo and Juliet* into an opera seem to have been struck by nothing but the love duets; and the fine thoughts in which the work abounds are not only not within their grasp, but are altogether beyond the reach of music. To speak of modern times alone, *Romeo and Juliet* has during the present century been set to music by no less than five composers: among the Italians, by Zingarelli, Bellini, and Vaccai; among the French, by M. Gounod and the Marquis d'Ivry, whose *Amanti de Vérone*, originally produced at the Théâtre Lyrique of Paris, was afterwards given with very little success at the Royal Italian Opera.

The *Merry Wives of Windsor* was taken by Balfe for the subject of an opera which he had engaged to write for Her Majesty's Theatre,—or King's Theatre, as it was called in those distant days. Balfe's setting of the *Merry Wives of Windsor* was entitled *Falstaff*, and the principal parts in the work were sustained by Grisi, Persiani, Ivanoff (the Russian tenor), and Lablache. The great, the enormous, Italian basso impersonated Falstaff; and with such a cast as had been secured for it the opera could not but succeed. It does not seem, however, to have made any great impression; for it has never been revived.

Probably the *Falstaff* libretto was faulty—a charge which could not be brought against the *Merry Wives of Windsor* as handled by the German dramatist, Mosenthal, and the German composer, Nicolai. The libretto of *Die Lustige Weiber* is, indeed, as clever as the music to which it has been set. It abounds in situations which invite musical treatment, and in each of the three acts the incidents are worked up to an effective dramatic finale.

In counting up those of Shakespear's plays which have been converted into operas, we must not forget *Othello*, which, in the hands of Rossini, became a true operatic masterpiece; or, at least, a true operatic masterpiece in the Italian style.

To speak in particular of one more Shakespearian opera, is the music of Nicolai's *Merry Wives of Windsor* Shakespearian? Happily not; for the art of composing operatic music has made considerable progress since Shakespear's time. So, it may be said, has the art of placing pieces of all kinds on the stage, surrounded by beautiful and appropriate accessories. Still one has a rough idea as to how a Shakespearian piece should be dressed; and, whether the costumes fixed upon be those of the time at which the action of the piece takes place, or those of Shakespear's own time (the latter was the rule at Shakespear's theatre), it can be said in either case that they are "Shakespearian." In regard, however, to the music, it would be absurd to imitate that of Queen Elizabeth's reign, and still more absurd to go back for examples of the style in which a Falstaffian subject should be treated to the period of Henry V. In setting

Shakespear each particular composer follows the bent of his own particular genius. Othello sings in florid Rossinian strains; Hamlet is gloomy after the latest manner of Ambroise Thomas; while Romeo is amorous with Bellini, passionate with Berlioz, or sentimental with Gounod. No composer has been quite successful in treating Shakespear's serious subjects. But Nicolai's light and joyous music is appropriate enough to the humorous incidents and lively dialogue of the *Merry Wives of Windsor*. The final scene of the forest, in which the unhappy Falstaff is terrified by demons, fascinated and frightened by wood-nymphs, and bewildered by the beauty of Mrs. Ford, is in all respects effective. The "forest melody" is not such a melody as Wagner was dreaming of when he wrote his celebrated passage on the nature of tune. But it is a very pretty and inspiriting melody all the same; and, like the harmonious sounds spoken of by Wagner, must, to be appreciated at its full value, be heard in the forest itself. Not, however, that it is ineffective in the overture, where, as final movement, it also has its place.

# CHAPTER XXXI.

### CARMEN.

SPAIN is a country inhabited by gipsies, smugglers, bull-fighters, and muleteers; on whom a semblance of order is imposed by soldiers only a little less undisciplined than the rest of the gaudily-attired, recklessly-behued population. The military have a disastrous habit of falling in love with the bright-eyed daughters of the gipsy-tribes, some of whom, like Carmencita or Carmen, the prettiest girl in Seville, make a pretence of earning a livelihood by working in the great cigar manufactory of the place. The cigar manufactory of Seville is an establishment which no one who has read Prosper Merimée's description of it, in the charming tale on which the opera of *Carmen* is founded, can forget. But description and reflection count very little in drama, especially drama prepared for musical setting; and of Mérimée's literary art there is no trace in the ingenious and highly-coloured, highly-characteristic libretto for which the Spanish tale of "Carmen"—worthy pendant to the Corsican tale of "Colomba" from the same pen—has served as a groundwork. Carmen makes a much freer use of the dagger than does the innocent Colomba of the stiletto. Corsican young ladies of good birth and breeding reserve the stiletto for great occasions, and meanwhile wear it in their stays in lieu of what used to be called a "busk." But the gipsy and the gipsyfied girls of the cigar manufactory at Seville are ready with the dagger on the smallest provocation.

Thus the playful Carmen, having had a quarrel with one of her young friends, has appealed to what Mérimée assures us is the *ultima ratio* of the Seville cigar girls, and has stabbed her antagonist. But the blow, however well-aimed, was merely the expression of a little momentary pique; and Carmen, when immediately afterwards she appears on the stage, shows herself petulant and wilful, but not malicious. Already she has had an opportunity of explaining her views on the subject of love, which, according to her philosophy, is an agreeable and delightful servant, but a most tyrannical master, and as such not to be tolerated. The question of reciprocity does not trouble her. If she loves, that is sufficient; and so much the worse for the loved one if he does not equally love her. The German poet who declares that, though a man may once in his life love without having his passion returned, yet that he who does so a second time is a fool at whom " sun, moon, and stars" must laugh, and who himself must laugh even if his love kills him, would have met with but little sympathy from Carmen. She can be affectionate, devoted, and for a time constant. But if she ceases to love she will not affect a sentiment she no longer feels; and she sets her face absolutely against the importunities of unrequited affection, which for her has no meaning. She can understand a man's killing her for not accepting his love; but she will not allow herself to be wearied and worried on the subject of a mysterious passion which comes and goes, and which can be neither forced nor controlled. Her theory, or rather her temperament (for it is to her temperament that the theory imagined for her by the ingenious librettists is due), seems to place her at an advantage in her dealings with men. But though the love she feels is of the kind which Stendhal in his celebrated treatise calls "*amour-goût*," yet the love she inspires is that terrible "*amour-passion*" which may cause heroic actions and also great crimes.

As for her external characteristics, they are completely in harmony with her mental and moral disposition. One can guess her probable actions from her appearance and demeanour as painted by Mérimée, or—what comes to the same thing—as exhibited on the stage by Miss Minnie Hauk, whose Carmen is a perfect realisation of

Mérimée's conception, If for a moment someone should suggest that the conduct of the captivating young gipsy does not bear the stamp of the purest morality, the idea, without being objected to, need not have more attention paid to it than it deserves. She is a beautiful graceful, sympathetic sort of savage, with much that is loveable in her, or she would not inspire so much love.

In the first scene, Carmen, after singing a quaint Spanish song, which, being called "La Habanera," may possibly be of Havannese origin, retires with her lively, unbusiness-like companions to the cigar factory, stabs one of them, as already mentioned, and is forthwith taken charge of by some dragoons who are doing the duty of police. The captain orders his men to fasten her hands together. But as she has already enchained the heart of the soldier appointed to watch her, this precaution avails nothing. In the prettiest manner possible, she makes José, the dragoon in question, admit that he loves her, sings him a very engaging air in the Spanish style, then appeals to him to set her free. Without much hesitation he consents. But when the guard appears in order to take her off to prison she re-assumes the handcuffs, and then slipping them off, as if by accident, disappears as the curtain falls on a very lively first act.

The second act, however, is still livelier. Here the scene is laid in a tavern, where gipsies are singing, dancing, and playing the guitar, while officers are listening, applauding, and making love to them. Carmen will have nothing to say to anyone. She is thinking of José, who, for allowing her to escape, has had to undergo two months' imprisonment. Suddenly José appears. Carmen sings to him, when all at once as she sings, and in harmony with her song, the recall is heard. The unfortunate dragoon, not yet altogether demoralised, thinks of going back to the barracks; but when Carmen tells him tauntingly to do so, and hints that he had better leave her altogether, he resolves to stay. For the attentions paid to her by José's officers she cares but little; and she equally rejects (though not so unequivocally as Don José, had he known of the circumstance, might have desired) the advances made to her by a famous bull-fighter, named Escamillo, who tries to please her by singing in a loud voice a very spirited tune which reminds one of the frequently Spanish Verdi. Carmen still loves no one but José, and if José does not love her in return so much the worse for him. But José is deeply enamoured of her, and agrees to go with her to the mountains, and there lead the life of a smuggler.

In his mountain retreat, Don José is visited by a virtuous peasant-girl, Michaela by name; a sort of Alice, who comes to him with news of his mother, and urges him in flowing and melodious strains to quit the gipsies and return to his home, when all will be forgotten. José does not quite see the force of these arguments, until at last, his mother being on the point of death, he goes back to his family.

Carmen, meanwhile, has become tired of a man who is neither good nor bad, and on his departure takes up with the bold bull-fighter. This occurs at the end of the third act. At the beginning of the fourth José re-appears, and is now ready to follow Carmen to the uttermost ends of the earth. But Carmen no longer loves him, and she tells him so. A bull-fight, moreover, is taking place, and when the air of the bull-fighter is shouted forth from the arena, José sees that this song fills Carmen's heart with joy. Thereupon he stabs her, calling her his "adored Carmen"; and when the victorious Escamillo appears to receive her congratulations and embrace her, she is dead.

*Carmen* is a stirring opera, full of movement and variety, for which a long life and a merry one might, from the first, have been safely predicted. The score would perhaps have been none the worse for a little more music of the cantalule style. But the wayward impetuous heroine is not the sort of young lady whom one can fancy singing scenas in set form, with introductory recitative, andante and cabaletta; and the work as it stands is doubtless what the composer as well as the author intended it to be. By its style it neither belongs to musical comedy nor to opéra bouffe. But it reminds one more of *La Périchole* than of the *Marriage of Figaro;* and a clever actress with a nice voice and some power of singing with expression, while quite unable to take the part of Susanna or of the Countess, might achieve a certain success as Carmen. If Miss Hauk sang less admirably than she, in fact, does, her impersonation of the passionate, capricious, fascinating and most original gipsy would reconcile her audience to any such deficiency, or rather would render them unable to perceive it. She enters into the spirit of the character, lives it, and never looks anything else but Carmen, from Carmen's entry until her tragic end. Her looks, gestures, walk, general air, and demeanour, all belong to one another and to the part; and as Carmen is the life and soul of the opera, it was, above all, to Miss Minnie Hauk's performance that the success of this very Spanish, very Bohemian work was in the first instance due.

## CHAPTER XXXII.

#### THE EVER-POPULAR MARTHA.

COUNT FREDERICK VON FLOTOW was born at Mecklenburg in 1812. Invited by his father to choose between arms and diplomacy, he returned an evasive answer and became a composer. He studied at Paris under Reicha, and was scarcely of age when he produced *Peter and Catherine*, which was executed by a company of amateurs at the Hôtel Castellan. After trying his hand once or twice more upon amateurs, he felt almost ready to meet the public at an open theatre. By way of transition, however, he had recourse to the Poles, whose misfortunes have been made the pretext of so many performances, and in 1840 brought out an opera called *La Duchess de Guise*, which was played at the Salle Ventadour for the benefit of the Polish exiles. *Le*

*Naufrage de la Méduse*—known in Germany as *Die Matrosen—Le Forestier*, and *L'Esclave de Camoens*, were Herr von Flotow's next works; all of which were produced at Paris, the first at the Théâtre de la Renaissance, the two latter at the Opéra Comique. *Stradella*, brought out at Hamburg in 1844, was Flotow's first thoroughly successful opera. It was played throughout Germany, and at Schwerin had the good fortune to please the Duke of Mecklenburg, who forthwith gave the composer the title of Chamberlain and afterwards appointed him Director of his Court Concerts. *Stradella* was succeeded by *L'Ame en Peine*, given for the first time at the French Opera in 1846, and subsequently performed in England at the Princess's Theatre under the title of *Leoline*. Since 1846 Flotow has produced nothing but *Martha;* but he has produced, and reproduced that work in so many forms, that it must have afforded him a good deal of occupation. Already in 1843 he had joined MM. Burgmuller and Deldevez in composing the music of a ballet called *Lady Henriette*. On the subject of the ballet a German libretto was written, which Flotow set to music and entitled *Martha*. He had adorned his work by introducing into the principal situation the beautiful national air known as "The last Rose of Summer"; and with this rose in his button-hole, the chamberlain of the Duke of Mecklenburg will no doubt go—at least, a little way—down to posterity. In arranging *Martha* for the

Italian stage the composer added two new airs, one for the contralto, the other for the baritone; and he made some further change in re-arranging it for the Théâtre Lyrique where, thanks in a great measure to Mdme. Nilsson's charming impersonation of the heroine, it was represented upwards of three hundred nights. In the German piece the action takes place in the reign of Queen Anne. The author of the Italian version has, for some inscrutable reason, gone back to the 15th century. Thus the characters in the Italian *Martha* wear, or ought to wear, mediæval dresses; though the heroine invariably attires herself according to the latest fashions, while Nancy puts on any riding habit that may happen to please her. In the French version the librettist has made the incidents of the drama occur almost in the present day. He no doubt believes, like M. Félix Clément, that statute fairs are really held at Richmond, and that "Tristan de Mickleford," is a probable sort of name for an English nobleman.

A work is sometimes more successful than its author, and *Martha* has certainly distanced Herr von Flotow in the race for popularity. We have not heard whether Herr von Flotow has been all round the world, but *Martha* has. It has, at least, been to every part of the civilized globe; and it might almost be said that where *Martha* is un-unknown civilization ceases. If this idea should ever occur to the composer and cause him undue elation, he can at once set himself to rights by reflecting that, after all, *Martha* has not been played so often nor in so many places as *Orphée aux Enfers*. To be sure, *Martha* is an opera, a *bonâ-fide* "work in music," whereas *Orphée* is only a piece of musical buffoonery; and it would be unfair to place such a graceful writer as Flotow on a level with Offenbach. Let us merely say, then, that *Martha* has had wonderful luck. What a *bonne fortune* for the work to have inspired such a singer as the late Mdme. Bosio with a liking for it, and, after her, two such singers as Mdme. Adelina Patti at the Royal Italian Opera and Mdme. Christine Nilsson at the Théâtre Lyrique. Herr von Flotow is to be pitied if he has not heard both these vocalists in his work. Hearing either it could never occur to him that the music of the principal part was pretty but trivial. He would think it charming from beginning to end, and through it the entire opera. Nor in the opinion of the great majority of opera-goers would he be far wrong.

The opera of *Martha* served to exhibit Mdme. Nilsson in a new character. This delightful vocalist soon ingratiated herself with the London public; soon came to be welcomed, the moment she appeared on the stage, with such applause as is reserved for special favourites only. A homely moralist has said that we should judge of our friends not so much by the impression they produce while they are with us, as by the impression we retain of them after they have left us. The moralist was quite right; and if he could only have heard Mdme. Nilsson, would have had the highest opinion of her, whose tones remain in the minds of her audience long after she has ceased to sing. She charms the public into subjection; exercising the same commanding influence over that not always tractable brute, that Una exercised over the lion. *Martha* is not a very significant opera; but it contains much lively and some graceful music, and not one single piece that can be called dull. It has been described as "a polka in three acts," and it has been said that the only true melody in the work is the borrowed one of "The last Rose of Summer." It is true that its choruses and concerted pieces are not above the level of dance music; and it is also true that "The last Rose of Summer" gives the opera a kind of beauty which would otherwise be wanting to it altogether. Flotow, however, when he appropriates an air knows how to turn it to account. The Irish melody is again and again introduced; and despise the unpretentious little opera if you will, the scent of the Last Rose " will cling to it still."

In Mdme. Nilsson's simple, unaffected, and charmingly expressive mode of singing this melody, lies the secret of *Martha's* success.

*Martha* is known to be Flotow's masterpiece. But as Flotow is not a great master his *capo d'opera* can only be so considered when weighed in the balance against his other works, *Stradella*, *L'Ame en Peine*, &c. It has already been pointed out that the little opera of

*Martha* as it now stands seems to have been the work of the composer's whole life. In Italianising the German opera based on the French ballet of *La Foire de Richmond*, he replaced the spoken dialogue by recitative, wrote a new air for the absurdly-named Plunkett, and a whole scene for " Lady Nancy."

The long-continued and apparently inexhaustible success of *Martha* is probably due in some measure to the effective distribution of music among the four leading personages. Four really good parts is about the maximum number that an opera can be made to contain, if each personage is to be suitably provided with solo airs, and if the voices are to be combined in duets, trios, and quartets, so that not one of them may for any length of time be left in the background. Nancy in *Martha* is not quite so interesting a character as her friend and patroness, the high-born Henrietta. But Nancy has a scena—composed for the late Mdme. Nantier-Didiée when the opera was first brought out in its Italianised form —which any first mezzo-soprano or contralto might be proud to have the opportunity of singing. Nancy, too, is constantly on the stage, and takes part in a large number of concerted pieces. In the music of this well-provided part the beautiful voice of the perfectly-singing Mdme. Trebelli is heard to excellent effect.

# CHAPTER XXXIII.

### AN OPERATIC CENTENARY.

It is to be regretted that no European character was given to the fêtes by which the Scala Opera House of Milan commemorated, in 1876, the hundredth anniversary of its establishment. If this theatre has really existed as a building for one hundred years, it may probably be regarded as by far the oldest edifice of the kind now standing. Our own large theatres— as Covent Garden, Drury Lane, Her Majesty's Theatre— have all been destroyed by fire once or twice; the company of the French Grand Opera has been burnt out no fewer than three times; and if the Scala Theatre has hitherto escaped the flames, the Italians should ask themselves whether they are acting wisely in publicly, ostentatiously, and in the face of the whole world, congratulating themselves on their good luck. When Fontenelle was approaching his own personal centenary, and friends complimented him on having attained so advanced an age, he used suddenly and mysteriously to impose silence upon them, observing that the Fates had forgotten him, and that it was desirable to keep the fact of his continued existence a secret. So with La Scala. If it has never yet been burned down, its time must now be at hand; and it is strange that believers in chance and in the evil eye, like the Italians, should venture to boast of the immunity this famous operatic theatre has hitherto enjoyed from the fate usually shared by opera-houses. Centenaries, however, are in fashion; and the Scala Festival would have been really interesting if it could have been made to include a few, not merely of the operas performed a century ago at the Scala Theatre, but specimens also of such works as were being played at the time in Italy, France, Germany, England, and Russia; for, strange as it may seem, Russia, in the year 1778, had an Italian opera to which a great Italian composer was attached. If, however, one hundred years ago Paisiello was composing for the Empress Catherine that first musical version of the *Barber of Seville*, which a generation or so later was to be entirely eclipsed by Rossini's immortal work on the same subject, it may be remembered that in our own time the Khedive of Egypt maintained an Italian Opera at Cairo, where as good singers were engaged as ever visited St. Petersburg in

1778, and for which the greatest Italian composer of our time is known to have written one of his finest works. Count Joseph de Maistre said that civilization ceased where the study of the Latin language ceased; and it may perhaps be held that the commencement of a certain sort of civilization is marked by the introduction of Italian opera. Italian opera is a product which has hitherto flourished almost exclusively under autocracies and despotisms. The petty potentates of Germany have often kept up excellent opera-houses; but one looks in vain for operatic theatres, or, indeed, theatres of any kind, in Switzerland. Even in the United States opera has never been permanently established; and in spite of occasional appearances to the contrary, Stendhal's prophecy that America, with all its liberty and all its commercial greatness, would never furnish a new home to the lyrical drama, has not hitherto been falsified.

Prussia in 1778—at that time a pure despotism, ruled as to its entire population, like Frederick's own orchestra, with the stick—paid more attention to operatic matters, though infinitely less to music as an art, than it does now. The king's knowledge of music seems to have been about equal to his genius for poetry; and as Voltaire, after he had quarrelled with Frederick, sneered at his Majesty's French verses, so musicians who had been employed in the royal band, and who had given the royal bandmaster private lessons, informed the world, after leaving the king's service, how indifferently his

Majesty played the flute. Sovereigns are perhaps more modest now. In any case they possess better taste than distinguished some members of their order towards the end of the last century. Joseph II. had the audacity to tell Mozart that in his *Marriage of Figaro* there were too many notes, which drew from the justly-offended composer the reply that it contained " precisely the right number." Frederick the Great, although barely able to read a score, used to conduct the orchestral execution of important works, and combining the functions of operatic manager with those of musical director, engaged his own artists, and when, whether from indisposition or from pure caprice, they declared themselves unable to sing, sent soldiers to arrest them and bring them by force to the theatre. The Empress Catherine, with all her faults, had too much womanly feeling and too much tact to impose commands or even counsels upon Paisiello, Cimarosa, and other musical celebrities whom she invited to her Court. Indeed, on one occasion when the Russian Empress made some observations to the famous Gabrielli, on the subject of the terms demanded by that primâ donna, pointing out to her that she was asking a higher salary than any Russian field-marshal received, the Italian vocalist is said to have replied that she "had better get her field-marshals to sing." No singer, however eminent, would have ventured to make such a remark to Frederick, who rather piqued himself on his ability to keep vocalists in their proper place. This, as no less an authority than Dr. Burney has informed us, he was able to do in more than one sense of the words. The king officiated when Dr. Burney was at Berlin, just a hundred years ago, as general conductor, " standing in the pit behind the *chef d'orchestre,* so as to have a view of the score, and drilling his musical troupe in true military fashion." If any mistake was committed on the stage or in the orchestra the king stopped the offender and admonished him; while if he ventured to alter a single passage in his part, the king " severely reprimanded him and ordered him to keep to the notes written by the composer."

Italy, however, a hundred years ago, was still the nursery of music. Her composers, as represented by Paisiello, Cimarosa, Guglielmo, Peroglese, and Piccini, visited the chief European capitals as those capitals are visited in the present day by the great Italian singers. Not that in the last century Italian singers abstained from making tours. But Italy now sends out singers alone, whereas a hundred years ago every country in Europe looked to Italy, not only for singers but also for composers, who travelled to the principal courts and the most celebrated opera-houses to superintend the performance of their own works. The Italian opera of those days was scarcely a more intellectual entertainment than it is now. So at least it would seem from an account of the operatic performances of his time left by an ingenious Italian author who was contemporary with Cimarosa and Paisiello. The operatic dramatist or librettist had already learnt not to allow himself to be hampered by conditions of time, place, unity, or probability. The ordinary incidents and scenes of the eighteenth-century librettist were "dungeons, daggers, poison, boar-hunts, earthquakes, sacrifices, madness, and so on." If husband and wife were discovered in prison, and one of them had to be led away to die, it was indispensable that the other should remain to sing an air, which, says the satirical historian of opera in the eighteenth century, "should be to lively words, so as to relieve the feelings of the audience, and make them understand the whole affair is a joke." It was further a rule in the *ars operatica* of that day, that "if two of the characters made love or plotted a conspiracy, they should always do so in the presence of servants and attendants." The prima donna of a hundred years since was, like our own cherished heroines of the soprano voice, in the habit of exacting remunerations which, though trifling compared with those of the present day, were already thought exorbitant. In the year 1778, as in 1878, the higher a prima donna could "rise in the scale the surer she was of having the principal parts allotted to her." The most backward country in Europe with regard to opera towards the end of the eighteenth century, and until after the French Revolution, was France; which half a century ago when

Rossini, Bellini, Donizetti, Meyerbeer, Auber, were all writing or about to write for Paris, was the first operatic country in the world. If the directors of La Scala had taken note, as they ought to have done, of opera as it existed in France just one hundred years ago, they would probably have presented a specimen scene from one of Gluck's operas and another specimen scene—a concerted finale, for instance—from an opera by Piccinni. The Italian capitals have never been the scene of those insane fends between rival composers and rival singers which London and Paris have time after time witnessed. Of all the fights between bodies of musical partizans— such as were waged by the admirers of Buononcini against those of Handel; by the adorers of Faustina against the worshippers of Cuzzoni; by the Maratistes, or enthusiasts on behalf of Madame Mara, against the Todistes, or fanatics in the cause of Madame Todi; and finally by the Gluckists against the Piccinnists—the contest carried on by these two latter parties was the most interesting because the most literary. The Handel-Buononcini disputes are remembered in literature by one famous epigram, of which the authorship is disputed, and by a few papers in the *Spectator*. The quarrel, however, between the Gluckists and the Piccinnists, took the form not only of theatrical rows, but also, and above all, of written controversy, in which most of the great French writers of the latter years of the eighteenth century engaged. Meanwhile, like so many rival singers whose respective admirers seem bent on tearing one another to pieces, the two rival composers were very good friends, and joined in expressing their astonishment that the French wanted songs written for them and yet could not sing.

In England, thanks especially to the intelligent patronage which Handel on his first arrival in this country had received at the hands of the aristocracy, the Italian opera, throughout the eighteenth century, was in a much more prosperous condition than in France, or, indeed, any part of Europe except Italy itself. A hundred years ago, as now, the best operas could be heard in London, executed by the best vocalists of the day. The artists—to give singers the name which they themselves have of late years assumed—did not demand such high salaries a hundred years ago as they do now, and the public paid less money for the privilege of hearing them. Stalls had not yet been invented; and places in the pit, which was then a fashionable resort, were only charged at half-a-guinea, or a smaller sum if taken beforehand. Subscribers unable to be present at a performance which they were entitled to attend, did not at that time let their boxes, but placed them freely at the disposal of friends. At the end of the performance the company in the pit and boxes used to meet in the coffee-room of the theatre, which, as the late Lord Mount-Edgcumb says in his memoirs, was "the best assembly in London." The character of operatic entertainments, considered in reference to the class of persons attending them, has doubtless undergone a change in every country. The directors, however, of La Scala, can only be expected in their centennial celebration to occupy themselves with changes of an artistic kind. The singers would be sorry indeed to see a full re-establishment of the operatic system of a century ago, and if they consented on one special occasion to appear in operas a hundred years old, we may be sure that they did so only on condition of being remunerated at current rates.

## CHAPTER XXXIV.

### DECLINE AND FALL OF THE TENOR.

SINCE the retirement of Signor Mario, not one of the numerous tenors who, season after season, have appeared at our opera-houses, has made sufficient mark to cause inquiries as to his whereabouts during the eight autumn and winter months which, in the eyes of operatic *habitués*, constitute the dull period of the year. We are all glad to hear from time to time that M. Faure is well, and that lucrative engagements have been offered to him. There may be some, too, who take an interest in the proceedings of Signor Graziani between the July of one year and the April of the following year. Among tenors—fallen as tenors are from their former "high estate"—Signor Nicolini has, undoubtedly, a certain number of admirers, though not enough to form a class worth the attention of the correspondents who keep us so well informed as to the doings of our most eminent soprani—light, medium, and robust. From a long list of basses—serious and comic—many good names could, no doubt, be cited; but not one that would carry with it anything like the weight which once attached to the illustrious name of Lablache. It may be said that Lablaches, Tamburinis, Marios, and Rubinis are not all to be expected at the same time. But it is a fact that those very artists, each in his own walk a type of excellence, did for many years form part of the same company; that in those days operatic troupes did not owe whatever importance they might possess to the prima donna alone; in a word, that operas were represented with more completeness—at least, as regards to vocalization—than can be secured for them now. Our orchestral resources have greatly increased during the past five-and-twenty or thirty years, and it would be impossible in the present day to assume, as in the year 1846, when the great secession from Her Majesty's Theatre took place, that only one operatic band of fine quality could be maintained in London. It is undeniable, too, that operatic vocalists abound, and that their numbers, counting only those of more than average merit, are constantly increasing. Yet if all Mr. Gye's and all Mr. Mapleson's singers were put together, it would be impossible to select from among them such a quartet as that for which Bellini composed *I Puritani* (Grisi, Rubini, Tamburini, Lablache), or that almost identical one (with Mario in the place of Rubini) for which, some years later, Donizetti composed *Don Pasquale.*

Lablache is one of the striking figures in modern operatic history; and his *Don Pasquale,* his Bartolo in the *Barber of Seville,* his Leporello in *Don Giovanni,* made a lasting impression on those who saw and heard him in those parts. As for Tamburini, is it not written in the annals of Her Majesty's Theatre that a violent demonstration was once made by the aristocratic *habitués* of that establishment, because, at the beginning of the season, when it was held that Tamburini should have been engaged, Coletti was substituted for him? We have Mr. Carlyle's authority for saying that Signor Coletti was a very superior person; though it appeared to this strange and not too sympathetic critic, that a baritone he chanced to hear on the occasion of his first and last visit to the opera, would have done well to adopt some profession more useful to the world than that of a dramatic vocalist. In any case, Signor Coletti was a singer of considerable reputation, which did not prevent his being held of no importance whatever, compared with the admired Tamburini. The remarkable thing, however, in the matter is not that one of two baritones should have been thought better than the other, but that the question of their respective merits should have been thought worth quarrelling about. Who, in the present day, can imagine a species of riot got up for the sake of Signor Graziani or M. Faure? Yet the Tamburini-Coletti disturbance attracted the attention of all London, and was thought sufficiently important to be made the subject of an Ingoldsby Legend.

If, in spite of the increased favour with which opera is generally regarded, we possess few eminent basses, and can name no baritones whose conflicting claims to supremacy would be likely to cause popular commotion, the case of the tenors is still more deplorable. Once the spoilt children of the lyric drama, these unhappy vocalists are now of no account whatever. Their chief airs, their final scenes, are either omitted by the conductor, or, worse still, are neglected by the public. When, as they frequently do, they commit suicide on the stage, they die, if not in silence, at least in solitude. There was a time when playgoers would no more have quitted a representation of *Lucia* without waiting for the dying strains of the hero, than it would now take its departure before the delirium of the heroine has set in. At present the moonlit cemetery has hardly been "discovered," the four horns have only just had time to prove their inability to play the few bars assigned to them, when the majority of the audience rise to depart; and long before Edgardo expires, that vacuum has been created in the audience department which nature and tenors equally abhor. If Gennaro's self-inflicted death is still witnessed by an unwilling, or at least by an unenthusiastic public, it must be remembered that in this instance the tenor scene is followed by a scene for the prima donna; and the prima donna is not only as great a favourite as ever, but is often the only member of an operatic cast to whom every sort of favour is shown. For her exclusively is reserved the admiration which was formerly shared by the prima donna, contralto, tenor, baritone, and bass.

In these matters there is no dictating to the public, but whatever the fact may signify, a fact it is that whereas Mdme. Patti, Mdme. Nilsson, Mdme. Albani, and Mdme. Gerster are sought for in all countries, and travel, in the character of stars, to the most distant lands, no one in any part of the world seems to care much for the voice of any tenor, baritone, or bass now on the stage. Thus the prima donna is assuming more and more every day the position which, immediately before the decline and fall of the ballet, was held in a sister art (though doubtless an inferior one) by the *première danseuse*. Tenor, baritone, and bass are still desirable and almost necessary, though, perhaps, not absolutely indispensable, for her complete success. But she, her singing, her acting, and, in some measure, her personal appearance, seems to be accepted as the chief end and object of operatic performances; and insensibly the delusion is gaining ground that instead of the prima donna having been educated to sing in operas, operas have been composed for prima donnas to sing in.

## CHAPTER XXXV.

### EXTINCTION OF THE BALLET.

THE world is growing old, or at least stiff, the times are out of joint, and Europe has almost given up dancing. Such is the complaint made by Mdlle. Sangalli in a work we have not read, but which is devoted to the celebration of the art she practises so well, and to lamentations over its decay. As a matter of fact, the ballet in England is a thing of the past. Many opera-goers of the present time have never seen a ballet-dancer of the highest merit. The older *habitués* recollect Taglioni and Fanny Ellsler. Plenty of middle-aged amateurs have seen, and, having seen, must necessarily have applauded, Carlotti Grisi; while younger men will certainly not have forgotten Rosati, whom we take to have been the last of the *ballerine*. Since Rosati, no *danseuse* of real eminence has appeared in London.

The glories of the ballet have almost died out on the Parisian stage. The army of dancers included in the *corps de ballet* of the Berlin opera-house is chiefly remarkable for its numbers; and we shall probably have to go as far as St. Petersburg to discover a *première danseuse* worthy in some measure to be compared with those of twenty and twenty-five years ago.

Meanwhile, dancing has not disappeared from our lyrical theatres. Years have passed since a regular ballet was represented at a London opera-house. *Divertissements* are still maintained as adjuncts to operas, and often amid the *coryphées* a third-rate dancer will appear in the character of *première danseuse*; but the ballet of Laporte's and Lumley's time is seen no more. So entirely, indeed, has it disappeared, that it becomes interesting to speculate as to whether this particular form of dramatic art can have ceased finally to exist. That seems impossible. *La Sylphide*, with Taglioni, *Esmeralda* with Carlotta Grisi, would still prove attractive if a Taglioni or a Carlotta Grisi could be found. But as a combat must cease when there are no more combatants, so ballet must come to an end when there are no more ballet dancers; and it is precisely because no *ballerina* is forthcoming of such remarkable excellence as belongs to some of our prime donne, that the mimetic drama with solo dances, and dances for two, three, or more personages in the principal situations, has, for a time at least, disappeared—and that at a time when the lyrical drama, with airs and concerted pieces, is more flourishing than ever. Without entertaining any very fanatical admiration for the ballet, we think, with Mdlle. Sangalli, that, like every other species of art, it should, if presented at all, be presented in perfection. The Royal Italian Opera, since its foundation, nearly thirty years ago, has never been celebrated for its ballets. It, indeed, owes its origin, at least in part, to the undue attention which the ballet had for years past received at Her Majesty's Theatre. Under Mr. Lumley's management, ballet, from being an inferior part in the ordinary operatic entertainment, was promoted to the first place; and operas of importance were ruthlessly cut down so that sufficient time might remain for the performance of long ballets. Singing was so systematically sacrificed to dancing, that it was scarcely possible to hear an opera of even the most modest dimensions in its entirety. Of grand operas there could, of course, be no question. If fragments of *Robert le Diable* were sometimes given, the most important feature in the shapeless jumble was the incantation scene with its brilliant dancing part for the abbess. When *Don Giovanni* was played, special attention was called to the fact that the *minuet* and *gavotte* in the ball scene would be executed by such and such dancers; and it happened more than once that in the cast of Mozart's greatest opera the principal performers were Ellsler and Cerito.

The most attractive operatic artists of the present day are the light *soprani* whom the various singing schools of the Continent produce in remarkable numbers. Formerly, however, it was not lightness of voice, but lightness of leg that ensured celebrity on the boards of our lyrical theatres. Far more valuable than the high stacatto notes, which excite such raptures on the part of modern *habitués*, were those *pirouettes*, *pointes*, and various steps of which the very names, if not absolutely forgotten, have at least ceased to convey any definite meaning. The *fanatico per la musica* has long been a recognized personage in Italy, and, indeed, in every other country; but it may be doubted whether such fanaticism was ever caused by music as was excited by dancing in that not very distant period when a London manager thought it worth while to engage, at one and the same time, four principal dancers, each as renowned in her own art as at the present time are Mdme. Patti and Mdme. Nilsson, Mdme. Gerster and Mdme. Albani in theirs. It was held, we believe, by Mr. Lumley himself, that the decay of the ballet in England might be dated from the days of that *Pas de Quatre* which he expended so much diplomatic talent in organizing. For the great dancers had their little vanities, and were troubled by questions of precedence, even as great singers are said to be in the present day; and it was the etiquette of the ballet that, in a combined step, the most important dancer who took part in it should appear last, and the least important first. Who, then, in the *Pas de Quatre*, should make the first entry or dance the first solo? It seemed impossible to decide this all-important point, when suddenly the ingenious manager suggested that the youngest should begin. This novel principle in stage-dancing having been accepted—probably through the suddenness with which it had been proclaimed—a new competition arose; and ultimately by balancing the claims of youth against those of talent, and the claims of talent against those of youth, it was found possible to effect a happy compromise. The *Pas de Quatre* was arranged; Carlotta Grisi and Cerito, Rosati and Lucille Grahn danced together, and the ballet was destroyed. United, they attracted all London. Singly, no one cared to see them; and as the *Pas de Quatre*, with four such "first ladies" in the quartet, could not be presented perpetually, but only once in a way as a special attraction, the public taste for ballet-dancing quickly diminished and soon became extinct. M. Lumley's triumph in the art of management proved one of those devices which, as Macbeth says,

> "being taught, return
> To plague the inventor."

A great deal might be written in favour of ballet-dancing. Much also might be said against it, and we should be very sorry to see it restored to the position of importance which it occupied at our operatic theatres in the days of Mr. Lumley and of the *Pas de Quatre*.

Nor can it be revived by mere literary advocacy. Letterpress is powerless in the matter; and if Mdlle. Sangalli wishes to see the ballet spring into new life, she must trust not to her pen, but to her legs and feet. She cannot write it, but she might possibly dance it into favour even in England, the least ballet-dancing country in the world. It is recorded of the first of the Vestrises—"the founder of the Vestris family," to adopt his own language—that when his son Auguste had offended the Parisian public, and felt called upon to make a public apology for his fault, he would not allow the young man to make a speech. "My son is no orator," he called out to the audience. Then turning to Auguste, he added, "Address them in your own manner; dance." Mdlle. Sangalli is not in the same position as Vestris the second; for while she has delighted thousands she has never given offence to anyone. But to her also one may say, "Address them in your own manner; dance." We are assured that Mdme. Sangalli's book is excellent. But her true eloquence is that of the leg. Let her speak the language of her art, and the public will listen to her with its eyes. The ballet has given us some graceful music, some tolerable subjects for lithographs and engravings; but with the exception of Heine's *Dr. Faust,* it has no literature.

## CHAPTER XXXVI.

### OPERATIC MANAGEMENT.

M. ARSÈNE HOUSSAYE, who had been for many years free from the cares of management, was persuaded by officious friends to undertake them anew. These gentlemen had probably free admissions in view, or believed that, from gratitude to them for their counsels, the future *impresario* would introduce them behind the scenes. In any case, they prevailed upon the ex-manager of the Théâtre Français to solicit the direction of a new lyrical theatre. M. Houssaye, as the result perhaps of a trying career, had become somewhat infirm of purpose, and no sooner had he applied for the theatre, the management of which he had been asked to undertake, than he repented of his rash act. The Minister of Fine Arts had received M. Arsène Houssaye's proposition with only too much favour. He procured the grant of the indispensable subvention, and had already proposed to sign the deed of concession, when the applicant himself called upon him to stop. M. Houssaye required time to reflect before accepting the doubtful benefit, coupled with certain responsibility, which it was proposed to confer upon him.

The favoured competitor had been chosen from among twenty candidates, all anxious to undertake the regeneration of French music. Some were bent on liberating it from the pressure of the "new school" with its imitations of Wagner. Others meant, above all, to free it from the corruption of opéra-bouffe. In any case, the work to be done was to be confided to M. Houssaye, who declined, however, to undertake it until he should have fairly considered the advantages and disadvantages of doing so.

Although M. Houssaye had not yet accepted the post offered to him, and, as a matter of fact, had formally refused to sign the agreement on the subject, the evening papers announced, the very day of his interview with the Minister, that he was about to become the director of a new operatic establishment. Early the next morning four *Dames de la Halle* called upon him, according to the custom in such cases, with enough bouquets of roses to fill a small cart—a compliment which the supposed new manager was obliged to pay for in gold. An hour or two afterwards a regiment of chorus-singers arrived, followed by light and dramatic soprani; tenors, florid and robust; baritones, basses, and solo singers of every description. Next came a composer with the full score of an opéra-bouffe: "the only style"—it was his own—"likely to succeed." This enterprising genius was followed by a serious composer with a still fuller score, who believed in nothing but "continuous melody" and endless recitative. The Wagnerite was succeeded by a master who wished to give new life to opéra-comique, which he audaciously proposed to render amusing, as in the days of Scribe and Auber. The future *impresario* was not required to accept all or any of the works brought to him without at least hearing them; and before the end of the day he found that he had a whole repertory of new operas on hand, not necessarily for production, but at least for consideration. Some of the composers were accompanied by singers; others, that there might be no mistake about the *tempi* or exact *nuances* of expression, offered to interpret their music themselves. Some of the lightest of the light soprani invited themselves to breakfast; and M. Houssaye's rooms, before the day was over, were full of candidates for engagements. Late in the afternoon two danseuses of unacknowledged eminence made their appearance. One was Mdlle. Azalia from Odessa, the other Mdlle. Ophelia from New York. More formidable than the artists who had preceded them, they were the bearers of regular letters of introduction; and

M. Houssaye relates, somewhat ungallantly, how, as he opened their notes of recommendation, he started awe-stricken at these "monsters besmeared with pearl powder."

During the next few days every five minutes brought a ring at the bell. In two days thirteen doctors called to beg the appointment of physician to the new theatre. M. Houssaye asked the thirteenth whether he thought it was the director's intention to engage none but invalids. Meanwhile, he did not content himself with passively undergoing the inflictions to which he was compelled to submit. He took active steps towards forming an efficient troop, and, first of all, engaged the services of a numerous and exceptionally beautiful *corps de ballet*, chosen from among the pupils of the Conservatoire. There was still some little difficulty about the selection of a theatre suitable for the production of works of all kinds. There was also a difficulty about the works themselves; and it is evident from M. Houssaye's own admission that he had no clear idea what to play. At one time he thought of Gluck's *Armida*, in which the principal part was to be taken by a "Russian Princess." Then he determined to put his trust in some new work written specially for the theatre. "But whose work," he asked himself, "should he take, and who should appear in it?"

That portion of M. Houssaye's epistle in which he speaks of the difficulty of deciding what sort of opera to bring out is very weak, and would certainly excite the derision of most managers. "It is so difficult," says this ingenious writer, but incompetent *impresario*, "to write a good opera, and so easy to write a bad one." "Besides," he continues, "when a good opera is really found, it is difficult to ensure its success, especially as public taste leans just now not towards opera but towards operetta." If such is really the case, why did not M. Houssaye, if he were resolved to direct an operatic theatre, determine to produce operettas? Because, in the first place, Offenbach had produced operettas in the most sumptuous style at the Gaieté, and in two years had lost one million of francs. Then it occurred to the timid speculator that Nestor Roqueplan, formerly manager of the Grand Opéra, had made a disastrous failure with a minor enterprise at the Châtelet. But what, above all, haunted him was the impossibility, real or supposed, of finding "a good opera." Some few that he heard were, he admits, suitable enough as regards music. "But what," he inquires, returning to his eternal questions, "is good music without a good libretto?" And even if the libretto as well as the music is good, you must, moreover, have good singers; and, finally, you must have "a good public, which, under present circumstances, is not to be counted on in France."

In private life it is sometimes difficult to stop a singer who has once taken upon himself the duty of "obliging" the company with a series of songs. It may be possible to engage him in conversation while another vocalist is smuggled to the piano in his place and behind his back. If the worst comes to the worst, he may be asked to stop. If things go beyond the worst, thus reaching that point outside the region of mere badness at which, according to the proverb, "they must mend," the police may be called in, and he may be given in charge as a disorderly person and the creator of a nuisance. But there is no way of dealing, otherwise than by persuasion, with the vocalist who sternly refuses to open his mouth for artistic purposes. Men, and even women, are familiar with all sorts of methods by which a silent person may be made to talk, shout, and, if need be, swear. No amount, however, of provocation or menace will extort a song from an unwilling voice. Nor can that end be obtained through the employment of brute force, though some may preserve a dim recollection of an opera scene in which an innocent young maiden, surprised by robbers, is compelled to sing. In the ballet of *Le Diable à Quatre*, too, the tyrannical basket-maker forces his pretty but mutinous young wife to dance by threatening her with a stick; and even in real life it is quite conceivable that a woman might by such means be induced to take active steps. Bears are forced, through the agency of physical pain, to cut extraordinary capers; and bears in human form may, as if to avenge their fellow brutes, use torture in their turn, and use it with effect, if all they desire is the performance of some species of dance. It would be very difficult, however, to drive a Taglioni or a Carlotta Grisi through a *pas* against her will, and no summary process has yet been discovered by which a vocalist can, in spite of himself, be forced to sing. An attempt was made some three or four years ago at Cincinatti to extort a song from the throat of a reluctant baritone; but, although first the mildest and ultimately the harshest means were resorted to, nothing could be got out of him. The baritone was entreated personally. His friends were appealed to. At last the police were sent for, and he was given in charge. Still he would not sing. As far as that baritone was concerned, not a single sound was heard, not a solitary note; and after many fruitless endeavours to prevail upon him to break silence, the manager of the company to which the obstinate vocalist belonged felt himself bound to submit to circumstances and to his fate.

Properly understood, every story bears some kind of moral, and a short account of the disagreement between the baritone who would not sing and the manager who wished to force him to sing may prove instructive both to managers and to baritones. It appears, then, that on a certain day the *impresario* of the Cincinatti opera-house proposed to tempt the public with two distinct performances, one of which was to be given in the afternoon, the other in the evening. The director had, perhaps, a change of tenors. But he seems to have been but poorly supplied with baritones, and, as a matter of fact, the baritone, against whom the strong arm of the law was invoked, was called upon to sing twice the same day. Never had such a thing been heard of since the night when, after hearing *Il Matrimonio Segreto* for the first time, the Emperor Joseph II., delighted with the work, gave a supper to all concerned in its performance, and ordered it to be repeated. The Cincinatti director, however, was not Joseph II., and the baritone whom he required to sing twice in the same day did not feel disposed to pay him homage at the expense of his own comfort, to say nothing of his voice. The baritone, then, refused to make the two appearances, and the "spirited *impresario*," after entreating, remonstrating, and threatening, finished, as we have said, by giving him in charge of the police. It may be presumed that the baritone had already taken part in the afternoon performance, and that it was for practical disobedience in regard to the evening performance, not for theoretical disobedience in regard to either of them, that he was given into custody. He seemed doomed, in any case, to spend a certain portion of his time in a Cincinnatti lock-up; and but for the intelligence of a superior official, who happened to understand that a refusal to sing *Vi raviso* in the character of Count Rodolfo or *Il balen del suo sorriso* in that of the

Count di Luna could scarcely be an offence against the criminal law, he might have been incarcerated until the arrival of the magistrate next morning; for in such a mysterious and previously unheard-of case as that of wickedly and feloniously declining to undertake two baritone parts in one day, it can scarcely be supposed that bail would have been accepted.

The Cincinatti *impresario* probably intended to prosecute the unwilling baritone under some section of a law corresponding to our Master and Servant Act. The relations, however, between master and servant are not precisely those which exist between master and artist; and even in the case of a servant objecting to do double work it is by no means easy to see how the grievance could be remedied by the intervention of the police. The immediate object, moreover, of the director was not to get the recalcitrant singer fined so many dollars and sentenced to so many days' imprisonment for being silent, but to have him ordered there and then, by supreme authority, to put on his costume, appear on the stage, and perform his part. If, as was asserted, the baritone had broken his contract, there would, of course, have been ground for a civil action. But, apart from the question of law, by what moral or physical process did the manager think it possible that a man bent on not singing could be made to sing? "Could he," asked a writer who called attention to the case in an American journal, "have induced a policeman to drag the baritone on the stage, and to club him violently whenever his turn came to sing, it is quite possible that more or less noise would have been drawn from him. But noise is not music; though, unfortunately, the converse of the proposition is sometimes true." It seems just possible that the irritated manager, remembering that police magistrates had power under certain circumstances to punish singers, may have hastily concluded that wilful and wrongful abstention from singing might be regarded as a punishable offence. But though the singing of some noisy professional vocalists might fairly be described as a kind of nuisance committed in a licensed establishment, no such nuisance could be dealt with through the criminal law; and the generally harmless practice of *not* singing, whether in public or in private, has never been condemned even by the most sanguinary codes.

Two historical personages, however, of the first importance—Frederick the Great and Napoleon—are known to have had almost as much trouble as the Cincinatti manager himself in their endeavours to make refractory vocalists sing. Nor were these potentates always successful in their endeavours; though far from contenting themselves with the humble and quite inadequate machinery of the police, they did not scruple to have recourse to military forces. If a prima donna whom Frederick was really anxious to hear pretended to be ill, he first sent a physician to her, and if there was nothing the matter with her, caused the medical visit to be followed by a visit from a party of soldiers, who escorted or, if necessary, carried the indisposed one to the theatre at which she was required to appear. In this fashion the celebrated Mdme. Mara is said to have been borne to the Berlin opera-house on a mattress, when she refused to get up. Napoleon, more than once, put under arrest singers who did not wish to accompany him on a campaign. And when Mdme. de St. Huberti accepted an engagement in London, in lieu of the Paris engagement pressed upon her by the Emperor, orders were given—though in vain—at all the seaports to prevent her departure. Neither King nor Emperor, however, with or without the aid of soldiers, can compel singers to sing against their will. Only one cure for such unwillingness is known. It consists in offering the part of the vocalist, who, for no matter what reason, is unable to appear, to a rival vocalist of equal pretensions and of about the same degree of merit.

## CHAPTER XXXVII.

### MUSICAL AGENTS.

A QUESTION was raised a few years ago in the United States as to whether a diplomatic representative was fitly employed in negotiating theatrical engagements; and an answer was given, somewhat hastily, in the negative. Mr. Washburne, late Secretary of the American Legation at Paris, had been advertising in the "New York Clipper" for a "first-class, bare-back, male and female rider," for the "Great American Circus, Paris, France — the palace circus of the world;" and the "New York Nation" declared that, in thus constituting himself the agent of "a spirited American circus proprietor," he sank beneath the dignity of the service to which he belongs. It can be shown, however, that diplomatists have long, and almost from time immemorial, been in the habit of doing agent's work for artists and managers of good position. Operatic celebrities have been particularly favoured in this respect. A great Minister of State, Cardinal Mazarin, introduced, or aided powerfully in introducing opera into France. The engagement of Cambert as director of music at the Court of Charles II. was effected by diplomatic means. Gluck, more than a century later, was induced to visit Paris by the representations of a secretary of the French Embassy at Vienna—that du Rollet, who arranged for Gluck, on the basis of Racine's *Iphigéni*, the libretto of *Iphigénie en Aulide;* and Picinni, at the instigation of Mdme. du Barry, was secured at Paris as opposition composer through the instrumentality of Baron de Breteuil, the French Ambassador at Rome, working in co-operation with the Marquis Caraccioli, Neapolitan Ambassador at Paris.

The *New York Nation*, too, might have remembered that the great Montesquien, when he was in England, had not thought it unbecoming on his part to interest himself in the welfare of the French artists who occassionally arrived in England with recommendations addressed to him; and that the illustrious Locke did not occupy himself so exclusively with the human understanding, as to have no time to bestow on the material interests of foreign *danseuses*. Locke was not, indeed, one of those practically epicurean philosophers of whom M. Arsène Houssaye discourses so agreeably in his

"Philosophes et Comédiennes." He had no general taste, either for the public performances or for the private society of ballerine; but a certain Mdlle. Subligny, having come to him with a letter of introduction from the Abbé Dubois, he is known to have made himself useful, and therefore, no doubt, agreeable to her during her stay in England.

Some junior attaché may remind us that Locke was a metaphysician, and had nothing whatever to do with diplomacy. He had, indeed, no official connexion with foreign affairs. But Montesquieu was a person of some political importance; and he did not think it unworthy of his position to help French artists of all kinds, and, in certain cases, to bring to their performances as many of the English nobility as were willing to attend. About the same time, at the suggestion of the Regent of Orleans, a Minister of State, M. de Maurepas, made overtures to Handel in respect to a series of performances which it was proposed that his celebrated company should give at the Académie Royale of Paris. M. de Maurepas wished, like Mr. Washburne the other day, to secure for Paris the best available talent; and he looked to Handel's opera-house for singers, as M. Washburne looked to the circuses of the United States for "bare-back riders."

As regards later times, we need only consult Mr. Eber's "Seven Years of the King's Theatre" to see that, immediately after the Peace of 1815, all the offers of engagements to artists of the Paris opera were made through the medium of the English Embassy at Paris, or by special missions with which diplomatists of distinction were glad to be entrusted. The committee of noblemen who aided Mr. Ebers in his management, treated, through the English Ambassador at Paris, with the director of the Academy, or with the Minister of Fine Arts; and though they failed to secure, by these elaborate means, the services of artists who, in the present day, would be engaged by an exchange of telegrams in less than an hour, they placed on record the fact "that they had employed their influence with the English Ambassador at Paris at the commencement of the season to obtain the best artists from that city; but it appearing that the Academy was not disposed to grant *congés* for London, even to artists for whose services the Academy had no occasion, the committee had determined not to again meddle in that branch of the management."

Examples could easily be multiplied of willingness on the part of the diplomatists to act as agents, if not of spirited "circus proprietors," at least of operatic and other managers. Perhaps, indeed, it is the fact of Mr. Washburne's having exerted himself on behalf of a circus proprietor that makes his fellow-countrymen anxiously inquire whether the dignity of diplomacy has not been compromised. It has been seen that diplomatists have always been accustomed to do agent's work for singers and dancers; and there is, indeed, a certain fitness in engaging on behalf of art the friendly services of a gentleman whose allotted occupation is to watch over the preservation of peace, and to patch it up by means of negotiations and treaties on those numerous occasions when it gets broken. But Mr. Washburne does really seem to be the first member of an embassy or legation who has proclaimed himself ready to do business for an equestrian director; and it may be held that, in these as in other matters, the line must be drawn somewhere, and that, in regard to managers, it should be drawn above, and not below, the level of circus proprietors. Mr. Washburne may reply that circuses are at least as deserving of encouragement as theatres devoted to opéra-bouffe or even ballet; and that a well-conducted circus will afford better amusement than an ill-conducted opera-house. Let Mr. Washburne, moreover, quote Dr. Johnson, who, when Boswell told him somewhat timidly that he had been to see a man ride on three horses, did not reply as he did to someone else who informed him that he had been to hear a woman preach, that such performances were curious rather than edifying, and that he would as soon see "a dog walk on his hind legs." Far from treating the achievements of the equestrian with contempt, the learned doctor made answer and said: "Such a man, sir, should be encouraged, for his performances show the extent of the human powers in this one instance, and thus tend to raise our opinion of the faculties of man. He shows what may be attained by persevering application; so that every man may hope that by giving as much application, though he may perhaps never ride three horses at a time or dance upon a wire, yet he may be equally expert in whatever profession he has chosen to pursue." Mr. Washburne knows already, and his critics may be requested to take the truth to heart, that many a famous *virtuoso* does no more than is claimed, in the above passage, for the skilful circus-rider. Let Mr. Washburne, then, pursue in all tranquillity his search after the "bare-back riders" for the "Palace Circus of Paris, France." He may justify his conduct in doing so by the traditions of his profession, and by the eulogium pronounced on circus-riders by the great Dr. Johnson.

The theatrical and musical agent is not, as some vainly imagine, a product of these latter days. In M. Edouard Fournier's excellent "Ancient History of Modern Inventions and Discoveries," the honour of having originated the lucrative profession of artistic middleman is claimed for one Barthélemy Laffémas, *varlet-de-chambre du roi, natif de Beau-Semblant en Dauphiné*, and author of a work on "The means of driving away beggary, constraining the lazy, and employing the poor." The aforesaid king's "varlet" also devoted himself to promoting the cultivation of the mulberry-tree, with a view, no doubt, to silk-worms, who would have spun for him, even as the persons registering their names at his general agency were to work for his benefit. The ingenious Afémas, as to whose project for establishing agencies of various kinds M. Fournier gives us but scanty details, found a successor in a certain La Blancherie, who, about the year 1788 formed a vast plan for interchanging the industrial and artistic productions of the various nations in Europe. He even formed, in connection with his enterprise, a journal which he entitled "Correspondance Générale des Sciencs, de la Littérature et des Arts." The newspaper failed, together with the association of which it was to have been the organ. Nor is the collapse of the whole undertaking difficult to account for. It had scarcely been started when the French revolution broke out. A few years afterwards all Europe was plunged into war, and the international idea, as conceived by La Blancherie, became for the time, from the mere force of circumstances, an absurdity. The hostile relations which ensued, put a violent end to all notions of friendly reciprocity between the different countries of the civilized world. It was not until thirty or forty years after the general peace that the international idea revived. The revival may be said to have been fitly symbolized by the Hyde Park Exhibition of 1851, the first of those International Exhibitions which have since been held again and again in every capital of Europe. Impossible in La Blancherie's time, they had now been rendered possible by the invention of steam locomotion, the establishment of a vast system of railways in England and on the Continent; by the substitution of steam vessels for sailing ships between the English and Continental ports; and at the same time by a belief that the long peace which had existed with but slight interruptions since 1815, would endure almost indefinitely. In spite of a few campaigns, severe while they lasted, but rapidly brought to a close, Europe, of which not long ago wars seemed to be a normal condition, has seen but little fighting during the last twenty-four years; and La Blancherie's idea of a "General Correspondence," in regard to industrial and artistic matters, might really in the present day have a fair chance of success.

## CHAPTER XXXVIII.

### LIBRETTI.

If the Three Graces had their little rivalries on the subject of personal attractiveness, it was not to be expected that the Nine Muses, with so many claims and counter-claims to pre-eminence, would ever get on well together. Nor do the "sister arts," as poetry, painting and sculpture, architecture, music, and dancing are sometimes called, form a very happy family. The bigger sisters would willingly combine to treat with contempt the nymph of the "light fantastic toe." Sculptors and architects have always been at war; sculptors maintaining that architects are but builders of a larger growth, while architects of pretension maintain that sculptors should be merely the decorators of their edifices, putting in this niche a statue, over that portico a group, on that wall a bas-relief, the whole under the direction and subject to the approbation of the great constructors-in-chief. Poets and composers have always agreed—we will not say like cat and dog, but at best like husband and wife. Music, "married to immortal verse," has seldom lived happily with its mate. The verse of true love does not invariably "run smooth"; or its smoothness is so unbroken that the result is a monotony of rhythm as distressing to the composer as lines in which the accent is, for musical purposes, constantly misplaced. In a word, a poem, estimable as such, may be and often is entirely unfitted for musical setting; just as a very fine fellow in his way may yet be unsuited to unmarried life. To escape the necessity of making too many concessions to the "poet," properly so called, many composers take as "words for music" such doggrel as they may, without reproach, add to, take away from, or otherwise alter, so as to bring it into conformity with their musical phrases. These are the composers who say openly that they would as soon set to music a copy of nonsense verse, or the statistics of Japan, as the finest lyric poem. One may compare them to domineering wives, who would rather have to deal with a husband of feeble temperament, ready on all points to give way to them, than with one of firm character, who, in matters of importance, would show that he had a will of his own. There are poets, on the other hand, who cannot bear that their words—of which, as they fondly hold, not one syllable ought to be lost—should be adapted as a fine flowing melody on which they will, for the most part, be gracefully borne along, but in which, also, they will run the risk here and there of being submerged. It must be admitted, too, that occasionally a poem does get lost in the music composed to it; and that even in cases where the composer is by no means superior to the poet whom he has seemingly overcome. Balfe, for instance, powerfully aided by Mr. Sims Reeves, has made the air to which he has set " Come into the garden, Maud," far more widely known than even the little poem by which it would seem to have been inspired; though, as a matter of fact, Balfe's pretty melody is borrowed, almost note for note, from Verdi's *Macbetto*. No one, in any case, would argue from the wider popularity of Balfe's music, as compared with Tennyson's words, that Balfe is the greater man of the two.

The misadventures of poetry in connection with music have been, indeed, considerable; and if now and then music has not served poetry quite well, it must be admitted that poets, temporarily disguised as librettists, have often served music very badly indeed. As with ill-assorted couples, there have been faults on both sides. But there have, at least, been examples enough of happy unions between words and music to show that music and words can, under particular conditions, be made to agree. Meyerbeer's setting of Heine's *Du Schönes Fischermädchen*, Schubert's setting of Goethe's *Erl-König*, are instances in point. Meyerbeer does not eclipse Heine, nor Schubert Goethe. In each case the composer has first borrowed inspiration from the poet, and secondly has given new force and new beauty to the poet's verses.

In spite of the many beautiful things that have been written by Milton and others on the natural alliance between music and poetry, the examples of "music married to immortal verse," have been but rare; and, as a rule, it is found that poetry and music only agree on condition, as in so many other unions, of one party to the alliance obeying the other. Our best English opera in a purely literary point of view is, beyond all question, *The Beggar's Opera;* which, notwithstanding the beauty of many of the melodies introduced, can scarcely, in spite of its name, be accepted as an operatic work. On the other hand, our most successful English operas, in a musical point of view—for instance Balfe's *Bohemian Girl* and Wallace's *Maritana*—are based on libretti whose literary value is beneath estimation. It does not, of course, follow from these examples of two kinds that a well-written opera-book must of necessity be set to poor music; nor that it is immaterial whether "words for music," provided only they be singable, testify to the wit or to the dulness of the author. But poets know very well that neither ideas nor images, nor beauties of versification, can be better appreciated through being sung to elaborate orchestral accompaniments, with repetitions of phrases and portions of phrases, instead of being read or recited. Composers, too, would rather like, as the ground-work for their music, a tolerably rhythmical poem of no particular meaning, which they could treat according to the requirements of a musical conception, demanding certain musical developments, than be tied down to the mere musical illustration of a fine poem, whose literary beauties could not be brought out unless the musician deliberately resolved, as the French say, to "efface himself." If from the lyrical poet we turn to the dramatist, the successful writer of plays will be found less willing even than his more musical brother, the song-writer, to march hand-in-hand with the operatic composer. Indeed, when opera was first introduced into England, or, at least, from the time when, under the influence of Handel, it first gained a large measure of public support, the dramatists of the day combined to attack it, and would gladly have crushed the "new-fangled" importation, which they did not altogether dislike, but which, they believed, diverted public attention from their plays. The views entertained on this subject by the generality of literary men, have been unconsciously summed up by Béranger, in his witty lament over the decline of the convivial song, eclipsed, as it undoubtedly has been, for all persons of musical taste, by airs and romances. With less truth the great chansonnier (whose lyrics, if neglected as songs, will always be remembered as perfect odes) maintained that as the old French song—love song, drinking song, or song on a subject of the day—was dying out in the presence of the drawing-room air with pianoforte accompaniment, so the drama itself was disappearing before the more dazzling but intrinsically inferior charms of the opera. The drama, like the song, concluded the genial but sometimes inaccurate satirist, was perishing, and he added :

> "Si nous t'enterrons
> Bel art dramatique,
> Pour toi nous dirons
> La messe en musique."

Men of energy and genius are almost always egotistical, in virtue of the very qualities which ensure their success; they see no salvation out of the paths they themselves are following. By a sort of courtesy to his brother poets, Béranger included the drama among the forms of art which he should like to see preserved; but in his heart he cared only for the convivial song sung to a ready-made French tune—the song which is remembered by its words, as Mozart's "Finch an dal vino," also a convivial song, is remembered exclusively by its music.

Great creators may be excused for their prejudices, when these are merely the dark shadows of a strongly-marked talent developed in one particular direction. But for the humbler critic, impelled by no overpowering bias, a similar apology can scarcely be made; and an opportunity, therefore, may here be taken of calling attention to an hypothesis put forward by Mr. Ward, author of a new and generally admirable "History of English Dramatic Literature," in explanation of the decline of our national drama, which he attributes in part at least to the introduction of opera. Considering what our national drama was in the reign of Elizabeth and until the time of the Great Rebellion—considering too, how, many masterpieces it produced under the Restoration—Mr. Ward's statement that the progress of the English drama "could not fail to be affected by the success of the foreign growth within the walls of English theatres," is to make a very serious accusation against one particular dramatic form. What Mr. Ward calls a "hybrid species," besides being attacked during the last two or three years by a certain number of musicians, has but rarely—in England never—been much esteemed by dramatists. Without entering into one of those æsthetical arguments, which are always decided according to the taste and previous conviction of each of the disputants, it can be shown by historical evidence, not indeed that opera is or is not an inferior form of the drama, but certainly that opera has never injured the drama. Opera, as an entertainment for all classes of the public, is scarcely more than 200 years old; and it is obvious, therefore, that up to the time of the Restoration, the English national drama cannot have been in any way affected by the musical drama of Italian origin, to which the name of opera was given.

The first operas produced in England were, indeed, brought out under the Commonwealth, when ordinary dramatic performances were no longer tolerated. An exception was made in favour of musical representations on the strange ground that music was an "unknown tongue," and on the perfectly sound plea that works in which music was to be the chief attraction would probably be free from such licentious dialogue as the puritanical censors of plays might without difficulty have pointed to in nearly all the dramas of the time. The operatic performances which took place in England under the Commonwealth could not have injured the national drama, since stage-plays with spoken dialogue had been absolutely suppressed; while it is quite possible that they may have helped to maintain the national taste for the theatre, which had so strongly manifested itself up to the outbreak of the civil war. When the national drama came back with the monarchy—no longer "national," it may be said, inasmuch as it was now only the drama of a class—the brilliant dramatists of those days never suspected that their success was diminished by the favour accorded to the opera. Locke, Purcell, Cambert (master of Charles II.'s band and the composer of *Ariadne*), Grabut (who set to music Dryden's *Albion* and *Albanius*) were all at this time producing operas, and other musical works more or less in operatic form. Charles II.'s court, too, is known to have patronised music, and especially French music, to a marked degree. Yet it never occurred to the dramatists of the Restoration that there was anything in the opera that could interfere with the well-being of the spoken drama. It might, perhaps, be maintained that during the early part of the eighteenth century, English opera, and French opera as naturalized in England, suffered much from the superior merit of our English comedies. In any case Wycherley, Congreve, Vanbrugh, and Farquhar never troubled themselves about the rivalry of operatic composers; nor was it discovered that the musical drama was the natural enemy of the spoken drama, until the writing of plays had fallen into the hands of Steele and Addison, neither of whom possessed dramatic genius, and of such authors as Ambrose Phillips, who, strictly speaking, was not a dramatist at all, but only a translator of French plays. Our drama was already very nearly dead when our principal comedy writer was the sentimental Steele, when Addison's *Cato* was the great tragedy of the day, and when Ambrose Phillips's adaptation of Racine's *Andromaque* was lauded as a work of high original genius. It was just at this period, however, that the great outcry was raised against opera, and above all Italian opera, then newly introduced into England.

The notion of making Handel answerable during his reign at the opera-house for the poverty of our drama as exhibited at other theatres, is indeed very far-fetched. Nor even in the present day could it be maintained that the English drama suffers to any appreciable extent from the patronage accorded by the aristocracy to Italian opera. As a matter of fact Italian operas, supported in part by subscription, are given in London every year, for a period of from three to four months; but this is not enough to account for the decline of the drama, if the drama is really in falling condition. Looking abroad, we find that periods of literary activity have also been periods of great musical activity. In Germany the time of Goethe, Schiller, of any number of philosophers, and of Heine, was also the time of Beethoven, Schubert, Weber, and Mendelssohn. In France, too, Rossini, Auber, and Meyerbeer were producing their masterpieces at the Académie, when Victor Hugo and Alexandre Dumas were writing for the *Théâtre Français*, and when Scribe's inexhaustible pen was keeping every play-house in Paris supplied with new works.

In dealing with this question of the injuriousness of opera, Mr. Ward, like a careful dialectician, keeps two arguments in reserve, so that, unable to support himself in respect to one, he may fall back on the other. If opera has not directly harmed the drama, it has at least, he says, had indirectly a bad effect upon it by encouraging dramatists to depend too much upon scenery, pageants, and other operatic devices. Yet it is difficult to see no traces of this influence in the simple dramas and mild comedies produced in the present day. But musical readers need scarcely be reminded that opera, as cultivated in England, cannot, for the best or worst reasons, have any sort of effect upon our national drama. Opera, except as an exotic, and for a few months every summer, has no existence in England ; and when opera flourishes among us as a plant of national growth, we shall assuredly find it accompanied by a vigorous national drama. Each may borrow new life from the other, but by neither will the other be overshadowed.

## CHAPTER XXXIX.

### OPERATIC AND THEATRICAL ANOMALIES.

After describing at length, and with much minuteness, the stage and scenic arrangements of the Paris opera-house, St. Preux, in *La Nouvelle Héloïse*, adds that a prodigious number of machines are employed to put the whole spectacle in motion, that he has been invited several times to examine, but that he is not curious to learn how little things are performed by great means. The little things, however, of the stage, have always possessed much interest for theatre-goers; and both in *La Nouvelle Héloïse* and in the *Musical Dictionary* Rosseau himself, in spite of St. Preux's disclaimer, devotes much attention to them. "Imagine," writes Julie's lover to the object of his affection, an " enclosure fifteen feet broad, and long in proportion; this enclosure is the theatre. On its two sides are placed at intervals screens, on which are curiously painted the objects which the scene is about to represent. At the back of the enclosure hangs a great curtain, painted in like manner, and nearly always pierced and torn, that it may represent, at a little distance, gulfs on the earth or holes in the sky. Everyone who passes behind this stage, or touches the curtain, produces a sort of earthquake, which has a double effect. The sky is made of certain bluish rags, suspended from poles or from cords, as linen may be seen hung out to dry in any washerwoman's yard. The sun, for it is seen here sometimes, is a lighted torch in a lantern. The cars of the gods and goddesses are composed of four rafters, secured and hung on a thick rope in the form of a swing or see-saw; between the rafters is a coarse plank on which the gods sit down, and in front hangs a piece of coarse cloth, well dirtied, which acts the part of clouds for the magnificent car. One may see towards the bottom of the machine, two or three foul candles badly snuffed which, whilst the greater personage dementedly presents himself singing in his see-saw, fumigate him with incense worthy of his dignity. The agitated sea is composed of long angular lanterns of cloth and blue pasteboard, strung on parallel spits, which are turned by little blackguard boys. The thunder is a heavy cart, rolled over an arch, and is not the least agreeable instrument heard at our opera. The flashes of lightning are made of pinches of resin thrown on a flame, and the thunder is a cracker at the end of a fuse. The theatre is, moreover, furnished with little square traps, which, opening at the end, announce that the demons are about to issue from their cave. When they have to rise in the air little demons of stuffed brown cloth are substituted for them, or sometimes real chimney-sweeps, who swing about suspended by ropes till they are majestically lost in the rags of which I have spoken."

Contemptible, however, as towards the eighteenth century was the character of stage decorations, both at the Paris opera and the Comédie Française—and doubtless, therefore, at nearly all the French theatres—the art of presenting threatrical pieces suitably and magnificently was not at that time by any means in its infancy. It was rather in its decadence.

During the reign of Louis XIV., the sun and moon were so well represented at the French opera that, as St. Evremond informs us, the Ambassador of Guinea, assisting at one of its performances, leaned forward in his box when those orbs appeared and religiously saluted them. In the days before Gluck and Mozart the opera at Vienna was chiefly remarkable for its size, and for the splendour of its scenery; and in a well-known description of an operatic performance at Vienna addressed by Lady Wortley Montague to Pope, we are told that "nothing of the kind was ever more magnificent," that "the decorations and habits cost the Emperor

£30,000 sterling," and that "the stage, built over a large canal, divided at the beginning of the second act into two parts, discovering the water, on which there immediately came from different parts two fleets of little gilded vessels that gave the representation of a naval fight."

When opera began to be treated seriously as a form of musical art, these spectacular varieties were abandoned. But in Rousseau's time the French opera was remarkable neither for its scenery nor for its singing. In the eighteenth century the Italians already thought more of the music of their operas than of the decorations to which, at an earlier period, they had accorded the first place. The stage effects of Servandoni and Brunio, who were at once architects, sculptors, and painters, are said to have been marvellous. Many of the Italian theatres had been constructed so as to admit of the most elaborate spectacular representations.

Mr. Edward Fournier, contrasting in his *Vieux Neuf* the poverty of our modern stage representations with the richness by which those of ancient times were distinguished, sets forth that the Farnesius Theatre at Parma, built for dramas, tournaments, and spectacles of all kinds, contained at least 50,000 spectators. Servandoni was for some time scene-painter and decorator at the opera of Paris; but a stage which, as Rousseau speaking through the medium of St. Preux has told us, was "fifteen feet broad and long in proportion," could not afford the Italian artist fit scope for his designs; and he accordingly left Paris for Dresden, where Augustus of Saxony, Mr. Carlyle's *Augustus the Strong*, enabled him to work on a grand scale, and to produce pieces in which four hundred mounted horsemen could manœuvre with ease.

It was not until three-quarters of a century later that horses, or even a single horse was destined to appear on the boards of the Paris opera-house.

To Meyerbeer, or perhaps to Meyerbeer and Scribe conjointly, belongs the doubtful honour of having introduced live horses in the musical drama. But long before Marguerite de Valois rode on the stage in the opera of *Les Huguenots*, a real horse had, in the year 1862, appeared before an ordinary theatrical audience in the character of Pegasus. As poets, according to an inhuman creed, make better verses for being kept without money, so it was held that the unhappy Pegasus ought, until the end of his performance, to be deprived of oats. The sensation of hunger gave, it is said, "a certain ardour" to the movements of the poetic courser; and the sound of corn shaken in a sieve had the effect of making the proud but famished steed neigh, snort, and stamp in a style thought worthy of Pegasus himself.

The white horse which figured in the first representation of *Les Huguenots*, at our Royal Italian Opera, without being precisely a Pegasus, had often served as hack to one of the greatest of English writers. It was, or had been, the property of Mr. Thackeray, and answered to the name of "Becky Sharp."

From the work in which Servandoni in the eighteenth century introduced at Dresden theatre 400 horsemen, to the one-horse opera of *Les Huguenots*, the step is indeed a long one. Nor does it seem to mark a progress, though, as a matter of fact, the history of the theatrical spectacle is something quite apart from that of the musical or of the poetical drama.

Opera has never profited by being represented with great scenic magnificence, nor by the attempts so frequently made to increase the interest of the work performed by introducing realistic or absolutely real accessories. The original stage Pegasus may perhaps have learnt to deport himself in a becoming manner, and it has been seen that precautions were taken towards that end. But the live goat in *Dinorah* always misbehaved itself until, ultimately, at the Royal Italian Opera, Mdme. Adelina Patti found herself obliged to discard her unruly pet, and to sing Dinorah's charming song either to a purely imaginary animal or to a stuffed figure.

At a Paris theatre an attempt was once made to give reality to a pastoral scene by bringing on to the stage a flock of live sheep which, however, frightened by the lights and the clamour of the audience, lost no time in going astray, so that at the second representation it was found necessary to replace the live sheep by paste-board imitations.

The insufficiency of the stage arrangements at the Paris opera, when Rousseau was expatiating on the artistic poverty of that establishment, may be explained in some measure, not only by the smallness of the stage, but by the manner it which it was blocked up by the aristocratic section of the audience, who sat in rows on either side of the singers, while the baser portion of the public stood in the pit which, until a comparatively recent period, was unprovided with seats. Often the occupants of the benches on the stage took quite a different view of the representation to that formed by the up-standing spectators in the *parterre;* and ideas were sometimes exchanged between the two great divisions of the public with an irritating effect, and with results which occasionally took the form of open violence. This actor or singer, under this absurd arrangement, stood in the midst of his audience ; and when, as sometimes happened, the remarks made by those on the stage caused him to turn round, he was accused of showing disrespect to the audience in front of the orchestra. At times under this arrangement a piece was hissed by one division and applauded by the other. It was not always the aristocratic section which showed itself in the right. *Le Grandeur*, by Brueys and Palaparet, was received with hisses from the stage, with applause from the pit. Molière's *Ecole des femmes*, which delighted the pit, found no favour in the eyes of the too fastidious but not sufficiently intelligent patrons of the seats on the stage, one of whom, at each fresh burst of laughter, is said to have exclaimed, with a shrug of the shoulders, "Laugh away! laugh away! you fools in the pit!"

The benches on the stage of the Paris opera were abolished, at the instance of the Count de Lauragais, who, it has been surmised, may have felt annoyed at Sophie Arnold's being stared at and spoken to by the frequenters of these seats. This munificent patron of the operatic art—and of operatic artists—paid, in any case, a sum of 12,000 livres by way of compensation for the loss sustained by the theatre in consenting to the abolishment of the *banquettes*.

At our English theatres the spectators who were allowed to take seats on the stage did not, as in France, place themselves prominently before the public. The practice, however, of admitting so many visitors behind the scenes, and of allowing them to remain on the stage while the performance was actually going on, could not but be attended with many inconveniences, one of which is mentioned by Mrs. Bellamy, in a well-known passage of her memoirs. A Mr. St. Leger, as Mrs. Bellamy passed before him, kissed her on the neck, and received a box on the ears in return. Lord Chesterfield rose in his box and applauded. His example was followed by the whole house; and at the end of the play Major Macartney, deputed by the Viceroy, waited on Mr. St. Leger, and requested him to make a public apology.

This incident had an important effect in bringing about a reform which had long been advocated.

Many reforms or innovations supposed to be of the present day are but returns to ancient practices. There is much in Herr Wagner's musical system—including the use of horses on the stage—which is not by any means so new as is generally supposed. There was novelty at one time in bringing the orchestra before the public, instead of keeping it out of sight as was done in the early days of the drama and quite lately at the Wagner festival of Beyreuth. The custom, too, adopted at Beyreuth of proclaiming the approaching representation by sound of the trumpet, though apparently new in the present day, is not so new as the system of distributing programmes, which dates only from the time of Dryden. In France the custom of naming the artists on the bills of the performances is still modern, being not quite a hundred years old. On the 9th September, 1779, the actors of Paris held a meeting, at which they adopted a petition begging the Mayor of Paris not to force them to print their names on the programmes. It was held by the profession that it was to the advantage of theatres generally that actors should remain anonymous; for if, in an important part, a favourite artist was to be replaced on a given evening by an artist of no great popularity, the public, it was argued, would not be prevented by such a substitution from attending. It was not until 1791 that the Paris opera adopted the custom of announcing the performers' names. However the general interest of the stage may have been affected, it can scarcely be said that artists, as individuals, suffered from the change; for under the old system they were frequently hissed, not by reason of their own incapacity alone, but because the public was disappointed at finding them cast for parts in which it had been expected to meet actors of greater popularity.

On one occasion an irritated amateur rushed from the Paris Opera-house and began to beat an unfortunate ticket-seller, from whom he had purchased his place. The cause of the gentleman's anger was at once understood.

"*Est que je savais qu'on lâ cherait le Pontheieu?*" cried the ticket-seller; for it was the singing of Pontheieu that excited the opera-goer's wrath.

Talking of hisses I may here mention that an actress of ability in her time, Mrs. Farrel, after being hissed in the part of Zaria, the heroine of the *Morning Bride*, especially in the dying scene, rose from the stage, and advancing towards the footlights, expressed her regret at not having merited the applause of the audience, and explained that having only accepted the part to oblige a friend, she hoped she would be excused for not playing it better. After this little speech she assumed once more a recumbent position, and was covered by the attendants with a black veil.

Such incidents as the one narrated by Mrs. Bellamy

were doubtless of frequent occurrence at the French theatres; not that they always took so serious a turn. On one occasion a dancer was listening to the protestation of an elderly lover who was on the point of even kissing her hand, when as he stooped down his wig caught in the spangles of her dress. At that moment she had to appear on the stage, and did so amid general laughter and applause; for she carried with her the old beau's wig or scalp, as if by way of trophy. The applause was renewed when a bald head was seen projecting from the wing in search of its artificial covering. Stories are told, too, of imprudent admirers, who, after exciting the jealousy of a machinist or "carpenter," did not take the precaution to avoid traps, and, as a natural consequence, found themselves at the first opportunity shot up to the ceiling, or sunk to the lowest depths beneath the stage.

The abolition of the *banquettes* at the Paris Operahouse, though due in one sense to the Count de Lauragius, who indemnified the actors for the loss of a valuable perquisite, may be attributed also to the representations made on the subject by the actor Lekain who played, moreover, an important part in connection with the reform of scenery, of costume, and of stage accessories generally.

Molière, in his opening scene of *Les Fâcheus*, and Voltaire, in several of his works, ridiculed the custom of allowing spectators to take their places on the stage.

The actors cannot but have known this practice to be absurd and, in an artistic point of view, most injurious. It may be doubted, indeed, whether the French for so many centuries would have respected the least respectable of the three unities, that of place, had they not been absolutely forced to do so by the conditions under which their actors performed, and by the absolute impossibility, with a narrow and crowded stage, of changing the scene.

Although the honour of reforming stage costume—to the extent, at least, of doing away with flagrant anachronisms in dress—is claimed for London, it was not to a great tragedian but to a very distinguished ballet-dancer that this reform was really due. In the early part of the eighteenth century, Roman, Greek and Assyrian warriors appeared on the French stage in a conventional military costume, which seemed to be considered suitable to warriors of all nations and all kinds. The dress consisted of a be-laced and be-ribboned tunic, surmounted by a cuirass, and of a powdered wig with tails a yard long, over which was worn a plumed helmet.

Mdlle. Sallé, the ballerina who first undertook the herculean task of rendering stage costumes reasonable and natural, proposed, in defiance of the prevailing custom, to give to each person in a ballet or other dramatic work the dress of the country and period to which the subject belonged. Mdlle. Sallé was a friend of Voltaire, who celebrated her in an appropriate verse, and she carried with her in 1784, when she visited London, a letter of introduction from Fontenelle to Montesquieu. Appearing at Covent Garden Theatre in a ballet of her own composition on the subject of *Pygmalion and Galathea*, Mdlle. Sallé dressed for the part of Galathea not in the Louis Quinze style, nor in a Polish costume, such as was afterwards adopted for this character at the Paris Opera-house, but in drapery imitated as closely as possible from the statues of antiquity. It was announced on the occasion of Mdlle. Salle's benefit at Covent Garden that "servants would be permitted to keep seats on the stage." This, however, was an exceptional arrangement. Endeavours were already being made in England to confine theatre-goers to their proper places in front of the house, and on many of the playbills of this period the following notification appears:—"It is desired that no person will take it ill their not being permitted behind the scenes, it being impossible to perform the entertainment unless these passages are kept clear."

Strange mistakes sometimes arose from the author's name not being announced. At the first performance of the tragedy of *Statira*, Pradon, the writer of that work, took his place among the audience to judge freely of its effect. The first act was a good deal hissed, and Pradon was about to protest, when a friend whispered to him not to make himself known, but in order to conceal his identity to hiss like the others. Pradon hissed, when a mosquetaire at his side asked him why he hissed a piece that was excellent, and the work of a man who held a distinguished position at court. Pradon, annoyed at his neighbour's interference, replied that he should hiss if he thought fit. The mosquetaire knocked his hat off. Pradon struck the mosquetaire, and receiving a beating in return, left the theatre insulted and injured, but not morally hurt.

A tragedy, in six acts, by M. de Beausobre, called *Les Arsacides*, had been formally accepted at the Comédie Française by some mistake. A large sum of money was offered to the author on condition of his withdrawing the work; but it had taken him thirty years to write the piece, he was now sixty years of age, and he was resolved to see it played. The tragedy was hissed from beginning to end. The actors wished to finish the performance at the beginning of the second act; but the audience were so amused with it that they insisted on hearing the whole. The next day the author went to the theatre and assured the actors that if they would give him one more rehearsal, and, above all, would allow him to add a seventh act, the work would have a glorious success. They prevailed upon him to accept an indemnity, and the piece was not played again.

The story is perhaps sufficiently well known of the celebrated English actor Powell seeking in vain for a supernumerary named Warren who dressed him, but who on this occasion had undertaken to play the part of Lothario's corpse in the *Fair Penitent*. Powell, who took the principal character, called out in an angry tone for Warren, who could not help raising his head from the coffin and replying, "Here, sir." "Come, then," continued Powell, not knowing where the voice came from, "or I'll break every bone in your body." Warren, believing his master to be quite capable of carrying out his threat, sprang in his fright out of the coffin, and ran in his winding-sheet across the stage.

Our dying heroes and heroines in the present day wait to regain animation until the curtain has fallen. Unless, however, they are supposed to be dead, they reappear in their own private character at the end of each dramatic scene which happens to have procured for them a marked approbation. A distinguished tenor, the late Signor Giuglini, being much applauded one night for his singing in the miserere scene of *Il Trovatore*, quitted the dungeon in which Manrico is supposed to be confined, came forward to the public, bowed, and then, not to cheat the executioner, went calmly back to prison.

A much more modern story of the confusion of facts with appearances is told, and with truth, of a distinguished military amateur, who had undertaken—for this occasion only—to play the part of *Don Giovanni*. In the final scene, where the profligate hero is seized and carried down to the infernal regions, the principal character could neither persuade nor compel the demons, who were represented by private soldiers, to lay hands on one whom, whatever part he might temporarily assume, they knew to be a colonel in the army. The demons kept at a respectful distance, and when ordered in a loud whisper to lay hands on their dramatic victim, contented themselves with falling into an attitude of attention. Possibly they may have remembered that according to the Articles of War, the soldier who lays hands on an officer is punishable with death.

Jules Janin, in the collection of his *feuilletons*, published under the title of *Histoire de le Littérature Dramatique*, tells how, in the ultra-tragic tragedy of *Tragadalbas*, an actor, in the midst of a solemn tirade, let a false set of teeth fall from his mouth. This was nothing more nor less than an accident; but the great tragedian showed great presence of mind, and also a certain indifference to the serious nature of the work on which he was engaged, when he coolly stooped down, picked up the teeth, replaced them between his jaws, and continued his speech.

At some French provincial theatre, where a piece was being played in which the principal character was that of a blind man, the actor to whom the part had been assigned was unwell, and it seemed necessary to call upon another member of the company to read the part. Thus the strange spectacle was witnessed of a man, supposed to be totally blind, who read every word he uttered from a paper he carried in his hand.

At an English performance of *William Tell* the traditional arrow, instead of going straight from Tell's bow to the heart—perforated beforehand—of the apple placed on the head of Tell's son, stopped halfway on the wire along which it should have travelled to its destination.

Everything, however, succeeded in Rossini's *William Tell* except the apple incident, as everything failed in Dennis's *Appius* except that thunder which Dennis recognised and claimed as his own when he heard it a few nights afterwards in *Macbeth*. Yet it has never been very difficult to represent thunder on the stage. One of the oldest theatrical anecdotes is that of the actor who, playing the part of a bear, hears a clap of stage thunder, and, mistaking it for the real thing, makes the sign of the cross.

## CHAPTER XL.

### THE LITERARY MALTREATMENT OF MUSIC.

MUSICIANS cannot help now and then being struck by the strange and not altogether explicable mistakes made by some of our greatest writers in connection with music. They may, perhaps, be reminded in return that if authors frequently make blunders—or, to be precise, write nonsense—on the subject of music, musicians have sometimes shown remarkable ignorance of literature. Ivanoff, the famous Russian tenor, on seeing Beamarchais's *Barbier de Séville*, at the Théatre Français, told Rossini, as an interesting piece of news, that the French had turned his *Barbier* into a comedy, and that it went remarkably well in its new form. Only the other day an eminent Italian vocalist in London, on being introduced to the eminent English vocalist, Mr.

## THE LITERARY MALTREATMENT OF MUSIC. 145

William Shakespeare expressed much satisfaction at making the acquaintance of our great national dramatist, adding aside to a friend, "Je ne le croyais pas si jeune." Passing from singers, whose chief business is the production of sounds, to composers who belong to the great family of artistic creators, it would be easy to cite instances of disregard shown by the latter in their musical settings for the sense and meaning of the words. An Italian composer, not finding the words and syllables of the *Credo* sufficiently numerous for the melody to which he was adapting it, is said to have interpolated here and there such words as *ah* and *non*. Thus treated, his profession of faith became *Credo, non Credo, ah non Credo in unum Deum*. Another, as if to show that he, at least, understood the literal meaning of his words, introduced the orchestral accompaniment of an *Agnus Dei* in the conventional instruments of pastoral music. Balfe, in fitting a melody to Tennyson's "Come into the garden, Maud," has strongly accentuated the first word, on which no accent should fall. It is true that the very fertile, though not always original, composer has borrowed his theme, note for note, from Macbeth's principal air in Verdi's opera of *Macbetto*, which may account for some manipulation of words. Wallace, in a trio of *Maritana*, composed to the words, " Turn on, old Time, thy hour-glass," has made " time " a word of seven syllables, and " hour " a word of two. A French vocalist under the first Republic found himself condemned, not to extend one syllable (and that syllable with an *i* in the middle!) over seven notes, but to deliver six syllables where the composer had only furnished music for one. In Montigny's *Déserteur*, one of the most popular airs begins with this line—

"Le roi passait et le tambour battait aux champs."

All mention of *Le roi* being forbidden, *la loi* was found a convenient substitute for the banished word; and in *Le Déserteur* "*la loi*" was described as passing in procession between lines of faithful soldiers. A singer who was unable to realise the idea of an abstract conception riding on horseback or in a carriage, replaced

"Le roi passait et le tambour battait aux champs"

by—

"Le pouvoir exécutif passait et le tambour battait aux champs."

But the greatest sinners of all in connection with music are our own librettists. In the English version of *Dinorah*, Corentin, the Breton peasant, having to say in verse, and to a particular tune, that some men are brave while others are not, is made to state the case by means of symbols in the following terms:—

"A was born to live in war and thunder,
B is otherwise, and so is C."

The author of these curious lines makes the bad character in Sterndale Bennett's *May Queen* say, in reference to the heroine's beauty, at the beginning of the trio:—

"Can that eye a cottage hide?"

The meaning of the strangely inverted inquiry is, "Can a girl with such eyes as yours consent to remain hidden in a cottage?"

Much better, as regards simplicity and sense, than "A was born," &c., or "Can that eye a cottage hide," are the following lines written by an ingenious Frenchman as an additional verse to "God save the King." When, at the time of the Restoration, Louis XVIII. was conveyed from Dover to Calais on an English man-of-war by the Duke of Clarence, afterwards William IV., a banquet was given at Calais in honour of the English Lord High Admiral, "God save the King" was sung, and this new stanza was tacked on to the anthem for the occasion:—

"God save Clarence
Who brings her king to France.
God save Clarence!
He maintains the glory
Of the British navy.
Oh! God, make him happy;
God save Clarence.

The rhymes in these remarkable verses to a French ear, or rather to a French eye, are probably not bad. But it must be admitted, that, however perfect to the eye, they leave something to be desired by the ear. The words might easily enough be sung to the tune of "God save the King," but it is difficult to imagine the singer giving them with much spirit.

In *Arsinoe*, the "first opera," according to Addison, "that gave us a taste for Italian music," Clayton, who afterwards wrote the words for Addison's *Rosamond*, and whose works were regarded by Steele as a sort of "music of the future," before which Handel's paltry productions must eventually sink into insignificance, had to set the following verses:—

> "Queen of Darkness, sable night,
> Ease a wandering lover's pain;
> Guide me, lead me
> Where the nymph whom I adore,
> Sleeping, dreaming,
> Thinks of love and me no more."

In the "repeat" of the melody which Clayton fitted to these lines, or to which the lines had to be more or less satisfactorily adjusted, it suited the composer to stop at line the fourth, so that the singer ended the piece, without completing it, by exclaiming—

> "Guide me, lead me,
> Where the nymph whom I adore."

With a similar disregard of the meaning of the author, Shield, who composed a century later than Clayton, travestied Shakespeare by punctuating him as follows:—

> "O happy, happy, happy fair,
> Your eyes are load-stars,
> And your tongue sweet air."

But to return to Mr. Clayton. "The style of this music," he had explained in an address to the public, "is to express the passions, which is the soul of music." Clayton, apart from music, was probably a clever and agreeable man; and taking him at his own valuation, or judging him perhaps by his general ability, the contributors to the *Spectator* came to the conclusion that he was all he believed himself to be. They could follow Clayton in his forcible arguments, and in the indignation he expressed at Handel's venturing to introduce a foreign entertainment into England, while Handel's music, on the other hand, said nothing to them. They did not hesitate to give the publicity of the *Spectator* to a letter in which Clayton not only proposed to start concerts of British music—or rather of his own so-called Italian music "grafted upon English poetry"—but declared "that favouring our design is no less than reviving an art which runs to ruin by the utmost barbarism under an affectation of knowledge." The good opinion which Addison and Steele had formed of Clayton as a musician, reminds one a little of the admiration felt for Berlioz, and indirectly for Berlioz's music, by Heine and Théophile Gautier, who could not fail to be charmed by Berlioz's wit. It reminds one much more of the popularity enjoyed by Thackeray's Sir George Thrum, the sturdy representative of native musical talent, whose "downright English stuff" was contrasted with the "infernal twaddle and disgusting slop" of

Donizetti. Without being a musician, Thackeray was artist enough to perceive the difference between the music of Donizetti, an Italian composer of the second class, and that of Sir George Thrum, a composer of no class.

Thackeray, with genius and intelligence equally developed, could not write absurdly in however small a degree on music or on any other subject. But he could make mistakes; and it once occurred to him that Beethoven had composed a very beautiful piece called the *Dream of St. Jerome*, of which no mention is made in any catalogue of Beethoven's works. Beethoven might have produced a new piece under that title, but as a matter of fact he did not. In due time, however—a proof that Thackeray's conception had nothing ridiculous in it—the dream became a reality, and *St. Jerome's Dream*, by Van Beethoven may now be purchased of all respectable music-sellers. It is said that one day an admirer of Thackeray and of Beethoven, anxious to learn which of Beethoven's compositions had given so much pleasure to the great novelist, asked timidly, but with an air of conviction, at a West End shop, for Beethoven's *Dream of St. Jerome*. After a little delay, and probably a brief consultation, the answer returned to the enterprising amateur was to the effect that the *Dream of St. Jerome* might be had in a few days, but that it was for the moment out of print. It had, of course, been explained that the perfectly imaginary work was spoken in the "Adventures of Philip" (Chapter XXXII.), and, as if to do honour to Thackeray's fancy, a piece, or portion of a piece, by Beethoven was engraved under the title which Thackeray had probably heard applied half in pleasantry, half in earnest, to some other piece by the same master. In families where music is much cultivated, a composition may easily get to be known by a name of which the signification will be by no means apparent to those unacquainted with its private origin.

After all, Thackeray's musical mistake is no worse than a literary mistake made for the first time many years ago by the great Wagner, and dutifully repeated again and again by his faithful followers. Figaro, in *Le Barbier de Séville*, says, as he improvises the words of his air (in the situation where Rossini has placed *largo al fattotum*), *Ce qui ne vaut pas la peine d'être dit on le chante.* Herr Wagner and the Wagnerites for *Ce qui ne vaut pas la peine d'être dit*, substitute *Ce qui est trop sot pour être dit;* and assign the remark as improved by themselves, not to Beaumarchais's Figaro speaking in jest, but to Voltaire speaking seriously in his own character.

Thackeray is not the only novelist of the present day who to an unknown piece of music has given an unknown name.

Very different, however, in character from these errors as to the titles of works, or as to the existence of works which were never composed, is a mistake which disfigures one of the masterpieces of modern fiction. In the novel in question "a perfect accord of descending fifths" is dwelt upon with a sort of rapture. Now, irrespective of all rules on the subject, it would be sufficient to try an "accord of descending fifths" on the piano, to see whether or not the thing is even tolerable. It is to be feared, however, that in the highest literary circles a taste for sequence of fifths is on the increase. In a volume of very charming songs, by one of the most popular novelists of the day, the purple cover is ostentatiously adorned by a sequence of ascending fifths printed in notes of gold.

Attention having once been called to the matter, it need hardly be said that "sequences of fifths" in music are neither desirable nor undesirable, but simply not to be thought of. Lucy and Stephen no more sang such intolerable sounds than Jules Janin saw red lobsters—except, indeed, in his mind's eye—when, in a celebrated flight of fancy, he described the lobster as "the Cardinal of the Sea." Alfred de Musset placed Andulasians in Barcelona :

> " Avez-vous vu dans Barcelone
> Une Andalouse au teint bruni ? "

But the Duke of Clarence (" God save Clarence," &c.), went far beyond Musset, and proved himself, as a natural historian, at least the equal of Jules Janin. Growing enthusiastic about the clearness of the sea at Malta, His Royal Highness is reported to have exclaimed, "At twenty fathoms, sir, you could see the bottom red with lobsters, by G—d." There may be red lobsters in the sea (dead ones), as there may be sequences of fifths in music, but neither would be delightful.

In *Uncle Tom's Cabin*, not only musicians and amateurs of music, but all readers, must have been astonished to find one of the personages playing the piano " with an airy and bird-like touch." The bird as a pianist might form a companion picture to *la loi* as an equestrian.

Ouida, in a lively account of the sufferings to which the officers of Her Majesty's Brigade of Guards are exposed during the London season, makes one of these unfortunate gentlemen so far forget himself at an evening party as to propose to a young lady between two movements of a symphony. Ouida or her hero may have had peculiarly bad luck, but as a general rule nothing so formidable as a symphony is presented at an evening party.

To the poet a good deal is permitted. When, however, the poet appears in the character of a novelist, and introduces musical performances, he ought not to make his players execute a work under impossible circumstances. Haydn wrote music of nearly all kinds, but he never composed quartets " for three violins and a flute." We are assured in *Les Misérables* that on the occasion of Valjean's banquet, "three violins and a flute played in an undertone quatuors of Haydn."

It may be said that if Victor Hugo, in an admirable romance, has thought fit to misrepresent the character of Haydn's quartets, his object in writing *Les Misérables* was not to teach music. But, author of the finest romances, the finest lyrical poems, the only fine plays, and one of the best libretti of the period—his own arrangement of Esmaralda as an opera-book—it is to be regretted that he should encourage, by his example, a species of carelessness in which it is only too easy to follow him.

In England no disgrace is attached to a total ignorance of music and everything connected therewith. But when an author undertakes to enlighten the world on the subject of music and musicians, he ought not to mistake a celebrated singer for a painter. Nor, in speaking of the vocalist so entirely unknown to him, ought he to assume an air of familiarity with the man in that pictorial character which never belonged to him; nor, above all, to make errors of this kind in a book, treating not only in a general manner on music, but also in a special manner of " music and morals." In a work published under the title just cited, the author transports us, " through the kindness of Dr. Liszt," to what he calls a *levée*—held late in the evening—at Chopin's rooms in the Chaussée d'Antia. Among Chopin's visitors is Adolphe Nourrit, the famous tenor, whom Mr. Haweis mistakes for a painter. "Adolphe Nourrit," writes our author, "the noble and ascetic artist, stands apart. He has something of the grandeur of the middle ages about him. In his later years he refused to paint any subject which was wanting in dignity." That is more that can be said of our guide to morals in connection with music. Painting, after Liszt, a gathering at Chopin's, he produces a flagrantly incorrect copy of a very flashy original. Nourrit is said to have suggested to Meyerbeer the scene of the great duet which closes so effectively the fourth act of *Les Huguenots*, and to have given valuable hints to Donizetti for *I. Martiri*. He, in fact, showed himself in many ways an "artist," but not, as Mr. Haweis imagined, an artist with the brush. The unfortunate man, when he found his powers as a singer forsaking him, committed suicide. He was at no period of his life a painter.

Mr. Haweis does not think much of the opera as a form of art. He has a perfect right to argue that the musical drama is neither drama nor music, and, in spite of its existence, that it cannot exist. But as a writer on music and the connection between music and morals, he ought not to represent Mendelssohn as condemning the moral tendency of a scene in Meyerbeer's *Robert le Diable*, when the scene which Mendelssohn refers to in the letter quoted in *Music and Morals*, belongs to Auber's *Fra Diavolo*. Besides confounding *Robert le Diable* with *Fra Diavolo*, and mistaking one of the first operatic singers of his time for a painter of religious pictures, the same writer declares it to be " well-known that the opening to the *William Tell* overture was written for a celebrated violoncello at Vienna," whereas it is notorious that *William Tell*, overture and all, was composed for the Grand Opera of Paris. A writer who makes such mistakes as these, cannot fail in the course of 500 and odd pages to make a great many more of the same kind. In fact he speaks of the " yodelling " of Polish peasants; describes the infant Gluck as " William Christopher *Ritter* Von Gluck " (as though Gluck had been born a knight); makes Mozart's canary sing " in G sharp " (whereas all the poor bird did was to sing an air in which G sharp occurs); cites Œcolampadius (a contemporary of Luther) as one of the biographers of Mendelssohn; and says mildly of Salieri, who was suspected of having poisoned Mozart, that he " did not appreciate him." The majority, however, of Mr. Haweis's errors are not at all amusing. He makes Mendelssohn die in 1847, and visit England in 1848. He assigns Beethoven's *Adelaida* to the year 1801 instead of 1794; and, after referring to the composer's passion for the Countess Giucciardi, observes that in the immortal song of *Adelaida*—composed seven ·years before—" we can almost hear the refrain of ' my angel !

my all! my life!' and such-like passionate utterances."

If an author who professes to instruct and enlighten the public in regard to music—and who is himself a cultivated amateur—commits blunders, not by the dozen or the score but by hundreds, it was scarcely to be expected that Charles Lamb, who did not care for music, would write very accurately about it. "Much less in voices," he says in his *Chapter on ears*, "can I distinguish a soprano from a tenor. Only sometimes the thorough bass I contrive to guess at, from its being supereminently harsh and disagreeable." It is to be regretted that the gentle Elia did not content himself with the simple and sufficient word "bass"; "thorough bass" meaning something very different from what he intended to express. Elsewhere, in *Imperfect sympathies*, Lamb, who frankly admitted that he could not distinguish a soprano from a tenor, speaks of the Hebrew enthusiasm of Braham, (who, it need scarcely be added, was a tenor), breaking out as he sang "When the children of Israel passed through the Red Sea." There are, however, no such words in the tenor part of the Oratorio.

Among other unfounded charges made against Prince Bismarck, the illustrious statesman has been accused of describing Beethoven's Sonata in A flat as "Beethoven's Sonata in A." In that interesting novel of contemporary political life, *For Sceptre and Crown*, the Prussian

Foreign Minister (A.D. 1866) cannot make up his mind to declare war against Austria. Much agitated, he calls upon the eminent pianist and politician Herr Von Keudell, to calm him by playing the funeral march, from—as the author, or at least as the English translator puts it —" Beethoven's Sonata in A." Prince Bismarck has more than once declared in the Prussian Chamber that he never said " might before right "; and that his famous remark about the efficacy of blood and iron was not his own, but was quoted from a well-known German poem. It would be interesting to hear from Prince Bismarck's own lips that he never spoke of the piece which he probably knows as " the Sonata with the funeral march," as " Beethoven's Sonata in A."

Some writers, in dealing with musical matters, commit errors of so simple a nature that one scarcely likes to raise a laugh at their expense. The pedant who makes a mistake ought never to be spared. But there was at least no affectation of technical knowledge in the observation addressed to the chief of a French municipality, by a secretary who, commissioned to report as to the manner in which a local theatre was managed, wrote: " The conductor of the orchestra has not played a note since his arrival. If he contents himself with making gestures, I suggest that he be discharged."

Nothing droller than the above is to be found even in the great repertory of moral and musical blunders from which several choice specimens have already been presented. For the best collection of similar mistakes, brought together with derisive intention, Berlioz's *Les Grotesques de la Musique* may be consulted. It is to be observed, however, that whereas the English writer goes wrong only when he speaks of composers, singers, musical historians, and musical works, without showing any fundamental ignorance of music as an art, the errors which Berlioz thought worthy of his attention are those of persons to whom, musicians as they thought themselves, the first principles of music must have been unknown. It will be enough to quote from Berlioz's entertaining work the substance of two anecdotes. A young lady—says the French composer, whose literary productions everyone can admire—buying a piece of music at Brandus's, was asked whether the fact of its being " in four flats " would be any obstacle to her playing it. She replied that it made no difference how many flats were marked, as beyond two she scratched them out with a pen-knife.

Our second anecdote, after Berlioz, is of a dancer who, rehearsing with the orchestra and finding that something went wrong, thought the fault must be with the musicians. " What key are you playing in ? " he inquired. " E," replied the conductor. " I thought so," continued the dancer; " you must transpose the air; I can only dance to it in D." What would Berlioz have said if he could have seen, in one of the most beautiful poems in our language, these melodious but inaccurate lines ?—

> All night have the roses heard
>   The flute, violin, bassoon ;
> All night has the casement jessamine stirr'd
>   To the dancers dancing in tune.

It is scarcely necessary to point out that dancers, however accurately they may dance in *time*, cannot, unless they make music with their feet, dance in *tune*. Berlioz, by the way, as a great master of instrumentation, might not have liked the composition of the little orchestra—"flute, violin, bassoon." But the bassoon was adopted, years ago, into English poetry, and, thanks to Coleridge and to Tennyson, will remain there.

What, nevertheless, is to be said about Coleridge and the "loud bassoon," except that in the first place the bassoon is not loud? Out of the *Ancient Mariner* no one has ever heard a "loud bassoon." Having been long accustomed to it, however, people have got to like it, and now would not, on any account, see the loud bassoon replaced by the "tender trumpet" or the "gentle ophicleide"; which for the rest, would suit neither the rhythmn or the rhyme of the poet. There is, however, another solemn and serious instrument which might have served the poet's purpose. The trombone, since it has been associated with the statue of the Commander in *Don Juan*—who never speaks except to an accompaniment of trombones—has possessed an unearthly character; and, vigorously played, there can be no question as to its being "loud." If, indeed, it were permitted to take with Coleridge a tithe of the liberties which everyone is allowed to take with Shakespeare, some commentator of the *Ancient Mariner* would doubtless have re-written the last four lines of the " loud bassoon " stanza, substituting, more or less ingeniously, for " loud bassoon " the words " loud trombone."

The author of *Music and Morals* supposes the life of Mendelssohn to have been written by a contemporary of Luther. An anachronism, however, is a comparatively mild form of absurdity. Shakespeare is full of anachronisms and other inconsistencies. From *Macbeth* to *Joan of Arc*, all Shakespeare's serious characters quote Plutarch, and all his comic characters allude to affairs of the day—not their own day, but Shakespeare's. The old painters, too, committed anachronisms in regard to costumes and accessories of all kinds, including musical instruments. Apollo, the Muses, Orpheus, are represented playing the violin and other instruments by no means of their date; but, at least, they play them in a becoming manner. The instruments, too, are correctly drawn, and are those of the period at which the pictures were painted. In Paul Veronese's *Marriage of Cana*, in the Louvre, the musicians play on stringed instruments of various kinds, such as the viola and the violoncello. Domenichino's *St. Cecilia*, also in the Louvre, plays the violoncello; and it is to be observed that she plays from notes which are held for her by a young angel who bears a strange resemblance to the late Mr. Buckstone. Many artists in the present day paint impossible instruments, and represent musicians playing under impossible circumstances. A few years ago a picture might have been seen at Christie's, the work of the late Mr. John Philip, in which there was a violin without bridge or strings. Mr. Du Maurier exhibited some time since in *Punch* a most gracefully drawn sestett party in which the performers had no music before them. Joachim will play his own part in Beethoven's or Mendelssohn's violin concerto, without notes. It is the fashion just now for all our pianoforte soloists to play without notes. But the notion of concerted pieces being executed by all concerned without notes is preposterous. In a "music party," by an old Italian, Flemish, or French painter it would be as impossible to find players without notes as to find a violin without bridge or strings.

Are no mistakes made, it may perhaps be asked, except in connection with music? Are not the technical terms of pictorial art abused by critics of painting? Do not amateur strategists commit blunders in describing the operations of war? The answer to these questions is, that though everyone is liable to make mistakes, no one runs the risk of making ridiculous ones unless he travels beyond the region of what he knows, or has tolerable reason for thinking he knows. As regards music, Fielding, without being a musician, knew that those were impostors who decried the genius of Handel in the interest of his envious British rivals. Similarly,

Thackeray was not to be deceived by the laudations given by the Bludyers of his time to Sir George Thrum at the expense of Donizetti. But neither Fielding nor Thackeray thought it necessary to go into ecstacies about "accords of descending fifths." Mozart, moreover, Mendelssohn, Weber, Spohr, were able in their letters to speak of musical performances without resorting to technicalities; and there are excellent reasons why this rule—followed, as a matter of course, by the great masters in their familiar correspondence—should be observed by writers who know enough about music to employ musical expressions, but not enough to avoid employing them incorrectly.

## CHAPTER XLI.

### DICTIONARIES OF MUSIC.

The idea of making music and musicians the subject of a special dictionary is not by any means so new as some who have given a well-deserved welcome to the dictionary published under the direction of Dr. George Grove, seem to imagine. The first Universal Dictionary or "Cyclopædia" was published in 1541, at Basel, by Ringelberg; to be followed during the next hundred years by many works of the same kind, until, in 1621, the celebrated encyclopædia, by the German Alsted or Alstadius, called *Encyclopædia Scientiarum omnium* appeared. A century afterwards, Leibnitz pointed out how desirable it would be to amend Alsted's book, and himself wrote a paper of suggestions for its improvement and extension. Nothing came, however, of Leibnitz's proposition, and Alsted's encyclopædia remained a mere arrangement of a number of treatises or manuals within the limits of a couple of folios.

More comprehensive in its plan, though less complete as regards the treatment of various subjects, was the work of Ephraim Chambers, a Westmoreland Quaker, who published at London, in 1727, an English Cyclopædia (the cyclopædia of Alsted was in Latin), "or Universal Dictionary of the Arts and Sciences." Chambers's purpose, as set forth by himself, was "to consider the several matters, not only in themselves, but relatively or as they respect each other; both to treat them as so many wholes, and as so many parts of some greater whole." The cyclopædia of Chambers, translated into French by an Englishman Mills, and a German Sellius, became through Le Breton, the Paris publisher to whom the translation was entrusted, the starting point for the famous *Encyclopédie* produced under the direction of Diderot and D'Alembert. Le Breton had promised the two foreigners to procure for them the right or privilege of publishing their French version of Chambers in France; but he preferred, after obtaining the Government patent made out in his own name, to keep it for himself. Wanting in honesty, Le Breton had, at the same time, sagacity enough to perceive that Chambers's work might be much developed and much improved. He referred the matter to Diderot, who became inspired with the idea of treating the subjects brought together in Chambers's *Universal Dictionary* on a greatly extended plan, and in a thoroughly modern spirit. Le Breton approved warmly of Diderot's project, and the better to carry it out associated himself with three other booksellers, while Diderot for like reasons entered into a sort of literary partnership with D'Alembert.

Diderot, in the preface to one of the volumes of the *Encyclopédie* speaks contemptuously of Chambers, who, he says, took his materials from all possible sources without once acknowledging his obligations to others, and without introducing into his articles anything of his own. The well-deserved character here given to Chambers and his work shows how essentially that mere compilation of facts and opinions differed from Diderot's *Encyclopédie,* which consists of a mass of essays, in alphabetical order, on all kinds of subjects by all the greatest French writers of the eighteenth century. The *Encyclopédie* bears more resemblance to Bayle's *Dictionnaire Critique* than to those compendiums of universal information to which it is usually traced, and to one of which it certainly owes its direct origin. Chambers did not, of course, make any pretence to having mastered the immense variety of subjects comprised in his encyclopædia. He got his information wherever he could find it, though not by any means in the sense in which Molière " prenait son bien partout où il le trouvait." Chambers, as Diderot said, "put nothing of his own" into the brief notices, and sometimes mere entries, of which his encyclopædia is composed. Bayle, on the other hand, in his *Critical Dictionary* deals with every subject from his own point of view, according to his own lights, and in his own manner. The truth of Buffon's remark on the subject of style, cited so often, and in most cases so incorrectly, is strikingly illustrated by the lasting superiority in a literary point of view of Bayle's dictionary, and of the *Encyclopédie*, to the innumerable dictionaries and encyclopædias of similar design since published. Bayle's dictionary abounds in fables, some of which are not of a very edifying kind; and the scientific articles in the *Encyclopédie*, even had they been perfect when they first appeared, would now, a hundred years afterwards, leave as a matter of course much to be desired. A good deal of history, too, has been made since the days before the French Revolution; and countries have been discovered of which the existence at that time was not suspected. The *Encyclopédie* then has naturally and inevitably lost a great deal of such worth as may originally have belonged to it, if it be considered only as a storehouse of information. But as a collection of essays and treatises by the leading French writers of the eighteenth century, its value remains undiminished. It is at this moment the most readable, the most interesting, and in many respects the most instructive, of all encyclopædias. Each article was the work of a man, sometimes of a great man, who in the first place was an excellent writer, and who, whether or not he possessed a complete knowledge of his subject, had at least studied it for himself, and who in presenting the results of his study never failed to introduce, as Diderot might have said, "something of his own." Facts, in short, are the property of everyone—of Diderot, of D'Alembert, and also of the booksellers' hacks, to whose labours the cheap encyclopædic compilations of the present day are due. But a writer's style is, as Buffon put it, " the man himself," and cannot be reproduced unless his very words be borrowed.

If the cheap encyclopædias of the day consist merely of extracts and abridgements from more comprehensive and, above all, more authentic works of the same general character, all our best modern encyclopædias differ from the famous *Encyclopédie* of the eighteenth century by the manner in which scientific subjects, and other subjects of a special kind, are treated. Diderot, in selecting contributors for the *Encyclopédie*, aimed, above all, at surrounding himself with great writers ; whereas the editor of a modern encyclopædia, undertaken on a liberal scale, would make it his chief object to secure for articles of a scientific or semi-scientific character men who thoroughly understood the subject. The services of specialists are engaged, and the writings of specialists are, in many cases, disfigured by a too copious use of technical language ; while the value of their information is lessened for the general reader by a tacit assumption that the elements, and often much more than the elements, of the matter under study are already known to him. There are specialists, too, who do not possess, and who affect even to disdain, the literary qualities by which all the articles contributed to the *Encyclopédie* are distinguished. To say of an encyclopædia published in the present day that its articles were brilliantly written, but wanting in knowledge of the subject, would be to condemn it. That, however, does not alter the fact, that many a modern encyclopædia, however valuable as a work of reference, is, viewed as a whole, unreadable.

The *Encyclopédie*, on the other hand, could be read by anyone possessing ordinary literary tastes from beginning to end. Diderot, D'Alembert, Voltaire, Rousseau, Montesquieu, Marmontel, and the rest of the celebrated French writers of the eighteenth century, wrote nothing that was not interesting. Whatever subject they might be treating, they could not but arrest the reader's attention, and place themselves *en rapport* with him. To do this in dealing strictly with scientific matters would no doubt be as difficult as to captivate the general public by means of a mathematical demonstration. A fair number of "specialists" were, it may be said, engaged on the *Encyclopédie*; and this would naturally be the case in regard to literature and philosophy. But in a good many instances knowledge of the subject was not the distinguishing characteristic of the articles contributed to the *Encyclopédie*; and Diderot himself showed that, without undervaluing the sufficiently evident advantages of positive knowledge, he attached the highest importance in these matters to literary expression and literary form.

Rosseau, for instance, to whom musical subjects had been entrusted, was, soon after the publication of the first volume, accused of having made several serious mistakes. A pamphlet, entitled *Erreurs sur la Musique dans l'Encyclopédie,* was brought out; and in the preface to one of the succeeding volumes of the *Encyclopédie,* the editor, taking his contributor's defence, wrote that "M. Rousseau, who joins to much knowledge and taste in music, the talent of thinking and expressing himself with clearness, which musicians do not always possess, is too well able to defend himself for us to undertake his cause." In the preface to an earlier volume, Diderot had found it necessary to complain of a critic who had taken the somewhat unusual course of praising an article which he might fairly have blamed:

"A critic," says the editor, "has twice described the article 'Accord' as excellent, which makes one suppose that he has read it carefully and understands its subject. This article, however, otherwise very well done, needed, to be really excellent, a more exact enumeration of the fundamental chords. The writer had omitted the chord of the seventh or simple dominant, very different both in itself and its inversions from the chord of the seventh or dominant, otherwise called chord of the tonic dominant.

These are the mere elements of harmony, and there is no student whom the omission in question would not at once strike. Accordingly this error must not be attributed to M. Rousseau, author of this fine work; it is only necessary to read it and to understand the subject to see that it is a copyist's error. He has begged us to make this announcement. The necessary correction is made in the errata of the second volume."

The pamphlet exposing the errors committed by Rousseau in the musical articles he contributed to the *Encyclopédie* was published anonymously; but its authorship is indicated with sufficient clearness, though indirectly, in Diderot's preface to the sixth volume. Unfortunately for Rousseau, the writer who condemned his articles was no less competent a person than the famous French composer Rameau. Diderot, without naming the author of the pamphlet, reproaches him with having attacked a man who had praised him—thus breaking in a shameless manner the first and most essential rule of literary good fellowship; and in a note to the preface the reader is informed that the flattering pat on the shoulder which had been brutally responded to by a blow in the face is to be found in the article "Accompagnement," which makes mention of only two persons—a M. Campion, to whom a passing word is given, and Rameau, who is referred to again and again, and always in terms of high praise.

Nor was this the first occasion on which Rameau had expressed his opinion of Rousseau's acquirements as a musician. When the *Devin du Village* was brought out in 1752—the very year, by the way, in which the publication of the *Encyclopédie* volume by volume was commenced—Rameau declared that in spite of its weakness and incorrectness, the music was much better than anything Rousseau could have produced. That the libretto of *Le Devin du Village*, like those of his two other operas, *Les Muses Galantes* and *Pygmalion*, was really the work of Rousseau, has never been doubted. But when these three operas were produced, Rousseau's right to claim the music as his own was in each case questioned; and the correctness of his articles on musical subjects was similarly impeached, both when he was contributing to the *Encyclopédie*, and afterwards when, ceasing his connection with that work, he published under the title of *Dictionnaire de Musique* a sort of musical encyclopædia written throughout by himself.

On the principle of giving much to those who possess much, the world will no doubt continue to regard Rousseau as the composer of *Le Devin du Village*. But as his technical knowledge of music was promptly denied by the musicians of his time whenever he wrote critically on the subject, so when *Le Devin du Village* was produced, with a success which Rousseau's other efforts in the operatic line failed to obtain, several persons in a position to know the true facts of the case came forward to declare that the music was not by Rousseau at all.

Rousseau, in the *Confessions*, states with much detail

how the music of each piece in the *Devin du Village* occurred to him; how he at one time thought of burning the manuscript; how his friends persuaded him to do nothing of the sort; and how at last he wrote the libretto and sketched out the whole of the music in six days: so that when he arrived with his work in Paris he had nothing to add but the recitative and what he calls the *remplissage*, by which he apparently meant the instrumentation. When, however, *Le Devin du Village* was about to be produced at Fontainebleau, under the auspices of Madame de Pompadour, Rousseau attended no rehearsal except the last; nor did he compose the recitative, which was furnished in his absence by Jéliotte the singer.

The music of *Le Devin du Village* was, according to Rousseau's enemies, the work of one Granet, a composer of Lyons, who had asked Rousseau for a libretto. Rousseau supplied Granet with the libretto demanded, and in due time Granet composed the music and forwarded it in a parcel to "M. Rousseau, homme de lettres, demeurant à Paris." There were a good many Rousseaus then, as, now, at Paris; and one of them, Pierre Rousseau by name, was a man of letters. To him came the package of music, which he must have seen was not intended for him. Being, however, of a curious disposition, and possessing a good knowledge of music, he not only read the work himself, but showed it to a musical friend, M. Bellissent, one of the conservators of the Royal Library. When the two amateurs had studied Granet's music sufficiently, they made it once more into a parcel and sent it back to the post-office, whence it was forwarded to the Rousseau for whom it had been intended.

The idea that Rousseau had not composed the music of *Le Devin du Village* seems first to have been conceived at the rehearsals, from which he was absent—or perhaps at that last rehearsal at which he was present without making his presence felt. Rumours of plagiarism on a wholesale scale originating at the theatre reached the "chroniclers," correspondents, and other journalists of the period; and the accusation was made formally in the secret memoirs of Bachaumont, in the *Gazette de France*, and in several pamphlets of the time. According to one writer, the score of *Lè Devin du Village* was the work of an abbé, who, by reason of his sacred calling, preferred not to let his name be known; another said that a woman had written it; while Voltaire declared that it had been found among the papers of Gaultier, director of the Marseilles Opera in 1685. Rameau, in expressing upon the subject the opinion already cited, referred to a remark he had made five years before concerning Rousseau's *Muses Galantes*, in which he had recognised two different styles—that of a master in some of the pieces, that of an unsuccessful student in the others. He concluded that only the feebler portions of the work belonged to Rousseau, whom he regarded as incapable of writing good music, but quite capable of claiming as his own the music of others.

The success with which *Le Devin du Village* was played did but animate and envenom the discussion as to the authorship of the score. At last M. de Bellissent, the conservator of the Royal Library, spoke. He remembered perfectly the incident of the misdirected packet received by Pierre Rousseau; and Pierre Rousseau the journalist, known at the time as *Rousseau of Toulouse*, wrote a long and detailed account of the affair in the *Journal Encyclopédique* of December, 1752.

It is quite possible that Rousseau may have sketched the airs for *Le Devin* (which, as he tells us, occurred to him almost simultaneously with the words), and forwarded them to Granet for correction or for orchestration. Rousseau, however, denied the Granet story entirely, and he took one rather ineffectual means of proving that he was really capable of composing such music as that to which the libretto of *Le Devin* had been set. He reset the work; and in 1779, twenty-seven years after the production of the opera in its original shape, and one year after Rousseau's death, *Le Devin du Village* with the new music was brought out at the Opera.

"This experiment," wrote Grimm in his *Correspondence*, "had no success. With the exception of the first air, 'J'ai perdu tout mon bonheur,' which was feebly applauded, all the other new airs were hooted without the least regard for the memory of the author. At each *ritornello* of which the motive could not be recognised, the pit called out incessantly for the old music; and the pieces in which the author has changed nothing were alone received with the accustomed favour."

Whether Rousseau was or was not the composer of the music to which *Le Devin du Village* was originally and still from time to time is played; whether or not the errors pointed out in his contribution to the *Encyclopédie* were " copyist's errors," as Diderot asserted in one case, or whether, as in another case he implied, they were to a great extent atoned for by the clearness of his ideas and the beauty of his style, it is quite undeniable that this eloquent and impressive writer has left many admirable pages on musical matters. His connection with the *Encyclopédie* did not last very long; and Diderot, in his preface to the sixth volume, after setting forth that Rousseau was quite competent to defend himself against the criticisms of which his articles had been made the subject, announced that he would scatter his enemies in a work of his own: a " Dictionary of Music," which he was about to publish.

Rousseau's "Dictionary of Music" has, from a technical point of view, been quite as severely attacked as his musical contributions to the *Encyclopédie*. His *Dictionnaire de Musique*, as compared with the two great classes of modern musical dictionaries, is much what the *Encyclopédie* is to the two great classes of modern encyclopædias. The articles, though those of a scientific character are borrowed in substance from earlier works of the same kind, are all replete with Rousseau's own personal views and written in his own characteristic style. Our smaller musical dictionaries are for the most part dictionaries of musical terms, and like the smaller kind of encyclopædias are useful only as handbooks of reference. Musical dictionaries of the larger kind have hitherto presented the fault, from the " general reader's" point of view, of including a good many articles which, however learned and however correct, are unreadable except to those who approach them thirsting for information and determined to acquire it wherever and however it can be obtained. Rousseau—like Voltaire, whom he so little resembled, and like Diderot, with whom neither Voltaire nor Rousseau had much in common— never wrote anything that anyone capable of reading would have been unable to read. All three dealt at times and, indeed, frequently, with profound subjects. But neither of them was ever abstruse in the sense of being unintelligible. To expect a writer to treat such a subject— for example—as " Acoustics " with all necessary detail, and yet with sufficient animation to interest the first person into whose hands his treatise might chance to fall, would of course be absurd. But Rousseau either left such subjects aside or treated them quite superficially. His dictionary abounds in errors, but it affords excellent reading, to which anyone may turn with the certainty of deriving from it entertainment, and in the midst of scientific errors (by which if he is not a scientific person he will probably fail to be shocked) a great number of absolutely true artistic ideas.

Take, for instance, Rousseau's article on "Opera," which he defines as

> "a dramatic and lyrical spectacle designed to combine the enchantments of all the fine arts by the representation of some passionate action through sensations so agreeable as to excite both interest and illusion. The constituent parts of an opera," he continues, "are the poem, the music, and the decorations. By poetry the spectacle speaks to the mind, by music to the ear, and by painting to the eye; all combining through different organs to make the same impression on the heart. Of these three parts my subject only allows me to consider the first and last with reference to the second."

Rousseau regards music as of two kinds. As "an institution of nature" its effects are confined to the senses; to the physical "pleasure which results from melody, harmony, and rhythm." But besides this simple music, so strangely described as "an institution of nature"—the music of dances and songs, the "people's melody," as Herr Wagner might say—there is dramatic music; and, as "the essential part of a lyrical scene aiming principally at imitation," music becomes one of the fine arts, and is capable of "painting all pictures, of exciting all sentiments; of competing with poetry; of endowing her with new strength; of embellishing her with new charms; and of triumphing over her while placing the crown upon her head."

All this is admirable and quite in harmony with the latest and most approved operatic theory of the present day. Rousseau, however, now launches into considerations on the music of the Greeks, whose language he declares was "so accentuated that its reflections in a long declamation formed spontaneously as it were musical intervals, distinctly appreciable." "Their theatrical pieces were," he asserts, "a species of opera"; and it was for this reason, he paradoxically adds, "that they could have no operas properly so called." In a like style we are informed that "all their poetry was musical, and all their music declamatory." Song, in fact, with the Greeks was "hardly more than sustained discourse." They really sang their verses as they declared at the head of their poems; a practice which gave the Romans and afterwards the moderns the ridiculous habit of saying *I sing* when nothing is sung. That which the Greeks call the lyric style was "a pompous and florid strain of heroic poesy accompanied by the lyre." It is known that the Greek tragedies were recited or chanted, that they were accompanied by instruments, and that they had choruses. A Greek tragedy was thus, according to Rousseau, a sort of opera, but an opera without airs.

Rousseau, in his long article or essay on the opera, shows himself no great admirer of what is now called "absolute music"; not at least in connection with dramatic works. Readers of the "Confessions" know how much Rousseau loved the music of Italy. But that did not prevent him from expressing the enthusiasm he felt for Gluck when all the French writers who had previously praised the music of the Italians undervalued him in order to increase by force of contrast the merit of Piccinni. The introduction into opera of pleasing but inappropriate melodies had, said Rousseau, a corrupting effect, and was in itself a sign of corruption. It had been felt necessary to

"bring physical to the aid of moral pleasure, and to supply by the charms of harmony the lack of distinctness in meaning, and of energy in expression. The less the heart was touched, the more need there was to flatter the ear; and from sensation was sought the delight which sentiment could not furnish. Hence the origin of airs, choruses, symphonies, and all that enchanting melody which often embellishes modern music at the expense of the poem."

These views harmonise perfectly with much that Herr Wagner has written on the subject of opera. But Rousseau was by no means disposed to accept as suitable for operatic treatment those mythical subjects which find so much favour in Herr Wagner's eyes. Schlegel, in his *History of Dramatic Literature,* without considering the value which mythical subjects derive from their simplicity and universal significance, recommends supernatural subjects to the operatic composer, on the ground that beings of an imaginary world may more appropriately, or less inappropriately, be supposed to express themselves in song than the inhabitants of the world we live in, who, as we all know, use habitually the speaking voice. The question of the fitness of symbolical legends for musical illustration had not presented itself either to Schlegel or to Rousseau. Rousseau indeed objected entirely to supernatural subjects; his objection being apparently founded on a passage from Arteaga's *Rivoluzioni del Teatro Italiano*, which he quotes in one of his notes. " Gods and devils," Arteaga had written, " were banished from the stage as soon as poets discovered the art of making men speak with dignity."

"At the birth of the opera," wrote Rousseau, " its inventors, to elude that which seemed unnatural as an imitation of human life in the union of music with speech, transferred their scenes from earth to heaven and to hell. Not knowing how to make men speak, they make gods and devils instead of heroes and shepherds sing. . . . As there was no plot which, however intricate, could not be easily unravelled by the intervention of some god, the spectator quietly abandoned to the poet the task of delivering his hero from the greatest dangers. . . . A supernatural action had in it no human interest, and the senses refused to yield to an illusion in which the heart had no part. It would have been difficult to weary an assembly at greater cost than was done by these first operas."

Gradually, however, the musical portion of the lyrical spectacle became developed. In the early days of the opera,

"what better use," he asks, "could be made of a kind of music which could paint nothing than by employing it in the representation of things which could not exist? But since music learned to paint and to speak the charms of sentiment, it has brought into contempt those of the Wand; the theatre was purged of its mythology; interest was substituted for astonishment. The machinery of poets and carpenters was destroyed, and the lyric drama assumed a more noble and less gigantic character. All that could move the heart was employed with success, and gods were driven from the stage on which men are now represented."

If much, and, indeed, nearly all, that Rousseau wrote concerning operatic treatment accords with Herr Wagner's now well-known views, his ideas on the choice of a subject agree neither with those of Wagner, nor, above all, with those of Meyerbeer. It is not enough that supernatural stories be banished from the lyrical stage. All political deliberations, all plots, conspiracies, explanations, and recitals, are also to be avoided. The main object of the lyrical drama must be to depict "energy of feeling and violence of passion." Here once more Rousseau anticipates Herr Wagner's way of thinking; which he again does when he points out how, after a time,

"Music, able to walk alone, began to disdain the poetry she had to accompany. To enhance her own value she drew from herself beauties of which her companion had hitherto had a share. She still professes, it is true, to express her ideas and sentiments; but she assumes, so to speak, an independent language; and though the object of the poet and of the musician is the same, they are too much separated in their labours to produce at once two images resembling each other, yet distinct, without mutual injury. Thus it happens that if the musician has more heart than the poet, he effaces him; and the actor, seeing the spectator sacrifice the words for the music, sacrifices in his turn theatrical gesture and action to song and brilliancy of voice, thus transforming a dramatic entertainment into a mere concert."

M. Gustave Chouquet, writing in Dr. Grove's *Dictionary of Music and Musicians,* is surely in error when, under the head of "Dictionaries of Music," he remarks that "it is to Rousseau's literary ability rather than to his elevated views on æsthetics, that the enormous success of his dictionary is due." Enough has already been cited from Rousseau's dictionary to show that his views on æsthetical questions were as elevated as they were clearly expressed. It is not the æsthetical but the technical portion of his dictionary that leaves something to be desired. Rousseau's musical studies may have been defective; but music had occupied a large share of his attention, and he possessed in the highest degree what Diderot, in his apologetic note, called "the talent of thinking and of expressing his thoughts with clearness."

It has already been mentioned that Rousseau's *Dictionary of Music* was by no means the earliest work of the kind. It was the first, however, that obtained great success, and which enjoyed the honour of being translated into several languages. Rousseau had turned to account both the substance and the form of Brossard, who published a *Musical Dictionary* at Paris in 1703; though the arrangement of the work in alphabetical order might well have been suggested to him by the *Encyclopédie* itself. In 1701 a Bohemian organist, named Janowka, had issued in Latin, *A Key to Musical Knowledge,* with which Brossard does not seem to have been acquainted; and a much older work of the same kind had been produced by the Flemish musician calling himself Johannes Tinctor. But the first musical dictionary which made its mark in Europe, or in any one European country, was Rousseau's *Dictionnaire de Musique*; and Rousseau's dictionary, whatever its shortcomings may be, remains in a certain sense, and especially in a literary point of view, a standard work. No one would now turn to it for instruction on the subject of the musical art; but it will always be full of interest, as containing an eloquent exposition of Rousseau's views in regard to a number of musical questions, and very lively accounts of the musical performances of Rousseau's own time.

To France, then, belongs the honour of having published not only the first great encyclopædia, but also the first musical dictionary, destined to become famous. Germany, however, among other countries, possessed already musical dictionaries of her own. Walthern had had brought out, about 1730, a musical dictionary (of which the second edition appeared in 1732), entitled, *Alte und neue Musikalische Bibliothek oder Musikalisches Lexicon*. But in this work the French lead had been so far followed that the author had adopted a plan suggested by Brossard at the end of his dictionary, to which, according to M. Chouquet, it forms "a kind of complement." Rousseau's dictionary had the same effect which had been exercised by the dictionary of

Brossard in stimulating the zeal of new lexicographers. Its influence was chiefly felt in France. But it has been already mentioned that the work was translated into various languages; and, besides affording materials for several new dictionaries published at Paris, it was imitated by Reynvaau, of Amsterdam, in 1795, whose *Muzikaal Kunst Woordenbook* was never, however, finished. In 1787, G. F. Wolf brought out a *Musical Lexicon*. But Forkel's *Universal History of Music* had appeared in 1788; and in 1802 a *Musical Lexicon*, by Koch, was published at Frankfort, which was in a great measure based on Forkel's work, and was greatly superior in all respects to Wolf's *Lexicon*. Gerber, meanwhile, had, in 1790, issued a musical *Historico-Biographical Lexicon*, of which he produced a new edition, or to which, rather, he added a copious supplement in 1812; for the new lexicon contained so many references to the old one that for the sake of completeness it was necessary to have both.

Now, however, in the matter of musical dictionaries we see the example of Germany followed by France; for Gerber's first lexicon was the model of the *Historical Dictionary of Musicians* by Choron and Fayolle, published at Paris in 1810. This again was the model of Fétis's well-known *Universal Biography of Musicians*, a work which, though full of errors, especially as regards English musicians, is nevertheless the most complete work of the kind in existence. To give but one instance of the careless, confident ignorance and hasty assumption by which several of M. Fétis's articles on English musicians are characterised, it may be enough to mention that John Barnett and Sterndale Bennett are treated as one and the same person. Sterndale Bennett becomes the composer of the *Mountain Sylph*. He had, in fact, written a charming, romantic overture called the *Wood Nymphs*; and as an overture is usually the preface to an opera, M. Fétis concluded that the *Wood Nymphs* and the *Mountain Sylph* formed but one work, and Bennett and Barnett but one man.

In Italy, where musicians occupy themselves more with the composition and execution of music than with the literature of the art, no dictionary of music was published until 1801, when the *Dizionario della Musica* of the Abbé Giannelli appeared. A second edition of Giannelli's book was brought out in 1820. But this work was entirely superseded by Dr. Lichtenthal's *Diziouario*, of which the first two volumes are devoted to musical subjects of various kinds, while the last two consist of an historical and critical catalogue of musical works. For his materials Lichtenthal was much indebted to Gerber, and through Gerber to Forkel. But he added much matter of his own; and in the year 1823, when it was first brought out, Lichtenthal's musical dictionary was by far the most complete work of its kind. It was at once translated into French; and almost simultaneously with the French version of Lichtenthal's dictionary was published a new *Dictionnaire de Musique Moderne*, by Castil Blaze.

Castil Blaze's dictionary, which is written in a vivacious and often in an aggressive style, abounds in anecdotes and illustrations. It was apparently intended to replace Rousseau's dictionary which Castil Blaze was never tired of attacking. The sort of work done in his character of composer by this musician—who was at once composer, author, and critic—would have failed to gain him much favour in the present day. He claimed to know the taste of his countrymen, and to possess the art of rendering palatable to them unfamiliar works which, unless specially prepared for French audiences, would not, he maintained, have the least chance of success. *Der Freischütz* became in his hands *Robin Bois*; *Oberon*, *Huon de Bordeaux*. In arranging Weber's third great opera *Euryanthe* for the French stage, he kept to the original libretto, as he also did in arranging French versions of some of Rossini's operas, including *Il Barbiere*, *La Gazza Ladra*, and *Otello*. But he took upon himself to remodel both *Oberon* and *Der Freischütz*. It must be reckoned, on the other hand, in his favour that *Don Giovanni*, which Kalkbrenner had broken up and transformed with all sorts of variations and additions into a sort of medley, was restored by him to its original form. He has himself moreover informed the world how, when he first undertook to arrange *Der Freischütz* for the French stage, his respect for the opera prevented him from making in it the slightest change.

Castil Blaze's first version of Weber's great work was brought out in its original form at the Odéon in 1824, when it was violently hissed, or, as the Provençal adapter with true southern volubility expresses it, "sifflé, meurtri, bafoué, navré, moqué, conspué, turlupiné, hué, vilipendié, terrassé, déchiré, lacéré, cruellement enfoncé jusqu'au troisiéme dessous." The opera was of necessity withdrawn. But Castil Blaze determined to reproduce it in another form. He remodelled the entire work, cut out such portions of it as had excited the derision of the too difficult French public, introduced here and there compositions of his own, and presented this arrangement of what he himself knew well enough to be a masterpiece under the title of *Robin des Bois*. In its new shape the opera, which still consisted for the most part of Weber's music, had a run of 357 nights at the Odéon, and of sixty at the Opéra Comique. Its course, however, was suddenly arrested at the latter theatre in virtue of a regulation which had apparently been overlooked, to the effect that no work must be played at the Opéra Comique which had not been written specially for it. Thirty-two years afterwards Castil Blaze took *Der Freischütz* once more in hand. He restored what in his *Robin des Bois* version he had cut out; cut out what he had himself added, and produced this third version of Weber's masterpiece—which must have been identical or nearly so with the first of Castil Blaze's two versions produced in 1824—at the Théâtre Lyrique.

Berlioz had brought out at the Grand Opera in 1841 a version of *Der Freischütz* with recitatives furnished by himself. Some such addition was indispensable if the work was to be given at the Académie, where, by the unchangeable laws of the establishment, no work comprising even the smallest amount of spoken dialogue can be performed. But in justice to Castil Blaze, who has been much blamed for the liberties he took with the works of great composers, it should be remembered that he did his best to make the French public accept *Der Freischütz* in its native shape.

Before publishing his musical dictionary, Castil Blaze had brought out a volume entitled *De l'Opéra en France*, which is very methodically arranged, and treats successively of operatic overtures, airs, duets, concerted pieces, choruses, finales, and so on; with examples from celebrated operas of each of these forms. This work includes moreover a sort of treatise on the opera, in which much stress is laid on the defective versification of French operatic poets, or "paroliers" as Castil Blaze called them. In arranging a great number of German and Italian operas for the French stage he made many interesting and often valuable observations on the art of translation, on the importance both for the composer and the vocalist of "words for music" being thoroughly singable, and on the absolute insignificance —or want of significance in a dramatic sense—of ordinary melodies. He did not—to deal with this last point first—pretend that the spirited, sparkling air of Figaro in the *Barber of Seville* could be made to lose gaiety by being allied to words of a sombre character; or that the solemn monotones with ghastly trombone accompaniment pronounced by the statue of the Commander in *Don Giovanni* might be rendered light and lively by being sung to words of a humorous character. But possessing a wide acquaintance with operatic music and with the history of operatic composition, he knew that airs had often been borrowed from the church for the theatre, and from the theatre for the church; also that composers had sometimes used the same melody with equal effect both in a comic and in a serious situation.

Berlioz has replied in an insufficient manner to arguments of this kind by showing that a trivial and familiar tune such as that of *Maître Corbeau* cannot without striking incongruity be sung to words of a grave character, and conversely. This, however, was to base a general rule on extreme cases for which Castil Blaze had already provided by treating them as exceptions. To put Castil Blaze's proposition in a few words, he maintained that in most cases an operatic melody derived its dramatic character from the situation in which it was presented and from the words to which it was sung. In reproducing this argument again and again (and there is scarcely one of his numerous works in which it is not to be found), he may to some extent have been pleading his own cause. As if to demonstrate its truth in a crushing manner, he set himself the task of composing a mass with melodies borrowed from Rossini's opera. One of the works laid under contribution for this strange project, to which Rossini with characteristic good nature gave his sanction, was the *Barber of Seville,* from which Almaviva's graceful cavatina was borrowed; and if anyone objected to this selection that the Count's love-song did not possess a truly religious character, the ingenious adapter could at once reply that Rossini had taken that very air from a mass of his own composition.

The chief faults of French libretti as vehicles for musical expression proceeded, according to Castil Blaze, partly from the poverty of the French language and the number of little words (such as *le, de, que, ne,* &c.) contained in it; partly from the inability of the librettists to turn the language to the best lyrical account; and partly from the librettists' ignorance of music, and consequently of the conditions under which " words for music " should be written. Latin, Provençal, Italian, English, were not troubled, he pointed out, with the multitude of little words which embarrassed the march of French sentences and rendered translations into French verse impossible. How superior was English, in which two or three words will often express as much as five or six in French. *Pope's Windsor Forest,* for example, became in French *La Forêt de Windsor de Pope* ; "beauty's charms," "les charmes de la beauté." Castil Blaze held that "the parasitic insects which were devouring the French language" might be extirpated if writers (and especially poets) would make an intelligent study of ancient French and of Provençal, which were alike free from the pests in question ; and he himself published several poems, original and translated, including a version of Figaro's *Largo al fattotum*, in the Provençal language, accompanying them with appropriate French renderings in which "parasitic insects" were scarcely to be found.

Castil Blaze was nothing if not pugnacious. He had the courage of his opinions, and missed no opportunity of asserting them. He seldom put forward a view of his own without making war upon those who saw the matter in another light; and his *Dictionary of Music* resembles Rousseau's work by its polemical character, if in no other respect. M. Gustave Chouquet describes it as "in part copied from that of Rousseau"; but this is a mistake. Castil Blaze had two much belief in himself and too little belief in Rousseau—whom he regarded not merely as a poor musician, but as nothing less than an impostor in musical matters—to borrow anything from such a source. Like Rousseau's dictionary, the dictionary of Castil Blaze is full of the writer's own personality. Like Rousseau's work too, it can be read with interest apart from all question as to whether in the present day and with a view to positive information it can be studied with advantage.

Since Castil Blaze's work, several dictionaries of music have appeared in France, among which may be mentioned one by the Escudier brothers of a general kind, and another by Ortigues devoted specially to church music. It occurred moreover a few years ago to M. Félix Clément to produce an operatic dictionary, or *Dictionnaire Lyrique*, in which an account may be found of the plot, the principal musical pieces, the date of production, the circumstances under which it was produced, and so on, of every opera of note, and many of no note whatever. M. Félix Clément's operatic dictionary is indeed singularly complete. But, though furnished with a supplement, added after the great body of the work had been finished, it has already of necessity lost something of its value as a universal operatic lexicon.

We have seen that one famous musical dictionary was in its origin an offshoot from an encyclopædia, and as encyclopædias gave birth to dictionaries of special subjects, so dictionaries of special subjects have in due course been swallowed up by encyclopædias. M. Félix Clément's labours as an operatic lexicographer are to be found not only in his *Dictionnaire Lyrique*, but also in Larousse's *Grand Dictionnaire Universel du 19me Siècle*, which claims to be, and in fact is, a collection of special dictionaries. M. Félix Clément, however, figures to greater advantage in the late M. Larousse's vast work than in his own small but comprehensive volume. The operatic articles are almost the same in both dictionaries. But in the *Dictionnaire Larousse* musical illustrations are given, and the principal airs from each opera noticed are reproduced. The *Dictionnaire Larousse* moreover contains in addition to the aforesaid operatic articles a number of articles on national airs and French popular airs of various kinds, in all of which the notes of the melodies are given.

The last few years have seen the publication of a very interesting *Dictionnaire Universel du Théâtre* by MM. Goizet and Burtal, in which operas and operatic matters are incidentally noticed, and of a *Revue de la Musique Dramatique en France* by M. F. Crozet, which is in fact a dictionary of operas. M. Crozet's work, however, is very inferior to the work on the same subject and in the same form by M. Félix Clément.

Some years ago an excellent musical dictionary—certainly the best which had up to that time appeared in England—was published under the editorship of Dr. Stainer and Mr. W. A. Barrett, by Messrs. Novello, Ewer, and Co. Since Grassineau about the beginning of the last century brought out what was apparently the first musical dictionary published in England, dictionaries of music and of musical terms have been produced plentifully enough. Most of these works have had the disadvantage of being just what they pretended to be. Like dictionaries of spoken language, they gave definitions, explanations, and examples, but nothing more. The object, however, of the dictionary produced by Messrs. Stainer and Barrett was, as set forth by the editors, " to give sufficiently true outlines of matters of fact, to inform the amateur correctly, and intimate to the musical student the results to which his own reading would probably tend." In this musical dictionary, which is expressly called *Dictionary of Musical Terms*, great attention is paid (probably for the first time in an English work of the kind) to subjects which belong partly to the art or science of music, partly to other sciences. Thus a number of physiological subjects had been entrusted to Mr. Champneys, of St. Bartholomew's Hospital.

The honour of having invented the laryngoscope is claimed for Signor Garcia; and if singing-masters render service to physiology and surgery, the latter, it seems to be thought, may equally render assistance to the student of music, and above all of singing. In all modern musical dictionaries, in that of Messrs. Stainer and Barrett, as in the later larger and more comprehensive one issued under the direction of Dr. George Grove, the domain of music is held to include not only the science of acoustics and the method of manufacture employed in the construction of musical instruments, but also the anatomy and physiology of those organs of the human body which give forth and take in musical sounds. Beethoven knew nothing of acoustics; the great singing-masters of the eighteenth century had never studied the physiology of the voice; and neither composers nor singers in their endeavours to touch the ear of the public have yet found it necessary to make the organ of hearing the subject of careful and minute study, such as is suggested by the article on the "Ear" contained in Messrs. Stainer and Barrett's dictionary.

The editors, however, of our modern musical dictionaries err on the right side, if at all, in providing their readers with such information as this of which musicians and students of music have certainly no need. We have not met with any musical dictionary containing an article on the Hand; though the hand of the violinist is almost as fit a subject for special study as the voice of the singer, and very much more so than the ear of the auditor. For pianists some remarks from an anatomical point of view on the hand, and on the danger of over-exerting it, or of unduly stretching it, might really be useful. Schumann is known to have disabled himself as a pianist by having recourse to some mechanical contrivance which he had hoped would have the effect of increasing his powers of manipulation; and M. Castil Blaze, in a work on pianoforte-playing and the piano, tells a story of some friend of his who similarly lamed himself, as to his hands, by practising assiduously for a great number of hours without cessation.

In France, and on the Continent generally, the latest musical dictionary published is M. Arthur Pougin's supplement in two volumes to M. Fétis's *Universal Biography of Musicians*, in which it is interesting to see that M. Fétis's omissions in respect to English musicians have been in a great measure supplied. M. Pougin was already known by several interesting biographies of modern composers; and his supplement to Fétis's *Biography* contains articles on most living composers of eminence. Here will be found the fullest biographical and critical notices that have yet been given of the composers and executive musicians of Russia. M. Pougin has wisely accepted assistance from various hands; and the contributor who deals with Russian music, and especially with the Russian music of the present period, is a well-known musical critic who has paid several visits to Russia, and is quite master of the subject he treats.

Strange that Russia should possess a national school of composers, of whom three at least—Glinka, Rubinstein, and Tchaikowski,—are known throughout Europe, while England has but a few composers, who scarcely know where to get their works produced, and America no composers at all. Strange, too, that Russia should have produced a certain number of pianists and violinists who have also achieved a European reputation. Some explanation of this phenomenon may doubtless be found in the plentiful encouragement which in Russia music and musicians receive from the State. The one good thing

Russia has done for Poland has been to found scholarships at Warsaw for successful students of music, and to make an annual allowance to the Warsaw theatre, where at least one highly successful opera by a native composer, Moniuszko's *Halka*, has been produced. In Russia, meanwhile, the two opera-houses of St. Petersburg (one Italian, the other Russian), and the one opera-house of Moscow (half Russian, half Italian) are all richly subventioned. Both St. Petersburg and Moscow, too, have their " Conservatory " of music, to which the name of " Conservatory " has not been given in vain; since such musical talent as the country possesses has been fostered and developed in these institutions. In some countries, which are doubtless better governed than Russia, but in which the principle of State encouragement for art is barely recognised, or not recognised at all, talent of the musical kind must take care of itself, and get itself educated as best it can.

## CHAPTER XLII.

### GROVE'S MUSICAL DICTIONARY.

THERE is no lack in this or any other country of so-called "musical dictionaries," which are for the most part dictionaries of musical terms—the language of music being to many an unknown tongue. These guides to the meaning of words in common use among musicians are doubtless necessary. But something more was wanted; and this need has been in a measure supplied by musical dictionaries of a biographical kind. Then we have plenty of musical text-books, methods, and catechisms. But hitherto no work had been produced in dictionary or any other form to which that familiar abstraction, the "general reader," could refer for full and accurate information in regard to the lives of eminent composers, the history of musical instruments, the origin and gradual development of musical forms (such as the Symphony and the Sonata), the career of great singers, and so on.

Such a work will be found in *The Dictionary of Music and Musicians*, issued in parts under the editorship of Dr. George Grove. The list of contributors includes a great many distinguished names; and what is more important, the work comprises a large number of excellent articles. Encyclopædias, technical and biographical dictionaries, and all literary works of which the execution is entrusted to many different hands, are from the nature of the case very difficult to edit in such a manner that each subject shall receive precisely the amount of space due to it. The subjects which come first in alphabetical order obtain, as a rule, more than their fair share of attention; so that in almost all encyclopædias the letters of the first half of the alphabet have much more space allotted to them than those of the other half. The word Accent deserved, no doubt, the five interesting pages in which the subject has been treated by Mr. Ebenezer Prout; and the two pages on Accents from the pen of the Rev. Thomas Helmore, are certainly not without value. But the fulness with which these subjects are treated, could not but be exceptional.

The indispensable article on Accompaniment (with which Rousseau's too famous performance on the same subject might be disadvantageously compared) is the work of Mr. Hopkins, organist to the Temple; Mr. Franklin Taylor writes of the ornaments and graces called in French "agréments." Those who know of no Agricola but the illustrious general whose life has been written by Tacitus, will perhaps be surprised to learn that the annals of music preserve the memory of no less than six Agricolas or Agricolæ, whose merits are recorded in the *Dictionary of Music and Musicians* (*Fortunati nimium sua si bona nôrint!*) by Dr. Franz Gehring, of Vienna, assisted by Mr. J. R. Sterndale Bennett. The student of manners and customs, whether or not he cares for music, will be interested to hear on the authority of Mr. Julian Marshall, that a distinguished Italian singer of the eighteenth century, Lucrezia Agujari by her true name, used, being the natural child of a certain nobleman, to be always announced in the play bills as "La Bastardina" or "Bastardella." A notice of the Ancient Concerts is furnished by Mr. Charles Mackeson; under the head of "Arrangement," Mr. Hubert Parry describes and illustrates various forms of musical adaption; Dr. Francis Hueffer contributes biographical and critical notices of Adolphe Adam, Auber, Boïeldieu, and other French composers; Dr. Stone deals with the history, construction, and resources of the Basoon and other wind instruments; Mr. Dannreuther contributes a paper on Berlioz; Mr. William Chappell tells the story of the rise and progress of the publishing firm of Chappell and Co.; Mr. Hipkins traces the history of the house of Broadwood and Co.; and apart from other sufficient reasons, Broadwood and Collard among pianoforte manufacturers, Boosey and Chappell among music publishers, would be entitled to a place in Dr. Grove's dictionary by reason of their connection with eminent composers. The Chappells were associated with J B. Cramer, and in its earliest days with the Philharmonic Society; Boosey and Co. published for Himmel and Romberg, Rossini and Merchadante; Collard and Co. included at one time Clementi as a member of the firm. The house now known as that of Broadwood and Co. was established at its present address, Great Pulteney Street, nearly 150 years ago, by one Tschudi, a native of Zurich, who on the recommendation of Handel was made harpsichord maker to the Royal Family of England. It was not, however, until 1770 that the first grand pianoforte made in London was constructed by a Dutchman with the assistance of John Broadwood, who had married Tschudi's daughter, and who after a time succeeded him in the management of the business.

Invaluable to musicians and lovers of music, the new dictionary contains much that will be interesting to theatre-goers, opera-goers, and men of the world generally. From Beethoven to Bridgetower, the mulatto violinist for whom the Kreutzer Sonata was composed, and from Bridgetower to Britton " the musical small-coal man"; from Broadwood's pianos to the barrel organs of the street, no personage, no subjects or objects belonging to the world of music have been forgotten. Dr. Grove's article on Beethoven, both by the abundance and significance of its biographical details, and by the justness and firmness of its critical grasp, is the most interesting and, though occupying but fifty pages, the most complete account of that marvellous composer and exceedingly strange man that has ever been published.

The forty or fifty pages devoted to this greatest of the great composers would, as a separate work, form the best critical biography of Beethoven yet published. It is very succinct, very complete, and thoroughly interesting. Perhaps what chiefly distinguishes this study is the writer's appreciation of Beethoven as a man. As to his pianoforte-playing, we are told that "at a pianissimo he would crouch down so as to be hidden by the desk, and then, as the crescendo increased, gradually rise, until at the fortissimo he would spring into the air with his arms extended, as if wishing to float into the clouds." With regard to his personal appearance, we read that he now and then attempted to dress in the fashion, attiring himself in silk stockings, long boots and sword, a double eye-glass and seal ring. But Beethoven was seldom so eccentric as when he was endeavouring to behave like other people. He never wore good clothes at home, and when Czerny first called upon him his beard was nearly half an inch long, his black hair stood up in a great shock, his ears were filled with wool which had apparently been soaked in some yellow substance, and his clothes were made of a loose hairy stuff which gave him the look of Robinson Crusoe. Those who saw him for the first time, though they may have been startled by his personal appearance, were often charmed by the eager cordiality of his address, and by the absence of the bearishness and gloom which even then were already attributed to him. His simplicity and absence of mind were shown in many strange ways. He could not be made to see why his standing in his night-shirt at the open window should attract notice; and asked with perfect simplicity "what those d——d boys were hooting at?" At Penzing, in 1823, he shaved at the window in full view, and when the people collected to see him, changed his lodging rather than discontinue the practice. He once wanted to pay for a dinner which he had neither ordered nor eaten; and he forgot that he was the owner of a horse until the fact was recalled to his mind by the presentation of a bill for its keep. He cut himself horribly in shaving, was disorderly in many ways, and could not as a rule write a legible hand, though the signature to one of his letters to Mr. Broadwood, as reproduced in facsimile, is not only clear and legible, but is marked moreover by a boldness and a certain elegance. His letters, says "G.," contain no descriptions or grace of style; they were often clumsy and incorrect. But they were also often eminently interesting from being so brimful of the writer's personality.

We are assured that, like some other men of genius whose appearance would seem to belie the fact, Beethoven was "extremely fond of washing." He would pour water backwards and forwards over his hands for a long time together; and if at such moments a musical thought struck him, he would become absorbed and would go on until the whole floor was swimming and the water had found its way through the ceiling into the room beneath. Beethoven's hatred of etiquette is sufficiently shown by the fact that he abandoned a lodging, for which he had paid heavily in advance, because his landlord insisted on bowing to him whenever they met. In a like spirit he, on a celebrated occasion, pulled his hat over his eyes instead of removing it; he neither wished to give nor to receive salutations. There is no end to the characteristic stories told of Beethoven in a memoir which is no less remarkable for its instructive criticism than for its interesting anecdotes. Before quitting the subject it is right to express full concurrence in the views of the writer, when, in connection with Beethoven's household management, he says, "A man whose principles were so severe as to make him say of a servant who told a falsehood, that she was not pure at heart, and therefore could not make good soup; who punished his cook for the staleness of the eggs by throwing the whole batch at her one by one, and who distrusted the expenditure of every halfpenny, must have had much to contend with in his kitchen."

Two great composers, Gluck and Gounod, are dealt with in Part V. of the dictionary, which includes, moreover, an elaborate treatise on "Form" from the pen of Mr. Herbert Parry; notices of several minor composers such as the Russian Glinka, the Norwegian Grieg, the Danish Gade, and the half-Russianised Englishman Field—all the work of Mr. Edward Dannreuther; memoirs, biographical and critical, of distinguished executants, from Arabella Goddard to Frederick the Great; detailed descriptions of the flute and grand piano and of the various modifications introduced into the manufacture of those instruments; together with much musical matter of a miscellaneous kind. A French composer, M. Guirand, whose *Piccolino* was a few years ago brought out by Mr. Carl Rosa, is made the subject of a short biography by the editor, who also contributes a brief but sufficient account of the life and labours of the late Hermann Goetz.

Departing from his usual custom in respect to separate operas, the editor gives a full account of the circumstances under which Beethoven's *Fidelio* was produced, and of the changes to which the work was subjected by its not easily contented composer, until at last it received its present form. As to the unhappy English pianist and composer who settled in Moscow, then unsettled himself to wander about Europe and find his way to an Italian hospital, there to be discovered by some benevolent Russian friends, who took him back to Moscow where he arrived only to die, we are reminded by Mr. Dannreuther that both as a player and a composer he should be regarded as the predecessor and model of Chopin, who, together with all modern pianists, owes much to Field. "The form of Chopin's weird nocturnes, the kind of emotion embodied therein, the type of melody, its graceful embellishments, the peculiar waving accompaniments in wide, broad chords, with their vaguely prolonged sound resting on the pedals—all this and more we owe to Field." The music of John Field should be better known in England. Up to the present time it has been strangely neglected.

Englishmen are well acquainted with at least the name of the Danish composer Gade, though his charming little pieces for the pianoforte find but rarely if ever their way to London concert-rooms. The Norwegian Grieg is all but ignored in this country. His concerto has, it is true, been given more than once at the Crystal Palace Concerts, but his charming works for the pianoforte alone are never played in public, though all who have "ears to hear" would be delighted with them. "During the term of his studies he lived," says Mr. Dannreuther, "mostly in the romantic world of Schumann, Mendelssohn, and Chopin, whose works then gave the tone to the entire musical life of the town (*i.e.* Leipzig) and especially of the Conservatorium. He has since become aware of the older and newer masters, without, however, showing very distinct traces of their influence in his compositions. The characteristic Scandinavian features of Grieg's musical talent took a tangible shape soon after his return to the north. The Danish, Swedish, and Norwegian Volkslieder and dances absorbed his fancy more than the study of any great composer's works; and henceforth his compositions are marked with the stamp of a particular nationality more clearly than any man except perhaps Chopin." In his notice of Robert Franz, whose songs have only during the last few years begun to be appreciated in England, Mr. Dannreuther tells us that "detailed critical essays" have been published upon his songs, and arrangements by Saran, Schaffer, Ambros, Hueffer, and Liszt; and he might have added that attention was first called to them in England by Dr. Hueffer, who devotes a very interesting chapter to Franz's compositions for the voice in his well-known work on the "Music of the Future."

Everyone will read with interest the article on Frederick the Great, as a musician and a composer. Dr. Franz Gehring, of Vienna, writer of the paper in question, shows that the prince's first musical instructor was not Quantz, the flute-player, but Gottlob Hayne, the cathedral organist. At the age of sixteen, however, he began to learn the flute from Quantz, and was soon afterwards obliged to study that instrument in secret, since the king, his father, regarded music as a pastime unworthy of one who was destined to "rule nations." The musical prince was reduced to such shifts as engaging flute-playing servants (probably musicians who had served in military bands); and we may be sure he cultivated assiduously the art of playing pianissimo. On ascending the throne he established a court band at Berlin, and despatched the composer Graun to Italy with instructions to engage the best singers for the operatic theatre he proposed to found. Exaggerated accounts have been published of Frederick's lavish outlay on music. Dr. Gehring tells us that the salary paid Quantz amounted only to 2000 thalers, or about £300 in English money. But he also received fifteen ducats for each of his compositions; and 100 ducats for every new flute supplied to the king. Frederick played the flute four times a day. He also studied composition to some purpose, for when Quantz died without finishing a concerto on which he was engaged, the king was able to complete the work. Frederick seems to have played the pianoforte equally with the flute. We are told at least that he entertained a high admiration for Silbermann's pianos; and one can scarcely conceive a composer confining his attention to the flute alone. Frederick produced a march which was inserted in Lessing's *Minna von Barnhelm*. He also composed a *sinfonia*—i.e. orchestral introduction—for *Acis and Galathea*, and another for *Il Re Pastore*. In 1835 a search was instituted by King Frederick William III. which resulted in the discovery of no fewer than 120 compositions of Frederick the Great. Apparently, however, they were not worth much, since Dr. Gehring informs us that they were "interesting only from their history, and not suited for publication."

Mr. Hipkins contributes a valuable article on the ancient and modern construction of the pianoforte. There was at one time a marked difference between the action of the Vienna pianos and that of the pianos constructed in London and in Paris. We learn from Mr. Hipkins that the Viennese action is still adhered to in Austria for the cheaper grands, but that "the English (Broadwood) and French (Erard) are used for the better classes," and that their various modifications occupy the rest of the field of grand-piano-making in other countries. Pianists are often more attractive subjects of study than the instruments on which they perform; and everyone will read with interest the biographical sketch of Mdlle. Arabella Goddard, of whom it is little enough to say that she is "the most distinguished of English pianoforte players." This eminent artist was born at St. Servan, close to St. Malo, and at the age of six was placed under Kalkbrenner in Paris. She had afterwards a few lessons from Mrs. Anderson, and also from Thalberg in London. A Thalberg's recommendation she was placed in the hands of Mr. J. W. Davison, who "led her to the study of those great compositions, many of which she played in England for the first time." Mdlle. Arabella Goddard's success, unlike that of all other English pianists (unless we go back to the days of John Field) has not been confined to her own country. She passed the winter of 1854 and the whole of 1855 in Germany and Italy. "She carried her classical repertoire with her," says her biographer, "and was received with enthusiasm by some of the best critics in Germany." It might have been mentioned that one of the most laudatory articles of which Mdlle. Goddard's playing was ever made the subject, proceeded from the pen of Herr Rellstab, the celebrated Berlin critic.

Libretto, Lind, Lipinski, Liszt, "Lo! He comes with clouds descending," Macbeth, Magyar music, Mapleson, and Mendelssohn may be mentioned among the remarkable persons and things treated of in another part of this excellent dictionary. Libretto is a capital subject, and Dr. Hueffer has made the most of it. He lays stress on the fact that every really successful opera has been founded upon a good libretto; and his argument is strengthened by what at first looks like a weak point in it—his own statement that the best of Rossini's operas in the serious style is *William Tell*. This masterpiece rests undoubtedly on a "dramatic basis." But its libretto is a very poor production indeed; and by this no doubt may be explained the fact that *William Tell*, though the finest of its composer's works, has not been by any means the most fortunate. It was something very like a failure when first brought out; and for many years, until Duprez suddenly came forward and infused new life into the part of Arnold, it was customary at the Paris Opera-house to play nothing of *William Tell* except the second act. "You are in the bills again to-night, Maestro," one of the managers of the Académie is reported to have said to Rossini on meeting him in the street; "we play the second act of *William Tell*." "What, the whole of it?" exclaimed Rossini, who for many years found his admirable opera represented at the theatre for which he had written it by a mere fragment.

It may be taken as a canon in the art of libretto-writing that the interest should be centred in the principal female character. From *Il Barbiere* to *La Sonnambula*, and from *Faust* to *Carmen*, it may be seen that in all strikingly successful operas the prima donna plays a prominent part and the love interest is strong. It appears from Dr. Hueffer's list of eminent librettists that they have nearly all been Frenchmen; and he might have mnetioned—though the fact is by no means generally known—that the very effective libretto of Balfe's *Bohemian Girl* is nothing more than a translation from the French. It was written for the manager of Drury Lane Theatre by the late M. de St. Georges, who founded his work on the ballet of *La Gitana*—(itself derived from Cervantes' tale of *Gipsy of Madrid*)—and called it quite properly *La Bohémienne*, which the "poet

Bunn," very improperly, translated into *The Bohemian Girl*. The present writer was once asked immediately after the production of *The Bohemian Girl* to translate "I dreamt that I dwelt in marble halls" into appropriate French verse, and recoiling at the prospect of so formidable a task, found himself saved all trouble in the matter by M. de St. Georges coming forward with the original song as written by himself. The libretto of *The Enchantress*, composed by Balfe for Mdme. Thillon, was similarly due to M. de St. Georges; which did not prevent Mr. Alfred Bunn from claiming it as his own. Mr. Bunn seems, in fact, to have invented nothing except confused figures of speech, such as "When hollow hearts shall wear a mask, 'twill break thine own to see," "When the fair land of Poland was ploughed by the hoof," and so on. Many of the very best opera-books have been founded on ballets; and, apart from Wagner's libretti, which by their beauty and their significance stand alone, almost every fairly good libretto is of French origin. Dr. Hueffer awards well-deserved praise to Romani, but Romani's two most famous works, *La Sonnambula* and *Norma*, are both from the French. Two British dramatists fought not many years ago a tournament of the pen for the honour of having been the first to conceive the brilliant idea of turning the *Norma* libretto into a tragedy; they suddenly dropped their weapons when a newspaper writer at last informed them that Romani had based his opera-book of *Norma* on a French tragedy by Soumet. *La Gazza Ladra, Fidelio, La Favorita*—to take three well-known operas almost at random—are all founded on libretti derived from French plays; and with the exception of Wagner's operas, and of the thoroughly German *Freischütz*, it would be difficult to name any opera known throughout Europe of which the same might not be said.

In an interesting notice of Jenny Lind Mr. Julian Marshall gives the cadenza which she was in the habit of introducing in the final air of *La Sonnambula,* with valuable indications as to her precise manner of executing it. Equally remarkable is another cadenza of totally different character—reproduced in the same article—with which the "Swedish Nightingale" used to adorn one of Chopin's mazurkas. In the brief account of the famous Polish violinist Lipinski it might have been mentioned that this artist led for many years Prince Galitzin's private quartet—the Galitzin for whom some of Beethoven's latest quartets were composed. Dr. Hueffer contributes an elaborate account of Liszt's life and works, which possesses special value for English readers, inasmuch as in this country Liszt's compositions are all but unknown. The few that have been performed in England bear no proportion to the many which English audiences have never heard. The Liszt article is adorned with a portrait of the eminent virtuoso whom some regard as an admirable composer. The meaning of introducing " Lo ! He comes with clouds descending " in a musical dictionary will not at first sight be apparent to every one. It was worth pointing out, however, that the melody now associated with such solemn words was originally nothing more than a lively dance tune. The rule is not invariable, but solemnity and liveliness in music are often a mere question of time. There is nothing vivacious in " The Last Rose of Summer," and nothing sentimental in " The Groves of Blarney." Yet the music of the two songs is, as regards notes, identical. Under the head of " Macbeth Music " Mr. Chappell gives a full account of the various musical pieces written for the tragedy by Lock and other composers. Among the " Macs " the distinguished composer who succeeded Sir Sterndale Bennett, both as Cambridge musical professor and as principal of the Royal Academy of Music, is of course not forgotten. " Magyar Music " receives due attention; and the turns of melody, the graces, and above all, the closes characteristic of Hungarian national tunes are faithfully reproduced.

The origin of the " Marlbrook" melody might have been discussed at greater length ; and some of the many, and it is to be feared indeterminable, points connected with it could perhaps have been dealt with more satisfactorily. It must be remembered, on the other hand, that whole pages and entire chapters written on this subject have failed to elucidate the true authorship of the well-known melody—so boisterous when shouted by convivial spirits to the words of " We won't go home till morning," so touching when sung by the amorous Chérubin in praise of his well-beloved " marraine." M. Gustave Chouquet brings forward more or less distinctly all the reasons that have been alleged for believing the melody to be of this or of that origin. But he decides nothing and adds nothing to what was already known about the matter. Chateaubriand, hearing the tune sung by Arabs in Palestine, may have been and doubtless was quite wrong in suggesting that it had been carried thither by the Crusaders. But, unless Chateaubriand deceived himself in thinking that he had heard " Marlbrook " sung by Arabs in Palestine, it is not enough for M. Chouquet to tell us that the Crusaders could never have known it. The air known in France by the name of " Marlbrook " is popular in the present day throughout Spain ; and if Chateaubriand had been aware of the fact, it would perhaps have occurred to him that the Arabs might have picked it up in Spain during the period of their domination in that country, or that they carried it with them to Spain, and then returned, still preserving it. M. Chouquet is quite confident that " Marlbrook " is of French origin. But he does not prove his case. Nor in a subsequent article on the " Marseillaise " does he say anything to shake M. Castil-Blaze's apparently well-founded assertion that the melody of the great revolutionary song of

France is German, and borrowed from a German hymn. He contents himself with reproaching M. Castil-Blaze for his want of patriotism in asserting that Rouget de Lisle, when quartered as an officer at Strasburg, heard a well-known German hymn, and wrote to it the spirited words which were soon to be adopted by all France.

We learn from the article on "Mapleson" that the manager of Her Majesty's Theatre, before becoming an impresario, had studied both as a vocalist and instrumentalist. In the former character he appeared for some time in Italy; and his practical experience of the lyric stage has doubtless helped him greatly in his managerial labours. Nevertheless the most successful operatic managers have often been entirely ignorant of music. Barbaja, the great director of Italian opera in Rossini's time, was about as ignorant of music as a man who nevertheless could tell a good singer from a bad one might well be. He had begun life as waiter at the gambling saloon attached to the Scala Theatre; and thanks to a certain intuitive talent for reading the popular taste in the matter of operatic music—thanks also to remarkable ability as organizer and administrator—he advanced little by little until he became, first, manager of the Scala, then manager conjointly of the Scala Theatre at Milan and of the San Carlo Theatre at Naples, and ultimately manager of the Scala, the San Carlo, and of the Italian Opera-house at Vienna.

In another section of the Dictionary much space is

given to articles by Mr. Rockstro on Opera and Oratorio, Orchestra and Orchestration. Mr. Hipkins contributes a long and valuable paper on the Organ; and we are indebted to M. Paul David for an interesting biographical and critical notice of Paganini, which is accompanied by a quaint and characteristic sketch of the famous violinist from the pen of Sir Edwin Landseer. Then come Paisiello and Palestrina; and, to show that nothing escapes the comprehensive grasp of the editor, it may be mentioned that such minor subjects as Haydn's Bear Symphony, known as "L'Ours," and the same composer's "Ox Minuet," are duly dealt with. There is nothing very suggestive of harmony either in the movements or the utterances of a bear; and one can scarcely connect an ox with either the playing or the dancing of a minuet. For the meaning of these titles, however, the uninformed reader must be referred to the Dictionary itself.

Under the head of "Oxford," some curious particulars are given on the subject of Oxford and Cambridge musical degrees—the really curious thing being that composers of ability can be persuaded to take musical degrees at all. It is bad enough to have a Poet Laureate; but what would be thought of a poet who allowed himself to be dubbed "Doctor of Poetry"? One is not shocked, it is true, at the application of the doctor's title to the poet Watts; but what could be more grotesque than "Dr. Shelley" or "Dr. Swinburne"? except, perhaps,

"Dr. Beethoven" or "Dr. Mozart," "Dr. Rossini," or "Dr. Verdi."

In "Opera" Mr. Rockstro had a most difficult and most perplexing subject to treat. The history of opera cannot be traced in one unbroken line. It starts in Italy; then it is introduced into France. Next it pays a visit to England, and seems to have become naturalized here; when suddenly it disappears, and little is heard of it until Italian opera, as cultivated at the beginning of the eighteenth century, is brought over to England by Handel. Opera has a distinct history in Italy, in France, in Germany, and in England—to say nothing of Russia and a few of the smaller European countries, or of the United States and the Republics of South America. For a considerable time it makes progress in Italy. Then Italian composers and Italian singers go abroad, taking Italian opera with them. German composers, too, visit Italy, and, after studying there, return to their native land to produce, with modifications, operas which must still be regarded as Italian in character. At last the Germans who have studied in Italy become the rivals of the Italian masters. Then Gluck and Piccinni contend with one another in presence of French audiences, and, above all, of French critics. Finally it becomes the turn of the Italians to borrow from the Germans; and Mozart, so highly indebted for his melodic inspiration—or at least for his melodic forms—to [Italy, was so much before the Italians in regard to the composition of his orchestra and the construction of his musical pieces, that when Rossini wished to introduce into Italian opera the important reforms which must always be associated with his name he had nothing to do but turn to Mozart as a model.

Rossini was the first Italian composer who accompanied recitative with the full band, assigned leading parts to bass singers, made of each dramatic scene one continuous piece of music, and brought to something like perfection those highly varied, amply developed concerted finales which form so striking a feature in modern Italian opera. All these innovations were simply adaptations from Mozart. The history of Rossini's Italian career is the history of opera in Italy during the first half of the nineteenth century; for Rossini caused the works of his predecessors to be laid aside, while his own works and those of his immediate successors—and in every sense followers—continued to be played almost to the exclusion of all others until the Verdi period. For even Verdi, who in his later works studies dramatic consistency and dramatic effect more than Rossini studied them in his earlier works, must nevertheless be regarded as belonging more or less completely to the school of Rossini. The history of Rossini, Donizetti, Bellini, and Verdi, and of their doings in Italy, might be written continuously; but the operatic historian has his plans suddenly disarranged when he finds Rossini and the masters of his school visiting Paris and composing works for Paris opera-houses. Meanwhile the Grand Opera has been having a history of its own. So, too, has its relative, the Opéra Comique. Nor have composers been idle in Germany, where, before Rossini's time, Beethoven produced *Fidelio*; while towards the close of Rossini's artistic life Weber brought out *Der Freischütz*.

It would be useless to deny that a very complete history of the opera might be written without much being said about its development in England or at the hands of English composers. Mr. Rockstro must surely be joking when he speaks of the *Beggar's Opera* as a sort of typical work, representing in its happiest form the musical drama of England. It was, he says, "an embodiment of English art, pure and simple. The plot was laid in an English prison; dialogues were spoken as in an ordinary play, and the music consisted of the loveliest English and Scottish melodies that could be collected either from the inexhaustible treasury of national song or the most popular ballad music of the day." It may be, and no doubt is true, that "no English opera composed after the Italian manner was ever so cordially welcomed as the *Beggar's Opera*." Only the name of opera is here given to what is nothing more than a dramatic piece with incidental songs. It would, perhaps, be more correct to call the *Beggar's Opera* a vaudeville; for, as in a vaudeville, the music of the songs, instead of being composed specially for the words, is borrowed from the popular airs of the day. Mr. Rockstro himself points out that Dr. Arne, though he began by producing works in imitation of the *Beggar's Opera*, yet aimed at higher things than these, his great ambition being " the formation of a school of English opera based upon the then fashionable Italian model." Borrowing a libretto from Metastasio, he composed upon it his *Artaxerxes*. Its reception, we are told, was " extremely encouraging, and deservedly so, for it contained much excellent music, and was performed by a very strong company." Unhappily, its success bore no fruits; and this, we are assured, was due to " the interference of a certain class of critics—men, for the most part, with some amount of literary ability, but utterly ignorant of the first principles of art, and therefore knowing nothing whatever of the merits of the question they pretended to decide—who, having come to the conclusion that the English language was unfitted for recitative, reiterated this opinion until they had persuaded a large section of the public to agree with them." Probably, however, the public would not have agreed with them had Dr. Arne produced a series of really fine works. Mr. Rockstro's remark tells in some measure against himself when he ingeniously observes that "no further attempt was made to sing English opera throughout, though no objection was raised against the introduction of any amount of recitative, accompanied or unaccompanied, into an oratorio." This surely proves that the opinion expressed by certain critics as to the absolute unsuitableness of the English language for recitative had no weight with the public.

It has been said that in undertaking to write the history of Opera Mr. Rockstro set himself a hard task: indeed, to narrate continuously the growth and development of opera in the various European countries would be not merely difficult but impossible. Mr. Rockstro has attempted to solve the puzzle by breaking up the history of opera into a number of different "periods," of which he reckons altogether as many as twenty. To give some idea of Mr. Rockstro's method of division, it may be mentioned that in his ninth period he deals with the operatic work done by Handel; that in his tenth period he is chiefly occupied with Logroseino, the inventor of the concerted finale, and with other Neapolitan composers of the same time; that the leading figure in the eleventh period is Gluck, with whom, of course, is associated towards the end of the "period" Piccinni; and that the twelfth period is devoted to Mozart.

One cannot say of prima donnas as of French actresses in the days of Candide—that " on les adore quand elles sont belles, et on les jette à la voirie quand elles sont mortes"; but the most interesting of them, all the same, are those that are still with us. The notice, then, of Patti will doubtless find many more readers than those of that great dramatic soprano Pasta; of that eminent light soprano (singing, however, at a time when the distinction between light soprano and dramatic soprano was scarcely so marked as it is now), Persiani; and the "creator," so far as the Anglo-Italian stage is concerned, of the part of Violetta in *La Traviata*, Piccolomini. Those who estimate Mdme. Patti's age solely by her youthful appearance, by her vivacity, and by the freshness of her beautiful voice, must be under the impression that she numbers less years than she has actually counted. Those, on the other hand, who chiefly bear in mind the fact that this wonderful artist has been singing in London every season since 1861 may well suppose her to be older than she really is. Her precise age (beginning of 1881) is thirty-seven and some months. She is the youngest daughter of Salvatore Patti, an Italian singer, and his wife, also a singer, who, before her marriage, was well known in Spain and Italy under the name of Barili. Mdme. Patti was not, as Americans fondly imagine, born in the United States. She was taken to America when still a child, and there at an early age received instruction from her brother-in-law, Maurice Strakosch, who not only taught her to sing, but as soon as she was ready to appear on the stage wrote for her those ornamental passages and cadenzas which Rossini so aptly described when, in reference to Mdme. Patti's execution of the part of

Rosina in the *Barber of Seville*, he exclaimed, " Elle a joliment Strakosché ma musique !" Maurice Strakosch, all the same, rendered his sister-in-law excellent service, a fact which she herself would be the first to admit and indeed to proclaim. Mdme. Patti made her first appearance in public when she was very young. But though she made a good impression from the first, she was wisely withdrawn with a view to further study. When, however, she reappeared at New York in November 1859, she was only sixteen years of age. At this, her second début, she came out as Lucia—still one of her best parts. Though, of late years, she may have lost one or more of her highest notes, together with some little of her marvellous flexibility, she has, on the other hand, gained in calibre of voice and also in richness of tone. Mdme. Patti made her first appearance in England in May 1861, at the Royal Italian Opera as Amina; and before she had finished the slow movement of her first air she had already achieved a striking success, which went on increasing year by year and which is fully maintained to this day. Mr. Alexis Chitty, to whom the notice of Patti is due, keeps within the mark when he says that this admirable vocalist and actress is " quite at home in the works of Meyerbeer and Gounod," and that she has " considerable charm both of person and manner." He is unnecessarily cautious, moreover, in stating that she is " perhaps the most popular operatic artist of the time." " Perhaps," however, is a very convenient word in musical criticism.

Mrs. Julian Marshall, in her very interesting article on Piccinni, renders but the barest justice to that composer. She lays stress on the fact—if fact it be—that "Piccinni was no discoverer, but an accomplished and successful cultivator in the field of art." Yet she herself quotes Jomelli's "Questo è inventore." This, it is true, may have had reference only to his melodic invention. She does not omit to state that among his other improvements on existing operatic forms should be mentioned his extension of the duet, previously treated in a conventional undramatic way, and the variety and importance he gave to the finale, the invention of which, in many movements, is, however, due to Logroscino. Piccinni was a much better musician than Gluck, and it has been seen that he was in some respects a discoverer. Gluck has, in any case, outlived his former competitor. Nothing of Piccinni's is now ever heard: all previous Italian composers were indeed driven out of fashion by Rossini. But Gluck's *Orpheus* and *Iphigenia in Tauris* are still from time to time performed. Mrs. Julian Marshall quotes the jest of Sophie Arnould, who, seeing Mdlle. Laguerre come on to the stage intoxicated in the part of Iphigenia, exclaimed, "This is not Iphigenia in Tauris, but Iphigenia in Champagne." A mass of similar witticisms which passed from mouth to mouth during the Gluck and Piccinni contests might have been quoted. When Gluck and Piccinni were both working at an opera on the subject of *Orlando*, the Abbé Arnaud, one of Gluck's most enthusiastic admirers, said that the German would write an *Orlando* and the Italian an *Orlandino*. Marmontel, a fervent Piccinnist, was sitting a few nights afterwards next to the Abbé when Gluck's *Alceste* was being played, and to annoy him remarked, as Mdlle. Lesueur cried out at the end of the second act "Il me déchire le cœur!" "Ah, mademoiselle, vous me déchirez les oreilles!" "What a fortunate thing for you," replied the Abbé, "if you could get new ones." Nearly all the great literary lights of the day, including Marmontel, Laharpe, and d'Alembert, were on Piccinni's side. Rousseau, great writer but poor composer, has sometimes been counted among the Gluckists; but he certainly was not one of Gluck's partisans.

The history of the piano is fully and admirably treated by Mr. Hipkins. Pianoforte music is dealt with by Herr Pauer; and a special article on pianoforte-playing is also the work of the eminent pianist just named. The elaborate paper on pianoforte music may be recommended not only to disinterested amateurs, but also to interested "professionals" occupied with the difficult problem of finding suitable pieces for presentation to the public. Treating of contemporary pianists, Herr Pauer says of Anton Rubinstein that he is "a composer of Titanic force, yet capable of producing the softest, most ethereal tones," and that he is "the interpreter of all imaginable styles and schools." Dr. Hans von Bülow has, says Herr Pauer, "given many proofs of a prodigious memory, which is, however, not always faithful to the original text of the composer; and for this reason has not the same value for the earnest musician which the general public seems to attach to it. His undertaking to play the five most advanced and most difficult sonatas of Beethoven at one sitting, though in itself a prodigious feat, seems one of those exaggerations of the present time which are also to be found among less interesting and noble occupations than pianoforte-playing. Beethoven himself would have been the first to deprecate such undertakings as at once exhausting for the performer and wearisome for the listener. With regard to intelligence, knowledge, memory, and technical execution, Bülow stands deservedly very high, and the programmes of his recitals embrace the masters of all schools and styles." Further on Herr Pauer says that "with Liszt and Thalberg, Rubinstein and Tansig, the brilliancy of technical execution reaches its culminating point: with regard to rapidity, force, ingenuity of combination, and dazzling effect, it is not too much to assert that the highest point has been gained, and that with respect to quantity of notes and effects our present players are unrivalled: whether the quality is as good as it formerly was (abut 1825) may be questioned." Herr Pauer finishes his contributions on pianoforte music and pianoforte-playing by giving a list of the pianists who have "flourished" during the last century or so, beginning with Carl Phillipp Emanuel Bach, and ending with Mdlle. Janotha. About one hundred and eighty names are given; and some sixty of those belong to pianists who may be counted as of the present day.

As an excellent specimen of the articles on purely technical subjects may be cited "Pedal Point," by Mr. Frederick Corder, who, by the way, is not only a distinguished composer and an able critical writer, but also a dramatist and a true poet. It is illustrated by abundant examples from the works of Guido, Palestrina, Bach, Beethoven, Chopin, Schumann, Wagner, Grieg, and Bizet.

## CHAPTER XLIII.

QUARTETT CONCERTS, AND THE CLASSICAL IN MUSIC.

The Monday Popular Concerts may be regarded as one of the very few musical institutions which really flourish in England, and have taken root in the heart of our public. The experiment of offering the choicest musical classics to a mixed audience, paying them from a shilling to five shillings a head for the privilege of listening to them—or of being sent to sleep by them as many thought must be the inevitable result—did not seem very hopeful when it was first proposed. But there are liberals in art as in politics; and it is part of the liberal artistic creed that the people have a greater capacity for the enjoyment of works of a higher class than they are generally credited with. Nevertheless a heart of oak, and a purse triply lined with money, must have belonged to the man who first embarked in Monday Popular Concerts. Good music was, no doubt, to be heard in England before the days of Mr. Arthur Chappell. But it was not within reach of the people—by which is not meant the populace whose taste can only lead them to music-halls; but the great body of the public.

It must be admitted that without a certain amount of previous cultivation no one can appreciate the highest productions of art. This is especially true in regard to musical art. Music is a universal language; but it is only the simplest utterances in this language that are universally intelligible. Beethoven's choral symphony might equally appeal to the sensibilities of uneducated Englishmen, uneducated Frenchmen, and uneducated Russians, and, beyond impressing them all through the mere force of sonority, would say very little to either. A rustic audience, from no matter what country, would probably derive some pleasure from the pastoral symphony. The imitations of natural sounds would interest them—as the merest cockney might be interested by Shakespeare's bad puns, and by the trivialities, if not absolute flaws, to be found in so many of his masterpieces. If the subject under consideration were not the Monday Popular Concerts but music in general—and not only music in general but art in general—it would be interesting to consider what the chief elements of popularity are in those musical, artistic, and poetical masterpieces which have really become popular. Why does *Don Giovanni* attract large audiences more constantly than any other opera? Why is the Madonna della Seddia the chosen design for such numbers of cheap pictorial brooches. Why is *Hamlet* the play of plays to fill the shilling gallery on a Saturday night? Not, as one species of cant would have it, because the public have a blind traditional reverence for the works of Mozart, Raphael, Shakespeare; nor, as the cant of another kind puts it, because the general body of the public are, in their *naïveté* and sweet susceptibility, more open to grand impressions than their so-called superiors whose sympathies have been dulled by cultivation. The simple, direct explanation of the phenomenon in question is as regards opera, that a number of people like the tunes in *Don Giovanni* without appreciating the beauty of the entire work; as regards the design of the brooch, that they are charmed by the lovely face; as regards the tragedy of *Hamlet* that the story interests them apart from the poetry and philosophy in which it is clothed. The shilling gallery may admire *Hamlet* in all sincerity; but they cannot admire it so much as a Goethe, a Schlegel, or a Hazlitt, nor for such various, nor, above all, for such lofty reasons.

It would be interesting to know what the shilling public, on the nights devoted at St. James' Hall to Monday Popular Concerts, finds so much to admire in certain specimens of chamber music, full of very choice, but also very recondite beauties? say, for instance, the last quartetts of Beethoven. Perhaps, treating each concert as an entire performance, it may be affirmed that in each—as in the opera of *Don Giovanni*—there is something for the general public, and a great deal which speaks eloquently to the regularly instructed musician, and even to the self-educated connoisseur, but which, to the great outside mass, says only what the notorious sonata said to the celebrated French philosopher, who, listening, did not know what to make of it. "Sonate que me veux tu?" exclaimed jesting Fontenelle, and receiving no answer, concluded that the sonata of which he could make nothing must somehow be in the wrong. Without being blind worshippers of mere names, one may hope that the frequenters of the Monday Popular Concerts do not, when they find that they cannot place themselves *en rapport* with some work of great repute, at once make up their minds that the work is to blame. The sonata's reply to Fontenelle has never been made known, often as his triumphant, one-sided conversation with that unhappy piece of music has been repeated. But before giving any answer, it might well have said to him, in the name of all music, "Que me veux tu Fontenelle?" The true complaint of the philosopher against the sonata appears to have been that it could not utter witticisms or discourse to him on the "Plurality of Worlds."

The scheme of the Monday Popular Concerts, though it gives no place to frivolous *ad captandum* pieces, yet includes within certain limits a great variety of music. Music written merely for the sake of display—that is for the display of certain qualities on the part of the executant—is absolutely proscribed. At the Monday Popular Concerts the leading pianist will never play Thalberg's pianoforte fantasias; nor the leading violinists Paganini's variations on the *Carnival of Venice*; nor the leading violoncellist arrangements and disarrangements of popular operatic airs. One would be astonished, too, in the way of vocal music to hear at these entertainments any ordinary operatic air. At the same time there is no denying the fact that the vocal music is not always so strictly classical as the instrumental music invariably is. We have heard songs at the Monday Popular Concerts which might have made quidnuncs look aghast through their spectacles, and pedants shake their wigs in dismay.

Since the word classical has been used, let us ask the precise significance of that word in connection with music. The director of the Monday Popular Concerts does not employ it at all, and is to be applauded for it. He gives his concerts a name which implies that they take place on Mondays, and are addressed to the " people " in the full and proper sense of the word—the public of all classes. Nevertheless in describing them briefly, one must say that they consist of "classical" music; and for the sake of musical readers and musical artists in general, we should like to see this word properly defined.

We all know what the words "classic," "classical" ought to mean. A " classic " should be a work placed and maintained in the first rank, by the consent of the best judges of succeeding generations. After a certain lapse of years a work that has once been fairly recognised as classical, continues to pass as such without further question; and though no one—perhaps because no one—takes any further interest in it, will be so esteemed until the end of time. There was a period when the only classics in literature were the Greek and Latin classics; and by a pardonable abuse of language the term "classical" is still applied emphatically, if not exclusively, to those works and all their belongings. Thus "a classical education" has come to mean an education in Greek and Latin; "a prize for classics," a prize for proficiency in Greek and Latin; "a classical master," a master who gives instruction in Greek and Latin, and so on. A classic in our own literature is called "a British Classic"—as though it were to the real thing what Britannia metal is to silver, or British brandy to pure Cognac. And there is, after all, some meaning in this. For classics or not, the poets of the last two hundred years have not been tested like the poets of the last two thousand years.

There is a difference, too, between a reputation enjoyed in one particular corner of the earth, and a reputation spread over the whole civilized globe. "Civilization ceases," says Joseph Le Maistre with indisputable truth—whatever the significance of that truth may be—"where the study of the Latin language ceases"; and authors whose writings influence in different degrees all civilized men, and which have been exercising this influence for nearly twenty centuries, may well, indeed, be styed "classical."

In the drama and in painting, the word "classical" has a special and very restricted meaning. A "classical drama" is a drama founded on a subject already treated by one of the dramatists of Greece, or by exception Rome; (Corneille's *Horace,* for instance, is an adaptation from the Latin of Seneca). At the same time the French recognize in their drama a clearly marked classical form. A classical subject is to be preferred—either the subject or an ancient classical drama, or failing that any subject borrowed from antiquity; but the division of the drama into five acts and the observance of the three unities must in any case be insisted on. Indeed, in the present day, classicality in the French drama is, above all, a question of form. There is also, however, a question of classicality in language which I feel to be somewhat beyond my competency, but as to which I may, nevertheless, say a few words. The language, then, of a French classical drama should be in strict accordance with the teachings and traditions of the French Academy, of which Molière was never a member. It should be correct, chaste, not rich in metaphor nor fertile in imagery—unless, indeed, it be second-hand imagery, already approved by the Academy; devoid of humour, the servant of one idea—that idea being never to deviate into originality but to walk in the ancient ways, and after the manner of the French classical writers of the French Augustine period, and in constant fear of the French Academy. The classical drama in France is the drama as moulded by the classical writers of the French stage—or those who for a time were so considered. It is admitted now that the French classical drama is dying out, that it possesses none of the elements of vitality. What, then, is to be said of so-called classics whose existence could not be prolonged for two centuries? Simply that they are not classics at all.

In pictoral art there are two kinds of classicality. In one sense a classical picture is any picture painted on a subject from Lemprière's Classical Dictionary—a work which perhaps more than any other, after the Peerage and the Authorised Version of the Scriptures, deserves to rank as a British classic. David, the author of the naked Romulus in the Louvre, was at one time the head of this classical school of painting in France. But true classicality in the pictorial as in other arts consists in the study and imitation of what are generally recognized as the highest models; and whatever else a classical painter may be, a classical painter is certainly one who endeavours to follow in the steps of the great masters. Thus Ingres, the chief classical painter of modern France, devoted himself at one time exclusively to the study of Raphael, and was said to have familiarised himself with all that Raphael had produced down to the smallest sketch. Let it be added, that for classical painters, the true text-books are not the classical authors nor even Lemprière's Dictionary, but the Bible, the New Testament, and, in Catholic countries, *The Lives of the Saints*. Indeed, in representing what in literature would be called classical subjects, David was nothing less than an innovator.

As regards both the French classical drama and French classical painting, in place of the word "classical" the word "traditional" or "conventional" might well be used. If an artist in the present day so far forgot himself as to paint what is known as a classical landscape (a student fresh from the Ecole des Beaux Arts might do such a thing) it would be a good thing to explain to him that there is nothing classical at all in such productions. Readers are aware that a so-called classical landscape is a landscape *plus* a temple—the temple, however, may on occasion be omitted ; *plus* one or more human figures who are indispensable, inasmuch as it is only through the imaginary enjoyment of the beauties of the landscape by these imaginary personages that any real enjoyment of them can be obtained by the actual spectator of the picture. Such at least is the ingenious theory on the subject; which is about as reasonable—indeed less reasonable—than to pretend that no man thoroughly admires a pretty girl unless he sees some other man admiring her.

What a variety, then, of things classical there are in the world! The "classics" properly so called—the chosen reading of a large portion of educated society for the last two thousand years; the pseudo-classics of modern literature, in which the mere outside forms of the ancient originals are reproduced; the genuine classics of modern literature; the classics of painting, including the works of the old masters, and pseudo-classic imitations of their works; and finally the classics of music, concerning which it would be well to have clearer views than we actually possess. Hitherto writers have been able so give a far better account of themselves, their works, and their manner of working than painters; while painters have in these respects shown themselves superior to musicians. One may admit that it is not the proper business of a musician to deliver lectures for the enlightenment of the heathen. Nevertheless we should like to hear the answers of the first half-dozen persons who might be requested to explain what is and what is not classical music. In the opinion of myriads of young ladies—the most numerous class of musical students in this and all other countries—"classical music" is a name used to designate any kind of music in which there is more harmony than melody, more learning than inspiration, and which is generally dull.

Some hold that the classical in music corresponds to the "legitimate" in the drama. In the drama everything is legitimate that is in five acts. Is it true that in music everything is classical which is in the form of a symphony, a concerto, a sonata, or any other of the recognized forms which the great masters of instrumental music have systematically employed?

As a general rule no Italian music is considered classical—or at least not until a century or so after it has been composed. German music, on the other hand, is almost classical by birth.

Probably, a certain amount of seriousness is thought absolutely necessary in classical music; and though satire—thanks, no doubt, to the salt that is in it—lasts as long as any other poetry, it may be true that comic music and lively music in general are less permanently impressive than music of a serious cast. Meanwhile, in the absence of all definitions and laws on the subject, ask any member or dozen members of the concert-going, opera-going public whether Rossini's *Barber of Seville* is a classical work or not, and be sure he will answer in the negative. Yet it is Beaumarchais in music and as admirable a musical comedy as ever was produced. The claims of Mozart's *Marriage of*

*Figaro* to be considered classical would of course pass unquestioned. Possibly, too, the music of Mendelssohn's *Son and Strangers* would, doubtless, be declared classical even by those who have never heard it, simply on the ground that it is the work of Mendelssohn. If, indeed, "classical" were an epithet reserved for the work of all serious, earnest composers, it would at least be intelligible, however incorrect. As it is, that term is applied not only to the works of the great masters, but to all very serious and more or less learned music, written in observance of their forms.

However, musicians great and small, musical young ladies, amateurs of both sexes, and the public in general, will certainly agree in regarding the instrumental music performed at the Monday Popular Concerts as classical, though, as before observed, the director never makes use of the word in any of his announcements. If Mr. Arthur Chappell were bound by law to describe the exact composition of his concerts, it would be enough for him to say that they are made up of the finest examples of chamber music left by the great masters: Bach, Haydn, Mozart, Beethoven, Schubert, Mendelssohn. Nor are modern composers neglected—Schumann, for instance; whose works, whatever may be their merits, can scarcely as yet be styled classical. The Catholic Church does not canonize its Saints until 500 years after their death. It would be too much to ask for such a delay in the case of a composer claiming classical rank. But it is evidently of the essence of classicality that the title of the composer to the epithet of "classical" should be universally recognised, and that such recognition should be of long standing.

## CHAPTER XLIV.

### REASONABLENESS OF OPERA.

THAT the words of operas are often nonsensical is a charge easily made out. This concerns the public less than it does the composer, and after the composer the singers. But the composer, once satisfied with his subject, seems to care very little about mere verbal details; and, set to music, the finest poetry—if it lay within the province of the librettist to produce it—would inevitably be lost sight of. It is not generally known that Victor Hugo once wrote an admirable libretto on the subject of his own *Esmeralda*, which was set to music by a lady, who filled in regard to the poet the position usually occupied by the poet in regard to the composer. Victor Hugo's libretto, musically embroidered by Mdlle. Louise Bertin, did not meet with anything like the success which Scribe obtained for so many of his little books after cutting, clipping, amending, and adding to them in all sorts of ways until they were fit to serve as foundations for the splendid edifices of Meyerbeer.

If operas are not so generally unintelligible, and if the verses employed in operas are not invariably nonsensical, it must at least be admitted that the opera as an artistic form is full of absurdities. So it has long been said; but the chief of the alleged absurdities is neither greater nor less than the absurdity of employing verse in tragedy, or satirical dialogue (with sally and repartee following one upon another, like questions and answers in a book of conundrums) in comedy. The French, like ourselves, were very fond of ridiculing opera when it first appeared among them; and if there is one thing more ridiculous than another in opera, it is the declamation in pretentious music of trivial phrases which would find appropriate expression in the very humblest-spoken prose. To this fault a close analogy exists in the truisms and puerilities enveloped in gorgeous verse which are to be met with in the French rhymed comedies of every-day life.

There is a ball scene in M. Ponsard's celebrated piece *L'Honneur et L'Argent*, in which the hero—a virtuous well-dressed young man, who sacrifices his stomach to his outward appearance, but repents when hunger comes upon him—produces a great effect by rushing before the footlights, and exclaiming confidentially to the audience :—

"Je porte des gants blancs, et je n'ai pas dîné!"

or, as one would say in English—

"I wear white kids, and yet I haven't dined!"

If such a thing is to be said at all, at least one would think it should not be said in verse. But the comedy in question happens to be written in verse throughout, the audience accept it as a versified comedy, and there is an end of the matter.

The first great satirist of opera, who only satirised it because he admired it so much, and because it occupied so much of his thoughts—St Evremond—took care in his comedy of *Les Opéras* not to make everyone speak in music; only the principal character—the heroine—being represented as seized with an invincible operatic mania. This, of course, has an absurd effect; which was the author's intention. " I would rather die," says —or sings—the heroine in question, "than speak like the vulgar. It is a new fashion," she adds, " at the court, and since the last opera no one speaks otherwise than in song. When one gentleman meets another in the morning it would be insufferably impolite not to sing to him '*Monsieur, comment vous portez vous?*' to which the other would reply, '*Je me porte à votre service.*' If the first gentleman says to the second, '*Après dîner que ferons nous?*' the second will probably answer, '*Allons voir la belle Clarisse.*'"

St. Evremond liked and appreciated the opera more than enough to be aware that such a phrase as "Après diner que ferons nous?" could never without manifest incongruity be introduced into a musical drama. It amused him to push to the very last point of extravagance the newest fashionable mania of the day; and this he did so effectually that he at once—as anyone by referring to *Les Opéras* may see—exhausted all the forms of ridicule that can possibly be directed against one of the most admirable forms of the drama.

When Italian opera was introduced into England, Addison could no more let such a novel and tempting subject escape his satire than St. Evremond when it was introduced into France. But the first Italian or Anglo-Italian operas brought out in England were played in exceptionally comic style. The singers imported from Italy sang in Italian, while those of native growth answered them in English. At length, however, the audience got tired of only understanding half the opera, and according to a sarcasm of Addison's "to ease themselves of the fatigue of thinking, so ordered it that at the present the whole opera is performed in an unknown tongue." This was very good pleasantry; but if anyone tried to get at the meaning of an opera by simply listening to the words, he would probably come to the end predicted by Dr. Johnson for the man who should commit the fatal error of reading *Clarissa Harlowe* for the sake of the story.

Music can only be intelligible to those who have ears to hear; but it is at least more intelligible in opera than in any other form, except, perhaps, that of the simple ballad in which it is often less intrinsically important than the words. Operas must always appear absurd to those who will not understand, or at least will not accept the fundamental conditions of this particular form of art; but as before mentioned it is not more ridiculous to suppose a kind of drama in which all the personages sing, than to suppose another kind in which they all talk verse, or successively, as it sometimes happens, rhymed verse, blank verse, and plain prose—corresponding in operatic language to lyrical airs, narrative or dialogue pieces, and recitative. In every form of art there are conventions to be observed. We must have certain postulates to start with, and for operatic purposes it must be taken for granted that song is man's natural language. Herr Wagner, in one of the most ingenious passages of his *Opera and Drama*, argues seriously that men sang before they spoke—or at least that they uttered cries of emotion before they learned to express their wants in detail and with precision. This is at least more probable than that they addressed one another in verse or in the epigrammatic prose of modern comedy; but as no one can maintain that man's primitive utterances were supported by orchestral accompaniments, the theory which would make Adam the first tenor and Eve the first soprano, falls to the ground.

The operatic composer says virtually to the public, "Let me make the characters of my drama sing, and they shall imitate in their singing the true tones of passion, which through no language can be rendered more powerfully than through music." But there is another argument for the reasonableness of opera, drawn from the character of operatic entertainments as now actually given in the principal theatres of Europe. If we are to have immense threatres, and if we are to have large masses of men introduced on the stage, then the singing, not the speaking, voice must be used; first, because the speaking voice in an immense theatre is lost—nor can its tones be raised and lowered like those of the singing voice; and secondly, because masses of men speaking all at once would produce nothing but a confused noise, whereas singing in unison or in harmony they play their parts well enough and add in a remarkable degree to the completeness of the drama.

In the Greek drama the principal characters wore masks—not because the impersonators wished to conceal their faces, but because the construction of the mask enabled the sound of their voices to penetrate to a great distance. No sonorous mask is necessary for the singer, who should be able to sing loudly without shouting, and in the softest whisper without being inaudible.

Opera need not always stand on the defensive. The charges brought against it can easily be repelled; but it has claims of its own to put forward. If it were desired to establish an immense theatre in imitation of the theatres of antiquity, what sort of dramatic entertainment would be the most suitable? Evidently the opera, and opera alone—unless it be thought necessary to separate from opera its handmaiden, the ballet. The opera is the only form of drama through which audiences of many thousands of persons can be addressed; the only form of drama in which a crowd, an army, a deliberative assembly, can effectually join with voices as with gesture in the action of the piece. Finally, it is the only form of drama in which three or four persons uttering similar or diverse sentiments can, without perplexing the audience, be made to utter them at the same time.

The scene of Vasca di Gama before the Inquisition, in Meyerbeer's *Africaine*, would have a very poor effect in ordinary drama.

The prelates and other members of the tribunal, instead of singing would of course have to speak; and as they could not speak all at once, they would have to address the unhappy Vasco through a single representative, instead of crushing him, as in the opera, beneath the weight of their unanimous condemnation. It would be more natural, more real, that the inquisitor should speak in the name of his colleagues; but the sentiment and character of the situation are rendered in the opera as they could never be rendered in a spoken drama.

Such a scene, again, as that of the market in *Masaniello*, in which the sale of fish and vegetables, the chattering of the dealers, and the hurry and bustle of the crowd, are made through beautiful and appropriate music to form one harmonious whole—could only be faintly and imperfectly imitated on the non-operatic stage by a representation in dumb show; for spoken words would be worse than useless.

The meeting of the Cantons in *William Tell* is another magnificent subject for an operatic scene, which, treated otherwise than operatically, would be as flat and dull as the procession of a Temperance League. How, indeed, can the descent of the various bands from the mountains, and their gathering together in one vast agitated flood, be suggested and impressed upon the mind so forcibly as through music? Here the operatic composer has an opportunity, of which Rossini took magnificent advantage, of going to the very heart of the dramatic situation and bringing out its full significance.

The quartett in *Don Giovanni* and the quartett (somewhat on the same model) in *Rigoletto*, are examples which must occur to everyone of the power of music to give a simultaneous presentation of different conflicting emotions. In a spoken scene for four personages it is evident that if they are to be understood they must speak only one at a time; and in the drama by Victor Hugo, on which *Rigoletto* is founded, the King, the Dancing Girl, the Jester, and the Jester's Daughter are of course heard separately and singly. This, no doubt, is more or less in accordance with the conversational system of every-day life—in which, however, neither cues nor catch-words are recognised. But no spoken dialogue, however skilfully constructed, would impress the hearer as the concerted music impresses him with the whole intention of the scene—in which the recklessness of the King, the levity of the Dancing Girl to whom he is making love, the despair of the Jester's daughter whom he has betrayed, and the passion of the Jester who believes he has already accomplished his revenge—all find expression, and, what is particularly to be remarked, simultaneous expression.

It may not be considered an advantage possessed by opera over the drama, that only in opera can a mass of persons join in prayer on the stage. The admirable scene of the passage of the Red Sea in *Moses in Egypt*, preceded by prayer and followed by thanksgiving, could not in any case be adequately presented without the aid of music.

To give one more example of the value of music as dramatic language, and of its power as a dramatic agent: to express sympathy between two lovers more perfectly than through the harmonized *ensemble* of a love duet would be impossible. Here, with or without words, the most matter-of-fact critic would surely understand what was going on.

## CHAPTER XLV.

### TATRA FÜRED, AND THE MUSIC OF THE HUNGARIAN GIPSIES.

THE place which bears this remarkable name stands or lies at the very foot of Mount Lomnitza, the highest peak of the Carpathians. Better air, water, walks, scenery, society, and wine are to be found there than at most places. The shooting in the forests which surround the base of the mountain is not bad. Deer are plentiful; and from time to time a bear is tracked, hunted with picked deer-hounds, and ultimately brought down. There used to be robbers within reach, but they have been hanged or otherwise disposed of. I have seen an eagle flying high above the bathing establishment; I have danced at the Tatra Füred balls with a young lady from the Hungarian plains, who had a dowry of five thousand buffaloes; and a pretty Hungarianised

German girl, with an embroidered jacket and her hair in plaits, who waited at the *table d'hôte*, came in crying, the first day I arrived, because one of two cows belonging to her had been devoured by wolves. I remember that a subscription was got up there and then; and that enough was raised not only to calm Gisela's grief, but to make her confess that she would not much mind if her second cow were devoured by wolves on the same terms.

Tatra Füred, then, differs in many important respects from Brighton, Scarborough, Malvern, and the best watering-places, coast and inland, of our own country; where neither deer, bears, eagles, wolves, buffalo-girls, nor pretty, innocent, naïve, cowkeeping Giselas, are to be met with. Mount Lomnitza, too, with a not absolutely unattainable summit, upwards of eight thousand feet above the level of the sea, is an important feature in connection with Tatra Füred; which, however, possesses my particular esteem, not merely as a mountain watering-place, where those who arrive ill cannot help getting well, while those who arrive well cannot help enjoying their health; but as an out-of-the-way corner of the earth, where a great deal of natural wildness and much patriarchal simplicity and liberality of life are found in combination with most of the essentials and many of the adornments of modern civilisation.

There are no printed books at Tatra Füred; and during two short stays that I made there, I never saw a newspaper; though that may have been probably my fault, from not asking for one. A manuscript book exists, in which visitors to Tatra Füred inscribe their names, together with any remarks which may occur to them in connection with Tatra Füred, or anything else. Most of the entries were in Hungarian. One man, however, of an original turn of mind, but defective education, had written—

"Tempora mutantŭr et nos mutamur in illis."

The short mark over the *u* had been made by an Englishman, who added, in his own language, "Evidently no Latin scholar"; and from a signature beneath it, I learnt that this correction and reproof proceeded from no less a personage than Dean Stanley, who was then travelling through Hungary on his way to Mount Athos. I found in the hotel-book the names of two or three other Englishmen and two English-women; nor when I returned a year or two afterwards had that list been increased by more than two or three new ones. Indeed, at this moment Tatra Füred is probably the least known of places that deserve to be known; and since it costs as much money and occupies almost as much time to go there as to go to St. Petersburgh or Constantinople, it can scarcely, under any circumstances, become a favourite place of resort for English tourists.

A holiday traveller, once arrived at Vienna, ought to take the train for Cracow, and thence make the best of his way by the mountain roads to the highest range of the Carpathians, called "Tatri." In his progress and ascent, he will meet with interesting races of varying degrees of social and historical importance: Poles; the race of Polish mountaineers called specifically "Gorali"; Jews, costumed as such, at every inn on the Polish side; Gipsies with, and the children of gipsies without, costumes (otherwise rags), on every high road at intervals, when he has once entered Hungary; at the town of Käsmark, Hungarians of German race, who are as much Hungarian by sentiment as any Magyars; and finally, at the little watering-place of Tatra Füred, Hungarians of the purest type from all parts of Hungary.

Anyone going to Tatra Füred should take with him whatever he is likely to require during his stay; for he will find nothing there but a bathing establishment and a species of hotel consisting of a certain number of bed-rooms, a terrace, on which a band of gipsy musicians performs throughout the afternoon, and a long sitting-room where the visitors dine by day and dance by night. As to breakfast or lunch, most people (after an early cup of coffee before starting) seemed to take it half, or a quarter, way up Mount Lomnitza, or some neighbouring height, according to the line of country marked out for the daily excursion and the point fixed on beforehand for the halting-place.

But such ordinary every-day words as "breakfast," "lunch," "dinner," give no adequate idea of the feast on the mountain side, which—not vaguely, but as a matter of fact—is quite of an Homeric character. I never saw any animals roasted whole, or even in those huge pieces which the heroes of the *Iliad* were not too proud to place with their own hands over the embers of their wood fires. But the kind of fire—the kind of long spit, made from the nearest suitable tree, and supported at each end on large stones; the method of grilling—over the ashes of a wood fire, which if it still emitted flame would set light to the spit—were all as old as the hills on which this primæval sort of cooking takes place, and recalls the fire, the spit, the stones, the method of grilling of the Homeric poems. The Hungarians, however, as I have said, do not cook whole quarters of sheep and goats. Their favourite mountain-dish is called " robber's roast," and is prepared by skewering together in regular order a steak, a rasher of bacon, a slice of onion, and so on, in successive layers, along the whole length of the spit.

The bedroom accommodation at Tatra Füred used to be very limited; and I remember on one grand occasion a number of Hungarian gentlemen driving in from the neighbourhood and having to distribute themselves in twos and threes all over the place. A friend of mine formed a temporary prejudice against them on this account; observing that " he didn't like men who drove four-in-hand and slept three in a bed." I do not know whether the nobiliary code of Hungary says anything about sleeping three in a bed—or, let us say, three in a room. But some secret article certainly enjoins the driving of four horses; and in the stables of Hungarian country houses of any pretension this indispensable quartet—often neither more nor less—is always to be seen. As regards the three-in-a-room question, it must be remembered that the country houses in Hungary, as in Poland, are very far apart, and that their proprietors are exceedingly hospitable. Thus it frequently happens to them to entertain more guests than their houses, according to our notions, can accommodate. They offer them a friendly reception, pleasant society, and provisions in abundance; but they must manage as best they can—not only three, but sometimes half-a-dozen in a room—for the night.

No crush of this kind need be feared at Tatra Füred; certainly not by any foreign visitor, for whom a separate bed-chamber would at once be found.

Another objection made to the bedrooms at Tatra Füred is, or used to be, that they were separated by the breadth of a tolerably wide garden from the general rooms, devoted to the afternoon banquet and the evening ball. In the days when there were brigands in the land, ingenious advantage was taken of this distribution of apartments. A dozen men, one of whom had previously in the character of a hydropathic patient made a complete study of the place, came down, rifle on shoulder, from the mountains about half an hour after the dinner-bell had rung and surprised the **entire** assembly of visitors in the midst of their first appetite. The ladies at Tatra Füred do not dress elaborately. But they wear ornaments; and these, together with their watches, and whatever money they had about them, they were required to give up. The gentlemen were, of course, compelled to turn their pockets out. The robbers were at all the windows, and commanded the *table d'hôte* from one end to the other. Then, to prevent unnecessary damage and waste of time in the bedrooms, the ladies were encouraged to produce the keys of their drawers and boxes, which were entrusted to a couple of bandits who plundered the sleeping-apartments, while a third waited outside to keep watch and maintain communications with the nine still grouped around the dining-room. The whole affair was managed so quickly and cleverly, that the twelve brigands were away in the mountains, or in the woods at the foot of the mountains, with coin, jewellery, silks, furs, and other valuables, before the diners at the *table d'hôte* were ready for their coffee.

It was through an act of brigandage—if boot-stealing deserves so romantic a name—that I first made the acquaintance of a place which, though not very accessible, I have visited twice, and hope some day to see again. A waiter at an hotel in Cracow, whom, from his mysterious demeanour, I had mistaken for a silent patriot, but who turned out to be nothing more than a sly thief, had, after presenting bills on his own account to all the lodgers, and obtaining payment from most of them, risen early in the morning, and at one fell swoop carried off in a sack all the boots put outside the doors to be cleaned. Never shall I forget the horror-stricken look with which the honest old waiter, who had been commissioned to break gently the news of the boot-stealer's misdeeds, came and whispered to me that "they" were gone. When I inquired who, or what had gone, whether they had gone far, and in what direction, he seemed inclined to weep, and could only mutter in a subdued voice, " Stefan ! "

I cared very little about Stefan's having gone; but I was amazed when it was at length explained to me that he had taken my boots with him. I had an interview with the proprietor on the subject. But as he had lost the amount I had owed him for board and lodging—paid the night before, as if at his solicitation, to the brigand-waiter—I made no demand for a restitution, or rather, replacement of boots. They were riding-boots, however. I had need of them ; and as they were "gone" I was obliged to call in the nearest bootmaker to supply the loss. I found that the nearest bootmaker had already been engaged some time in supplying similar losses on the part of other lodgers in the same hotel; and it seemed to me that the job would altogether bring him in about ten or twelve hundred florins clear profit. Some of the plundered ones,—travellers, no doubt, of the light luggage school—had been left absolutely bootless; and the old waiter drew a pathetic picture of them as they lay helplessly in bed, or sat ignominiously in their stockings, until the fortunate bootmaker could spare time to attend to them.

I did not like to say anything against the bootmaker, who presented a most respectable appearance. But so also the bandit of the hotel had done; and after a time I could not help fancying that the bootmaker, who was profiting by the theft almost as much as the thief himself, might have taken an interest beforehand in its commission—might have agreed, that is to say, to pay to the thief, not a percentage on the amount of the theft, but on the amount of orders which, through the theft, might come to him. The hotel-keeper would not hear of this.

"The waiter," he said, was "simply a brigand from the Carpathian mountains." This fact would in no way have proved the absurdity of my supposition to anyone who had read Edmond About's *Roi des Montagnes;* but the hotel-keeper was probably not acquainted with that work.

Thinking no more of the bootmaker (who, if men are to be judged by their works, was not a bad man, for his boots were admirable), I asked whether there were really brigands in the Carpathians.

"The brigand who stole your boots is there for one," said the hotel-keeper; "you may be quite sure of that."

I determined to follow him: not to pursue him with a view of delivering my boots from captivity and him to justice, but simply for the sake of seeing the Carpathians, of whose existence in the comparatively close vicinity of Cracow I was thus formally reminded. I dare say I had had some vague idea before—especially when Cracow was visited from time to time by a sudden, violent, mountain-bred thunderstorm—that I was not very far from the Carpathians. But how many people in England know at this moment where the Carpathians really are? Who knew where Gallipoli and Balaclava were before the Crimean war? Who knew where Pont à Mousson, or even Sedan itself, was before the war of 1870?

To get to the Carpathians I found that the best thing to do was to hire a country carriage or cart for an indefinite time, at a defined rate—about ten shillings a day, as far as I remember. The driver was an intelligent man; which, however, did not prevent his informing me, before we had exchanged many words, that he was of noble descent—a fact in natural history which seemed to me more curious than important. What interested me much was to hear that his son, a boy of ten or twelve, was suffering from an attack of fever, of which the father said the mountain air would cure him, if he might be allowed to bring him on the excursion. The next morning, when the father drove up, with his son already installed on the box of the light, simply-constructed, peasant's *britska*, which was declared to be the only suitable vehicle for mountain roads, I thought, from the hot, sickly, enfeebled look of the child, that his parent was about to make rather a hazardous experiment with him. But the fatigue of such travelling as we were about to undertake could not be great; and though the prayers of the church are periodically offered up for "those who travel by land or by water," it has often occurred to me that the people really to be pitied, if not prayed for, are those whom their fate condemns to stay at home. If this "sick person," who was at the same time a "young child," remained at Cracow he would at least have no fresh air. As it was, during our first day's journey he had nothing else. The second day he began to eat. The third day he took enough interest in life to answer when he was spoken to. The fourth day he was lively, moderately voracious, and inclined to be talkative; and before a week, meeting with a *britska* returning to Cracow, we sent him home by it, cured of his fever and restored to something like his normal condition of health.

About eighteen months afterwards, in the flat country around Kieff, at the time of the general break-up of winter, when large tracts of ice and snow "thaw and resolve themselves" into temporary lakes, I was attacked with the same sort of malady from which I had seen the child of the Cracow coachman suffering, and which, under the influence of dry, fresh air, he had got rid of before my eyes. Instead, then, of taking the quinine which was prescribed for me on this, as it had been on previous similar occasions, I started in an open post-carriage for the Galician frontier; found myself, a few miles from Kieff, once more in the midst of winter, so that I was able to change my "cursed sort of carriage without springs"* for a sledge; and after three or four days of very easy travelling, during which I drank considerable quantities of hot tea, arrived almost well at the Hebrew town of Brody, in Austrian Poland. For some kinds of fever, then, dry, fresh air, whether of the mountains or of the steppes, would seem to be as certain a specific, and a speedier one (without any chance of a supervening headache) than even the never-failing quinine.

People on the Polish side of the Carpathians—to which I now return—seemed to think that no one could want to visit their mountain watering-places, except for the purpose of getting rid of some illness, or the consequences of an illness; and I was asked, on all sides, what "cure" I proposed to follow, and for how long. At the Polish watering-place of Szczawnica (pronounced "Shtchavnitza") natural mineral waters are to be had as offensive in taste, and probably as efficacious, as any as the most celebrated German springs supply. If in its

---

\* "A cursed sort of carriage without springs, which, on rough roads, leaves scarcely a bone."—Byron's apt description of the Russian *kibitka*.

native form no mineral water can be found sufficiently nasty for the taste of experienced amateurs, hot goat's milk may be added; the flavour of which, combined with the rotten-egg flavour of the favourite spring, gives a result of which those only who have tried it can speak with adequate disgust.

The Carpathians, more fortunate than the Alps, are beyond the reach of mere "trippers." Not that they are so very distant; but they are out of the beaten track. Probably no one, except a Pole or a Hungarian, ever went to Szczawnica or Tatra Füred, except as it were by accident—meaning to go somewhere else and taking one or both of these watering-places on his way. Occasionally, it is true, but only very rarely, a German professor is to be met with in the Carpathians, engaged in botanical, or geological, or ornithological, or even linguistic and ethnological researches. The slopes on the Polish side are inhabited by a race of mountaineers who, besides being more robust, are as frank and independent as the Polish peasantry in general are the reverse. Is their hardihood due to their personal habits as mountaineers, and do they owe their independence to the protection of the mountains? Or was it inherited independence of character that made them seek protection where they would be sure to find it, either against their own domestic tyrants, or against Tartar invaders? Mountains will not make the feeble energetic, but men of energy hard pressed will take to the mountains to defend themselves, when men without energy succumb; and a savant, who had started, and was examining from every point of view, this "question" of the Polish mountaineers, assured me that at the foot of the Carpathians he could find traces of every language in Europe. I was unable to follow him in his inquiries, which were chiefly based on the theory that, in addition to the Poles of the immediate neighbourhoood, fugitives of many nations, escaping from belligerents, had taken refuge in the mountains near Szczawnica. I remember, however, that just after the travelling professor had told me what various languages and remains of languages were to be found at the foot of the Carpathians, an old gentleman, who turned out to be an Hungarian, startled me by calling out, "*Sub quâ dominatione vivisne?*" to which, erroneously inferring that he mistook me for a member of some oppressed nationality, I replied "*Sub nullâ dominatione; liber sum!*" It soon became evident to both of us that the Latin language could only serve to conceal our thoughts; and we took refuge in French, which we, at least, pronounced on identical principles. German was at that time a proscribed tongue among patriotic Hungarians.

Besides the Latin-speaking Hungarian (who, however, is gradually dying out) the "goral," or mountaineer, and the "ross," or mountain horse (strange name for a useful animal, when one remembers that "ross" meant a superb war-horse in ancient Germany, and that "rosse" means a horse fit for the knacker in modern France!), the slopes of the Carpathians are remarkable for Jews, who, at Szczawnica, keep a row of lodging-houses, bearing curious distinctive signs, such as the Eel, the Angel, the Vulture; and for gipsies, who as infants roll naked about the ground, as children beg, and as adults mend pots and kettles, doctor horses, and play the violin. To see a gipsy child beg is worth the coin you must naturally give it after putting it through the whole of its admirably-dramatic performance. It will be plaintive, desperate, assume a famished expression, or burst out laughing, according to the apparent mood of the person for whose benefit the scene is being played, and who will, in any case, be appealed to with smiles or with tears until he parts with a piece of money. Of the tinkering and horse-coping gipsies I know nothing, except that at a country house near the mountains, where I passed a few days, a benevolent young lady made an ineffectual attempt to reduce a party of them to a settled mode of life, or at least to fix them in a settled abode. Regular work was provided for them, cottages were assigned to them, and during about three months they seemed to have become civilised. Their children actually went to school. One fine morning, however, they had all disappeared. Not a horse, not a tea-kettle was missing. They had stolen nothing; but a regular life and a fixed place of abode were just the very things they could not understand; so they migrated.

With the return of the cold weather, they came back to their cottages, did not attempt any explanation of their sudden departure, but resumed work, after a time to disappear again, leaving the amiable young lady much distressed at her inability to change their nature—to eradicate habits of some thousand years growth.

The violin-playing gipsies, however, like the singing gipsies of Moscow, have adopted something of the varnish of civilisation; and, what is still more remarkable, have, tempted by money, acquired the habit of making, and even keeping, engagements, doing stated work at appointed hours, and so on. Mr. Borrow declares that the only gipsies who have become civilised are the singing gipsies of Moscow; and he cites one in particular, who married a Russian Count. A relation, however (by marriage), of this most civilised of the gipsies told me one day that she used from time to time to insist on appearing in public without shoes and stockings,—and she was ultimately murdered by her servants, who thought she did not treat them in a civilised manner.

Liszt, in his fantastic, rhapsodical variations on the theme of *The Gipsies and their Music in Hungary*, represents them with justice as incapable of adopting civilised habits permanently. But the violin-playing gipsies of Tatra Füred are civilised enough to play together for so many hours every day during the season; and if they were to become what would be called " quite civilised "

—if, that is to say, they were to adopt ordinary dress and demeanour, and learn to play from notes—they would lose their distinguishing picturesqueness, both of costume and of execution, and would find themselves reduced to the cheap level of ordinary orchestral players.

Their actual method of studying, or rather picking up, the melodies which, when they have once adopted them, they play with so much of their own peculiar expression, is very primitive. I had the misfortune to occupy at Tatra Füred for an entire day the room next the one in which the gipsies rehearsed their music. They were at work on the *Trovatore*, which some facetious person had probably recommended to them as a gipsy opera; and as the chief of the band played an air on his violin the other first violins followed him, to the best of their ability, in a sort of procession which, in quick movements, became a race. There were a great many false starts, and when the players did get well off together they seldom went very far without a breakdown. But, after a time, if one fell out he had to come in again the best way he could. No one waited for him; and at last they had all in their own manner, learned, with their own modifications, what they had intended to learn. Verdi, perhaps, would not always have recognised it; but Liszt would, and would, moreover, have tried to explain how the Italian melodies had been altered in accordance with the principles of the special musical system attributed by him to the gipsies. I should have said that in supplying the harmony, they follow at their rehearsals, or rather experiments, a strictly tentative method. Certain notes are tried, and their effect not being found satisfactory, are replaced by others—whose effect is also not satisfactory.

But there must be an end to everything, and at last the notes of the accompaniment got somehow shaken into their proper places. The black-haired, bronze-faced, eagle-eyed gentleman who acted as conductor was content; and, sallying forth, armed with his violin, and followed by his band, took up his position on a platform, at the head of the dining-saloons, and introduced his new selection (the *Trovatore* was once new) to a partly-hydropathic and entirely-sympathetic public.

The gipsies play with great impulse, and with much exaggerated expression, and are alternately and very suddenly melancholy and joyful, plaintive and triumphant. To be appreciated, however, they should be heard, not in music with which one is already familiar, but in those native Hungarian tunes, which they have been in the habit of playing from childhood, and which they have appropriated and thoroughly adapted to their own taste. In this manner the gipsies, so to say, "gipsify" Hungarian and other music; but they do not, as Dr. Liszt persists in imagining, possess music, and a musical system of their own.

## CHAPTER XLVI.

#### THE BYEWAYS OF BOOKMAKING.

Every literature possesses a body of rules teaching the poet and the dramatist what to avoid; and an ingenious Frenchman once published a guide to novel-writing which contained positive directions for pursuing that craft, so that with a little application every novel-reader might become his own novelist—at once the creator and consumer of his own literary smoke. No one by studying the *Ars Poetica* could make himself, in however small a degree, either a versifier or a playwright. But the author of the guide to novel-writing did at least aim at showing how novels might be cut out and perfected, or rather designed piece by piece, and put together, not indeed like boots and shoes, but rather like garlands of artificial flowers or elaborate ball-dresses. Perhaps, however, the novel-writing guide might be most fitly compared to a cookery book. It gave instructions on the choice of a heroine as Mrs. Glasse, or La Cuisinière Bourgeoise, tells you what sort of fowl to pick out for your contemplated hash. It recommended for some purposes a tender hero, for others a tough one. There was a chapter on the art of serving up the heroine, or, in other words, of introducing her to the reader. Then the hero and the heroine had to be stirred up together after certain forms, according as they were disposed to harmonise like cream and the yolk of egg, or were of seemingly antagonistic natures, like oil and vinegar. Hints were furnished on the preparation of incidental observations; and the art of blending reflection with narrative was fully treated. Of course the villain was not forgotten— nor the story; and the intended novelist was strongly advised to make the latter "interesting." The weakness of the book seemed to consist in this: that if the aspirant to the enviable position of successful novelist could make his story interesting—which he was enjoined to do without being told in what manner—the rest was comparatively without importance. To profess to teach a man the art of writing a novel, and to tell him, among other things, that he had better make his story interesting, is as good a joke in its way as that of informing the aspirant to poetical honours that when he has at last finished his work he had better keep it by him for nine years. The counsel has, in each case, an ironical look. But scanty thanks would be forthcoming alike from the poet—warned that when he has followed a number of maxims on the subject of poetical composition, the best thing he can do with his poem will be to hide it—and from the novelist—who, after many useful rules have been impressed upon him in respect to novel-writing, is further assured that he must make his story "interesting." In an indirect manner the one is told as plainly as the other that teaching will be of no value to him.

If, however, authors cannot teach others how to conceive and bring forth works of art, they can sometimes explain how the idea and plan of their own creations first occurred to them. Edgar Poe has published a curious exposition of the genesis, or rather of the deliberate construction, of the *Raven*; an exposition, it must be added, which is not accepted by all his admirers as having been made in perfectly good faith, and which is declared to be not a synthesis, but virtually an analysis. The late Alexandre Dumas, too, has told us how the main idea of one of his most successful plays first came into his head. He was walking down the Boulevard, when suddenly it struck him that a man found in a compromising situation with a woman might save her reputation by killing her and declaring that he had done so by reason of her resistance. Out of that idea was developed the drama of *Antony*. The fact may be interesting. But neither the starting-point of Poe nor of Dumas could have been turned to account by one who was neither a poet nor a dramatist.

If, however, the secret of literary invention cannot be imparted, methods of borrowing literary materials with skill and success may easily be communicated. A regular school of plagiarism was maintained for a time in France, and among its pupils one of the most distinguished preachers of the seventeenth century, Fléchier, is said to have been included. Poetry, on the principle, perhaps, that "the poet must be born," does not seem to have been included in the course. Or it may have been thought that poets were already sufficiently accustomed to borrow images and ideas, and to reproduce in their own works whole passages from the ancients. Instruction in the art of plagiarism was in any case confined to orators; and the school was named "L'Académie des Orateurs Philosophiques," with Richesource, its founder, as "director." Richesource declared himself able to make "distinguished writers" of those even who possessed no literary talent; and he has left a work on the subject, in which his method is fully explained. *The Orator's Mask; or, The Manner of Disguising all Sorts of Compositions, Letters, Sermons, &c.* is its title; and the author explains at the outset that "oratorical plagiarism is the art that some employ with much skill for changing or disguising all sorts of discourses composed by themselves, or due to the pen of another, in such a manner that it becomes impossible for the author to recognise his own work, his own style, or the substance of his work, so adroitly will the whole have been disguised." The parts of the work which it is proposed to appropriate are to be arranged in a new order, words and phrases are to be replaced by equivalents. "An orator," the reader is told, "has said that an ambassador should possess probity, capacity, and courage. The plagiarist will say that he should possess courage, capacity, and probity." He would be but a poor plagiarist, however, who should chop and change in this manner; and the ingenious plagiarist will, it is explained, replace "probity" by "sincerity" or "virtue," "courage" by "force of soul," and so on. For "ambassador," "envoy" would, no doubt, be substituted; and "should not be without" would probably do duty for "should possess."

Richesource's Academy has long ceased to exist; but his method is still employed, consciously or unconsciously, by numbers of orators in the pulpit and at the bar. It appeared, too, from a case tried in London some twenty years ago, that professed plagiarists are sometimes employed "to destroy copyrights" as the evidence set forth; or, in other words, to treat literary matter which copyright formally protected so as, in the words of Richesource, to render it "impossible for the author to recognise his own work." In the case referred to, the most vulgar kind of plagiarism—the "plagiarism of commerce," it might be called—had been performed upon the substance of a guide-book which had been in a great measure transmuted, though not so thoroughly as to leave no trace of the process. Two words specially sworn to by the author—namely, "savage grandeur," had been taken whole by the plagiarist. A graduate of the "Académie des Orateurs Philosophiques" would probably have converted them into "wild magnificence."

The "art of extemporaneous speaking" taught by certain professors in the present day is probably nothing more than an application of Richesource's method of plagiarism. The story has been told often enough of the funeral oration pronounced in memory of the Duke of Wellington by the present Earl of Beaconsfield. That was a performance which Richesource would doubtless have condemned as inartistic, since neither the substance nor the style of the borrowed discourse was disguised. But if the "art of extemporaneous speaking" can be taught at all, one of its rules must be that when the speaker has nothing to say of his own he is to borrow from some one else.

In the drama plagiarism has been much more freely practised than in any other branch of literature. Managers, in fact, are bound at all hazards to entertain the public, and with that view, like the great manager-dramatist of France, "take their property wherever they find it." The origin of the piece is unimportant, provided the piece itself be suitable. The public, moreover, might be prejudiced against it if they were told that it had not been made expressly for them; and they would certainly listen with mistrust to a comedy which, professing to represent the manners of one country, was known, as first composed, to have depicted those of another. Then there are so many degrees in dramatic plagiarism, from the poet who borrows nothing but an undeveloped subject, or the idea of a subject, to the playwright who re-fashions other men's materials; and from the playwright to the adapter, who perhaps invents a few details, and to the translator who invents nothing, yet, in many cases, does not scruple to claim the work he has translated as his own creation.

The novelist who publishes as his own the work of another man is, unlike the dramatist under similar circumstances, looked upon as having committed a disgraceful action. About the time of the Crimean war it occurred to some foreigner, who had honoured England by making it his home, to publish, as an original story, a translation, or adaptation, of Gogol's *Dead Souls*. To suit the English taste the ingenious adapter had done his best to replace Russian manners by English manners, and had made a point everywhere of substituting English for Russian food. Thus, cold mutton and porter, or ham sandwiches and pale ale, were served to guests arriving on a visit in lieu of caviar and vodka. When this plagiarism on a large scale was exposed in the columns of the *Athenæum*, the publisher expressed his regret at having been made a party to a deception practised on the public, and the book was withdrawn. No such sacrifice would be made, nor could it in fairness be expected, from a manager enabled to satisfy himself that a work which he had announced as original was in fact a translation, more or less imperfect.

Mr. G. A. Sala has told us in the interesting column which he contributes weekly to the *Illustrated London News* that Paley's *Natural Theology* is freely translated from the Dutch. French bank-notes are, or used to be, adorned with an inscription to the effect that "the forger is punished with twenty years' hard labour." Paley must have felt something like the forger of a French bank-note when he undertook to teach morality by means which, as he was reminded every moment by the very work on which he was engaged, were immoral. In the opening chapters on contrivance and design, the watch which he represents himself as finding on a barren heath, he had, in fact, stolen. So in setting the Ten Commandments to music, old Haydn, with grim humour, stole a melody for the eighth.

Even Richesource, " disguiser " by profession, would scarcely have given his approbation to a method of " disguising " history invented by Le Père Barre, and practised, it may be hoped, by him alone. Gower, in the *Confessio Amantis*, had long before spoken of Menander as an historian, classing him with Josephus, Esdras, Ephiloquorus, and others; and had described Ulysses as a learned man, to whom Cicero taught rhetoric, Zoroaster magic, Ptolemy astronomy, Plato philosophy, Daniel divination, and Hippocrates medicine. These, however, are but trifling errors compared to the mistakes, or rather the misrepresentations, made by Le Père Barre in his *History of Germany*, of which some two hundred pages are adapted, with the most grotesque results, from the history of Sweden. Le Père Barre wished above all things to divert the reader; and as Voltaire's *History of Charles XII.* was much more entertaining than anything he could write, he embodied it, with some indispensable changes of name, in his *History of Germany*. He applied to the Emperor Rudolph Voltaire's remarks on King Stanislaus, and made Valdemar, King of Denmark, say and do precisely the same things as Charles XII. at Bender. This again would not have suited Professor Richesource, who limited his system of plagiarism to " philosophical oratory," and, for the most part, to the enunciation of abstract principles—the property, he seems to have held, of anyone who liked to take the trouble to utter them.

In connection with bookmaking meant to amuse, specimens of bookmaking intended to mislead might be cited. Of these the most notorious perhaps is that

*History of France* published under the Restoration, by Le Père Loriquet, with the initials of the Jesuits' motto, *Ad majorem Dei gloriam*, as epigraph. The edition, however, of the work in which Napoleon Bonaparte is said to figure as a certain " Marquis de Bonaparte, who gained important victories at the head of the king's armies," is not be found; and the late M. de Montalembert denied that it had ever existed. Scarcely less valuable than a copy of the missing edition of Le Père Loriquet's *History* would be that number of *Le Journal des Débats*, belonging to the same period, in which the following statement is said to be contained. "Bonaparte was never christened Napoleon. His true name was Nicholas. But this man wished that everything connected with his person should be extraordinary."

A very remarkable class of bookmakers are translators who will not be satisfied with merely translating. Voltaire said of translators that they were like servants who thought the masters they had the honour of waiting upon were the greatest persons in the world. Some servants, however, and some translators, think themselves quite as good as their masters. In a French version of Plautus, published in 1719, the playful translator, M. de Geudeville, declares towards the end of his preface that he has spared no pains "*pour mettre ce vieux comique à la mode.*" " I have followed my own inclination," he adds, " and I am convinced that true men of taste, a select band, will be much obliged to me for having endeavoured to divert them all the more." Auteroche, author of a rhymed translation of Virgil's Æneid, has altered scenes, characters, and motives. He does not, however, on that account consider himself Virgil's superior. On the contrary, he tells the reader that he feels sure Virgil would have done the same "if he had only had time."

It was reserved for a distinguished Russian nobleman, Count Orloff, to discover the means of acquiring a certain literary reputation without writing a line. He employed a number of French writers, many of them men of considerable distinction, to compose, under his direction, a History of Italian Music. The Count did not claim to be more than the originator of the work; but his name appeared in large letters on the title-page. To the same patron of letters belongs the undeniable merit of having first made known to the West of Europe the admirable fables of Kriloff. A number of song-writers and minor poets of the Restoration were engaged to put into French verse prose translations of the Russian fabulist's most important productions. Besides being well paid, these gentlemen are said to have been sumptuously entertained at the Count's table; and the work, when finished, was announced as having been executed under the Count's "presidency." In spite of Count Orloff's liberality and care, the enterprise did not turn out so well as might have been expected. Each of the poets (among whom Désaugiers, the famous *chansonnier*, and Rouget de Lisle, the author of the *Marseillaise*, may be mentioned) wished to show himself a second La Fontaine, and, introducing much matter of his own, destroyed the character of the original. One, moreover, in reproducing the *Elephant*, mistook a satire on triviality in criticism for a eulogium on the worship of the infinitely small.

A curious list of translators' mistakes, or mistakes made in translation, might be made out. Thus the Abbé Viel, writing of Canterbury, and misled by the word "canon," stated that the cathedral was surrounded by artillery. The primate of all England was apparently in his eyes a military ecclesiastic, like the former Vladika of Montenegro. Guizot, in his *Life and Times of Shakespeare*, has—writing in English—expressed a hope that Shakespeare may be more and more "traduced" for the benefit of the French. Authors' mistakes, however, belong only indirectly to the subject of bookmaking; nor is it always wise to point them out. Indeed, as a famous "printer's reader" once remarked in a poem on the subject of his own occupation, called *Corrector Typographicus* : to the man who corrects the errors of another

"Plus satis invidiæ gloria nulla manet."

Indignation was created a few months ago in a great

part of England and Scotland by an inquiry made in *Macmillan's Magazine* as to where Mr. Black found Beethoven's *Farewell*, or rather by a statement that no such piece existed. "Did the writer," it was asked, "never hear of the sonata called *Les Adieux, l'Absence, et le Retour*, and if so, had he not sense enough to know that Mr. Black must have been thinking of the first movement in that work?" Mr. Black's enthusiastic admirers do not seem to perceive that it is only when heroines thoroughly charming and life-like sit down to the piano, that one cares to know what it is they are playing. Young ladies of an inferior stamp might confound Beethoven's *Adieux* (a piece which would have sorely taxed the powers of the simple Miss Wenna) with *Beethoven's Farewell to the Piano* (an impudent and worthless forgery which is still current), or the Funeral March of the Sonata in A flat with the Funeral March of the Heroic Symphony, and no one would give a second thought to the matter.

Erroneous opinions cannot always be described as mistaken; though that young man may fairly be said to have committed a blunder who, having stated before a board of examiners that Charlemagne lived 800 years before Christ, and being asked whether he did not mean "after Christ," persisted in his original statement: adding, "I am sorry to disagree with you, but that is my opinion." Many authors cause a certain amount of confusion to their admirers by changing their opinions —their opinions properly so called. Numbers of writers have begun as Revolutionists to end as Conservatives. Victor Hugo, however, who for the last twenty-eight years has been an ardent Republican, gained his first reputation as a Legitimist.

Apart from errors made by themselves, a good many authors have been the causes of errors, sometimes very droll ones, made by others. Guarini's *Pastor Fido* has been included in a catalogue of religious books; we have the authority of Mr. Hill Burton for stating that Mr. Ruskin's *Notes on the Construction of Sheepfolds* were much asked for among the muirland farmers, and that great disappointment was caused by their discovery of the real nature of the work; Miss Edgeworth has herself told how her *Essay on Irish Bulls* was ordered by an Agricultural Association; Mr. Swinburne's *Under the Microscope* was classed by German publishers as a scientific work; and Henri Murger's *Scènes de la Vie de Bohème* is reported to have had a corner given to it by Herr von Sybel in his *Historische Monatsschrift*.

Probably index-makers have shown themselves quite as ingenious in misapprehending their authors' intentions as catalogue-makers themselves. The compiler of some Annual Record is said to have been much annoyed at finding that in his index, which he had entrusted to other hands, no reference was made to Parliamentary proceedings. So at least it seemed, until at last under the head of " Public Meetings," he discovered " Meeting of Parliament." A very industrious index-maker, who let nothing escape him except now and then the main subject of the sentence he was dealing with, made in his index the following entry :—" Greatness of Mind, instance of." This corresponded with a passage in the body of the work which related how a certain magistrate had declared that he had " a great mind to send the accused to prison without the option of a fine."

Errors arising from hasty and inconsiderate " cutting down" are to be met with, not in books (for an author always cuts himself down with remarkable tenderness), but in carelessly edited newspapers. A barrister of my acquaintance was much irritated at seeing it stated one morning in a London journal that he had defended an accused person, " who was accordingly convicted." The reasons for the man's conviction—apart from the manner in which his counsel might have defended him—were not given. In connection with eccentric journalism a story is told of a reporter—in the days when "descriptive reporting" had not yet been invented— who, being instructed to report an eclipse of the sun, and finding that no speeches were delivered on the occasion, wrote, in stereotyped phrase, that " the proceedings were entirely without public interest." A certain admiration must be felt for that inexperienced reporter who, being sent to the Divorce Court, caused much dissatisfaction in the office by merely writing the plain truth, that " the evidence was unfit for publication."

The errors in which so many books abound, and from which none, it is believed, are absolutely free, are due for the most part not to the writers of the books, but to the printers and to those literary officials of the printing-office called in France "correctors," but in England simply "readers." Not that there is any proportion between the mistakes which the "reader," in some hopeless endeavour to extract light from darkness, is liable to commit, and the mistakes made by the compositors, or by the author himself, which the reader is constantly setting right. But he is considered responsible not only for the blunders which he originates, but also for those, at least of a typographical kind, which he fails to correct. His duties, then, are arduous, and, indeed, can only be adequately performed by a man of considerable learning and ingenuity. Every profession should have its ideal; and the ideal of the printer's reader is well set forth in the following passage from a letter addressed to the French Academy by the "Société des Correcteurs des Imprimeries de Paris." "The functions of the corrector," says the letter, "are very complicated. To reproduce faithfully the manuscript of the writer, often disfigured in the first proof; to bring into conformity with the orthography of the Academy the manner of spelling peculiar to each author; to give clearness to the composition by the use of a sober and logical system of punctuation; to rectify erroneous facts, inexact dates, false quotations; to see that the rules of art are strictly observed; to perform, for hours together, the double operation of reading by the intelligence and reading by the eye on the most difficult subjects, and always on a new text, in which each word may hide a snare, since the author, carried away by his thought, has read not what has been, but what ought to have been, printed: such are the principal duties of a profession which writers have at all times regarded as the most important of those connected with the typographical art."

Admirably written! But where was the "correcteur" when, in a certain French Prayer-book, "Ici le prêtre ôte sa calotte" was replaced by "Ici le prêtre ôte sa culotte"? or when M. Guizot, who in the Chamber had exclaimed, "Je suis à bout de mes forces," was declared to have said, "Je suis à bout de mes farces"? or when a certain envoy was represented as having been "dévoré" when he had in fact only been "décoré," by the Bey of Tunis? There was intention, no doubt, in the apparent misprint by which M. de Caulaincourt, accused of complicity in the murder of the Duke d'Enghien, was called in the *Moniteur*, not Duc de Vicence, which he had just been created, but "Duc de Vincennes"; and the Spirit of Poetry would seem to have presided at the making of the famous mistake in Malherbe's verses, by which

"Rosette a vécu ce que vivent les roses,
L'espace d'un matin,"

became, through the poet's having omitted to cross his t's,

"Rose elle a vécu ce que vivent les roses," &c.

Where, again, was the "reader" when, in Alison's *History of Europe*, the printers were allowed to state that among the pall-bearers at the funeral of a great naval hero was "Sir Peregrine Pickle"? or when, in a work on *Gems and Precious Stones*, the quotation from the *Merchant of Venice*, "I had it of Leah when I was a bachelor," was turned into "I had it of Keats," &c. Or, once more, where was he when in a novel by the lively Comtesse Dash, the concluding phrase of the sentence—"pour bien connaître l'amour il faut sortir de soi," was allowed to appear as "sortir le soir"?

Printers will always manage to construct a grammatical sentence out of any assemblage of words entrusted to them. Unless the manuscript be absolutely and totally illegible, they will, in their own phrase, "make sense" out of it; though this so-called "sense" may be absolute nonsense, or, without being nonsense, something very different from what the author intended. It would seem that in some printing-offices the readers are so intelligent and so perfectly reasonable that they will tolerate nothing fantastic on the part of their authors. A poet is frequently seized in his flight and brought down to earth by his translator; and Mickiewicz used to say of one of his countrymen who had reduced him into French prose, that "God had sent him as a humiliation." Printers, too, will sometimes vex the poet's soul by " making sense " out of his most delicate imaginings. What must have been Mr. Tennyson's feelings on seeing, in the latest edition of his works, the line

"And followed by a hundred airy does,"*

turned into

"And followed by a hundred hairy does"?

On the whole, however, printers' readers render invaluable services to authors of all kinds; and it should not be forgotten that of the errors laid to their charge many are the work of the authors themselves or of their transcribers. In a volume by a lady whose writings have doubtless given a considerable amount of pleasure, the involuntary act or process which Johnson would have denominated "sternutation" is printed "stercoration." A French *correcteur* would have been bound to look for this portentous word in the Dictionary of the Academy—where he would not have found it. The English " reader " ought not to have passed it. But no " reader " can be supposed to have invented it.

Johnson in the definitions of his Dictionary is known to have allowed himself a certain latitude in the way of pleasantry. But it is scarcely probably that under the

* *The Princess*, canto vi. line 71.

head of "sit" he would have given this pretended quotation in illustration of one of the means of the word:—"Asses are ye that sit in judgment." The reference is to Judges v. 10, where we read, "Speak ye that ride on white asses, ye that sit in judgment." The transcriber seems to have copied out only the last six words of the passage, and the printer to have inserted " are " in order to " make sense."

Translators, considered as " traducers," have already been spoken of. But in connection with this subject a remarkable error, as illustrating the danger of carelessness in combination with a good dose of stupidity, may be cited from the notes to Bohn's edition of Gibbon's *Decline and Fall of the Roman Empire*, vol. vi. p. 472. Gibbon's text runs: " Bohemond's embarkation was clandestine, and, if we may credit a tale of the Princess Anna, he passed the hostile sea closely secured in a coffin." To this Gibbon gives a note: " Anna Comnena adds that, to complete the imitation, he was shut up with a dead cock; and condescends to wonder how the barbarian could endure the confinement and putrefaction"; to which Bohn's editor adds: " In M. Guizot's edition the translator, having mistaken the original English word, rendered it by *cuisinier*, and embellished the tale by shutting Bohemond up with the corpse of a *cook* instead of a *cock*. So it is that errors in history are perpetuated."

The mistakes of translators are more dangerous, and

also less amusing than misprints; while the drollest typographical errors are those which compositors make, but which readers correct, so that they never meet the public eye. A great writer of our time, among whose merits that of a clear handwriting is not conspicuous, in describing the Mount of Olives and his own brilliant discovery of the precise road taken by the Saviour on His triumphal entry into the Holy City, had abbreviated the word "Jerusalem" into "Jerus." But this hardly justified the compositor in presenting the sentence with this striking variation: "On reaching this rock we were at once unexpectedly greeted by a most magnificent view of Jones."

# INDEX.

## A.

ACADÉMIE Royale, of Paris, i. 12.
Academy of Music, the Royal, i. 12.
Accompaniments, first raised to importance by Monteverde, i. 6.
Actors of France, ask to remain anonymous, in 1779, ii. 135.
Addison's satire on opera, ii. 246.
Agents, musical, ii. 108.
   Barthélemy Leffémas held to be the first, ii. 113.
"Aïda," Verdi's masterpiece, i. 311.
   composed by Verdi for the Khedive of Egypt, ii. 1.
   description of the plot, ii. 2.
"Akbar," by Abbé Mailly, the first French opera, i. 7.
Albani, Mdlle., first appears at Covent Garden, i. 29.
   her impersonation of Elizabeth in "Tannhäuser," i. 222.

Albani, Mdlle.—*cont.*
   her impersonation of Lucia, ii. 31.
   her renderings of Wagner's characters, i. 206.
Alboni, Mdme., her *début* at Covent Garden, i. 21.
   an air in "Les Huguenots" composed for her, i. 254.
Alsted's Encyclopædia, ii. 164.
"Alte und Neue Musikalische Bibliothek und Musikalische Lexicon," by Walthern, ii. 184.
"Amber Witch," by Wallace, performed at Her Majesty's, i. 14.
"Ambleto" [Hamlet], Gasparini's, ii. 58.
Ambroise Thomas, M., his "Hamlet," ii. 50.
   his "Mignon," ii. 44, 47.
America, destitute of composers, ii. 197.
American diplomatist, and riding-circus agent, ii. 108.
Anachronisms, literary, artistic, and musical, ii. 161.
Angri, Mdme., succeeds Mdlle

Angri, Mdme.- *cont.*
   Alboni, at Covent Garden, i. 21.
Anna, Donna, the character analysed by Hoffman, i. 130.
Anthony, Plutarch's Life of, i. 54.
"Ariadne," a French opera by Cambert, i. 8.
Arditi, M., succeeds Sir Michael Costa as musical director, i. 29.
Auber's "Gustave III." i. 311.
Audience, absurd position of, in Rousseau's time, ii. 133.

### B.

BALFE's "Bohemian Girl," i. 299.
   his "Come into the Garden, Maud," borrowed from Verdi's "Macbetto," ii. 118.
   his "Falstaff," ii. 61.
"Balle in Maschera," by Verdi, produced at Covent Garden, i. 26.
Ballet, extinction of the, ii. 91.
   killed by a *pas de quatre*, ii. 94, 95.
   the best method of reviving it, ii. 96.
"Banquet of Don Pedro," by Shadwell, i. 115.
"Barber of Seville," of Beaumarchais, ii. 21.
   of Paisiello, ii. 21.
   Mdme. Patti's admirable rendering of Rosina in, ii. 14.
Barbier, M. Jules, dramatizes "Faust," i. 46.
Barre, M. Le Père, his extravagant plagiarism, ii. 279.
Beale, Mr., first manager of the Royal Italian Opera, i. 18.

Beaumarchais, M., his "Barber of Seville," ii. 21.
   the model for his Count Almaviva, i. 98.
Beausobre, M. de, compels the performance of his well-hissed tragedy, ii. 140.
Beethoven, his peculiarities of manner and dress, ii. 203.
   his "Dream of St. Jerome," due to Thackeray, ii. 150.
   his "Fidelio," ii. 206.
"Beggar's Opera," the best English literary opera, ii. 119.
   not really an opera, ii. 221.
Bellamy, Mrs., occasions the removal of stage seats for auditors, ii. 134.
Bellini, does not employ gipsy character, i. 301.
   never attempts ecclesiastic music, ii. 7.
   his "I Puritani," ii. 42.
   his "La Sonnambula," ii. 39.
"Benvenuto Cellini," by Berlioz, produced at Covent Garden, i. 22.
Béranger, M., his lament over the decline of ballads, ii. 120.
Berlioz's "Benvenuto Cellini," produced at Covent Garden, i. 22.
Bevignani, M., succeeds Sir M. Costa as musical director, i. 29.
Blancherie, M. La, starts an international art-production-interchanging society, ii. 114.
Blaze, M. Castil, his experiments with "Der Freischütz," ii. 188.
   his "Dictionnaire de Musique Moderne," ii. 187.
   his work "De l'Opéra en France," ii. 189.
   undertakes to compose a mass

Blaze, M. Castil—*cont.*
with Rossini's operatic music, ii. 191.
Bohemian "Faust," i. 169.
"Bohemian Girl," Balfe's, i. 299.
performed at Her Majesty's, i. 14.
Bookmaking, the art of, ii. 271.
Boot-stealing, anecdote of, ii. 260.
Bosio, Mdme., her charming impersonation of Catarina, i. 279.
Breteuil, Baron de, engages Sig. Picinni for France, ii. 109.
Brossard, M., his "Musical Dictionary," ii. 183.
Bülow, Dr. Hans von, his inexhaustible power, i. 228.
Bunn, Mr. Alfred, his performances as librettist, ii. 213.
Byron's "Sardanapalus," i. 140.

## C.

CAMBERT, driven from France, is received by England, i. 8.
his opera of "Ariadni," i. 8.
founds the regular opera in England, i. 8.
"Camp of Silesia," the part of the heroine written for Jenny Lind, i. 281.
"Camille the Coquette," purified American version of "La Dame aux Camélias," i. 307.
Caraccioli, Marquis, assists in bringing Sig. Picinni to France, ii. 109.
"Carmen," description of the opera, ii. 67.
sketch of the character, ii. 65.

Carré, M. Michael, dramatizes "Faust," i. 46.
Censorship, dramatic, in France, i. 106.
in Italy, i. 106.
Chambers, Mr. Ephraim, his Cyclopædia, ii. 165.
Chappell, Mr. Arthur, starts the Monday Popular Concerts, ii. 231.
Charles II. of England shelters Cambert, and founds the regular opera, i. 8.
Choron and Fayolle, MM., their "Historical Dictionary of Musicians," ii. 185.
Cincinatti, the obdurate baritone there, ii. 103.
Civilisation, its limit, according to Joseph le Maistre, ii. 236.
Clarence, Duke of, sees red lobsters in the sea, ii. 153.
"Classic," its import, ii. 235.
as applied to music, ii. 241.
as applied to the drama in France, ii. 236.
Classical music, what is it? ii. 239.
Clayton, Mr., his amusing efforts to wed melody with verse, ii. 148.
Clément, M. Félix, his "Dictionnaire Lyrique," ii. 193.
Clement XX., Pope, author of several libretti, i. 9.
Cokain, Sir Aston, his tragedy of "Ovid," i. 109-114.
Comedy, inappropriateness of verse to, ii. 245.
Commonwealth, the opera introduced into England during the, i. 8.
Composers, misuse of words by, ii. 145.
Composers and poets, ii. 117.
Concerts, Monday Popular, ii. 230.

"Continuous melody," according to Wagner, ii. 6.
"Conversion of St. Paul," a sort of opera of A.D. 1440, i. 5.
Costa, Sir Michael, musical conductor at Covent Garden, i. 20.
 his abridgment of "Lohengrin," i. 237.
 retires from the directorship of the Royal Italian Opera Company, i. 29.
Corneile, Thomas, versifies Molière's "Festin de Pierre," i. 108.
"Count Ory," by Rossini, produced at Covent Garden, i. 22.
Covent Garden, temporary home of the opera, i. 13.
 Sir Michael Costa musical conductor at, i. 20.
 burnt down, in 1856, i. 19.
 proposal to purchase Mr. Gye's interest in, i. 28.
 Mdme. Grisi gives her farewell performances at, i. 23.
 Mdlle. Albani first appears at, i. 29.
 Berlioz's "Benvenuto Cellini," produced at, i. 22.
 "Dinorah" produced at, i. 26.
 Donizetti's "I Martiri" produced at, i. 22.
 Gluck's "Orfeo" produced at, i. 26.
 Gounod's "Faust" produced at, i. 27.
 Gounod's "Romeo and Juliet" produced at, i. 28.
 Gounod's "Sappho" produced at, i. 22.
 "L'Africaine" produced at, i. 28.
 Meyerbeer's "L'Étoile du Nord" produced at, i. 24.

Covent Garden—*cont.*
 Rossini's "Count Ory" produced at, i. 22.
 Spohr's "Faust" produced at, i. 22.
 Verdi's "Balle in Maschera" produced at, i. 26.
 Verdi's "Don Carlos" produced at, i. 28.
 Verdi's "Il Trovatore" produced at, i. 24.
 Verdi's "Rigoletto" produced at, i. 22.
Cramer, Beale, & Co., actively support the formation of the Royal Italian Opera, i. 18.
Cromwell, Oliver, opera introduced into England in his time, i. 9.
 his reason for permitting operatic performances, i. 10.
Crozet, M. F., his "Revue de la Musique Dramatique en France," ii. 194.
Cruvelli, Mdlle. Sophi, appears at Covent Garden, i. 23.
Crystal Palace, Opera concerts given there, i. 24.
Csillag, Mdme., as Fidès, i. 255.
Cyclopædia, Mr. Ephraim Chambers', ii. 165.
"Cynthia's Revels," by Ben Jonson, i. 90.

## D.

Dancing, undue preponderance at one time given to, ii. 93.
Davenant, Sir Wm., introduces the Italian opera into England, i. 8.

## INDEX. 297

"Daughter of the Regiment,' Donizetti's, ii. 37.
Delafield, Mr., becomes manager of the Royal Italian opera, i. 17.
becomes bankrupt, i. 18.
"Der Freischütz," the legend of, i. 34.
M. Castil Blaze introduces the opera into France, ii. 188.
"Devil and Dr. Faustus," English version of "Faust," i. 45.
"Dictionary of Music and Musicians," by Dr. George Grove, ii. 200.
"Dictionary of Musical Terms," by Messrs. Stainer and Barrett, ii. 195.
"Dictionnaire Lyrique" of M. Félix Clément, ii. 193.
"Dictionnaire de Musique," by J. J. Rousseau, ii. 172.
"Dictionnaire de Musique Moderne," by M. Castil Blaze, ii. 187.
"Dictionnaire Universel du Théâtre," by MM. Goizet and Burtal, ii. 194.
Diderot, the plan of his grand "Encyclopédie," ii. 166.
"Die Lustige Weiber," Nicolai's, ii. 62.
"Dinorah," the most lunatical of operas. i. 285.
English libretto of, ii. 146.
produced at Covent Garden, i. 26.
Diplomatists who have acted as agents for operatic celebrities, ii. 108-111.
"Dizionario della Musica," by Abbé Giannelli, ii. 186.
by Dr. Lichtenthal, ii. 186.
"Don Carlos," by Verdi, produced at Covent Garden, i. 28.

"Don Giovanni," of Mozart, its symbolical character, i. 117.
described by Hoffmann, i. 119-127.
conflict of drama and military discipline, ii. 141.
Donizetti, does not employ gipsy character, i. 301.
his "Don Pasquale," ii. 35.
his "Elisir d' Amore," ii. 36, 38.
his "I Martiri," produced at Covent Garden, i. 22.
his "La Favorita," ii. 33.
his "La Figlia del Reggimento," ii. 37.
his "Lucia di Lammermoor," ii. 31.
his "Miserere," never yet heard in England, ii. 7.
"Don Juan," origin of the legend of, i. 64.
the legend of, discussed, i. 49.
description of Torelli's version of, i. 76-87.
French versions of, i. 76.
Goldoni's legend of, i. 55.
Italian version of, i. 74.
Spanish version of, i. 73.
as represented in England, i. 109.
Alfred de Musset's, i. 132.
Molière's comedy of, i. 71.
particular description of Molière's, i. 93-105.
of Mozart, i. 42.
of Poushkin, i. 146.
"Don Juan" and "Faust" compared, i. 43, 47.
Don Juan Tenorio, claims descent from the legendary Don Juan, i. 67.
"Don Pasquale," Donizetti's, ii. 35.
Drama, the decline of the, ii. 121, 123.

Drama—*cont.*
  real cause of the decline of the, ii. 124.
  origin of the musical, i. 3.
Dramatic plagiarism, ii. 276.
Dress of prime donne, inconsistent with characters depicted, i. 307.
Dumas, M. Alex., his "Dame aux Camélias" contrasted with "La Traviata," i. 305.

## E.

Effects, dramatic and operatic, compared, i. 291, 292.
"El Burlador di Sevilla," French translation of, i. 116.
"Elisir d' Amore," Donizetti's, ii. 36, 38.
Encores, inappropriateness of, i. 233.
Encyclopædia, Alsted's, ii. 164.
"Encyclopédie," origin of the famous, ii. 165.
  the excellent style of the writing, ii. 167.
  essential difference between it and modern works, ii. 168.
England, the Italian opera introduced into, by Sir W. Davenant, i. 8.
"Ernani," Verdi's, i. 290.
  description of the plot, i. 293.
Errors, literary, amusing instances of, ii. 284.
"Esmeralda," Victor Hugo produces a libretto for, ii. 243.
"Eurydice," the second, i. 6.
Eutychianus, his history of Theophilus of Syracuse, i. 48.
  his testimony to the truth of the legend, i. 173.

## F.

"Falstaff," Balfe's, ii. 61.
  performed at Her Majesty's, i. 14.
Farrel, Mrs., her apology for not dying better, ii. 136.
Faure, M., his success in "L'Étoile du Nord," i. 284.
"Faust," the legend of, i. 35.
  its gradual transformation, i. 160.
  legend of the printer John Faust, i. 150.
  his supposed connection with the legendary Faust, i. 175.
  his historical ante-types, i. 149.
  Widman's legend of, i. 154.
  the Bohemian, i. 169.
  the Polish, i. 156.
  Goethe's, i. 164.
  first produced on the stage, i. 177.
  Gounod's, i. 165.
  produced at Covent Garden, i. 27.
  Poushkin's, i. 145.
  Scheible's, i. 162.
  Spohr's, produced at Covent Garden, i. 22.
  Spiess's, i. 156, 160.
  as a ballet, i. 172, 176, 177.
"Faust" and "Don Juan" compared, i. 43, 47.
Fétis, M., his "Universal Biography of Musicians," ii. 185.
Feuds among musical partizans in London and Paris, ii. 83.
Feuillet, M. Octave, his "M. de Camors," i. 102.
"Fidelio," of Beethoven, ii. 206.
Fidès, in "Le Prophète," difficulty of the part, i. 255.

Field, Mr. John, striking peculiarities of his music, ii. 207.
"Fifths," sequences of, their intolerable character, ii. 152.
Fitzball, Mr., his " Flying Dutchman," i. 192.
Five-act operas, ii. 28.
Flotow, Count Frederick von, his birth and education, ii. 71.
his " La Duchesse de Guise," ii. 71.
his " L'Ame en Peine," ii. 72.
his " L'Esclave de Camoens," ii. 72.
his " Le Forestier," ii. 72.
his " Le Naufrage de la Méduse," ii. 72.
his " Peter and Catherine," ii. 71.
" Stradella," his first thoroughly successful opera, ii. 72.
" Martha," his last and greatest work, ii. 72.
" Flying Dutchman," the legend of, i. 40, 189.
of " Blackwood's Magazine," May 1821, i. 193.
description of Herr Wagner's, i. 210.
Fontenelle, M., his witticism on sonatas, ii. 233.
Forkel, his " Universal History of Music," ii. 185.
France, the opera introduced into, by Lully, i. 7.
five-act operas peculiar to, ii. 28.
Abbé Mailly composes the first French opera, i. 7.
Cardinal Mazarin aids in introducing the Italian opera into, i. 7.
" Fra Diavolo," Italianized by Auber himself, i. 285.

" Fra Diavolo "—*cont.*
produced at the Lyceum, i. 25.
Frederick the Great, Gottlob Hayne his first musical instructor, ii. 208.
his method of drilling vocalists, ii. 81.
has Mdme. Mara forcibly carried to the stage to sing, ii. 107.
his musical compositions, ii. 209.
French versions of " Don Juan," i. 76.
Frezzolini, Mdme., the first Leonora in " Il Trovatore," i. 297.

## G.

GABRIELLI, Mdlle., her brusque rejoinder to the Empress Catherine, ii. 80.
Gasparini's " Ambleto " or " Hamlet," ii. 58.
Gautier's ballet of " Giselle," i. 179.
Gerber, his " Historico-Biographical Lexicon," ii. 185.
Geudeville, M. de, is proud to make Plautus entertaining, ii. 280.
Giannelli, Abbé, his "Dizionario della Musica," ii. 186.
Giliberti, Onofrio, renders "Don Juan " into Italian, i. 74.
the author of Don Juan's " catalogue of lovers," i. 96.
Gipsies, introduced into very many operas, i. 301.
not introduced by Rossini, Donizetti, or Bellini, i. 301.
their musical peculiarities, i. 300.

Gipsies—*cont.*
 the singing, of Moscow, ii. 268.
 the violin-playing, of Tatra Füred, ii. 268.
Gipsy begging in Hungary, ii. 267.
"Giselle," ballet by Gautier, i. 179.
Giuglini, Sig., contributes to the success of "Les Huguenots," i. 253.
 allows his courtesy to override "the situation," ii. 141.
Gluck, his rivalry with Picinni, ii. 226.
 his "Orfeo," produced at Covent Garden, i. 26.
Goethe's drama of "Faust," i. 44, 164.
 gives personality to Margaret, i. 164.
 his opinion of setting "Faust" to music, i. 165.
 his "Wilhelm Meister," ii. 44.
Goizet and Burtal, MM.; their "Dictionnaire Universel du Théâtre," ii. 194.
Goldoni's legend of Don Juan, i. 55.
Gomez, the Brazilian composer, i. 290.
Gounod's "Faust and Margaret," i. 46, 165.
 produced at Covent Garden, i. 27.
 his character Marguerite, i. 180.
 his "Romeo and Juliet," ii. 57.
 produced at Covent Garden, i. 28.
 his "Sappho" produced at Covent Garden, i. 22.
Grabbe, Herr, his tragedy of "Don Juan and Faust," i. 42, 44.

"Grand Dictionnaire Universel du 19me. Siècle," by M. Larousse, ii. 193.
Granet. M., the supposed composer of Rousseau's "Le Devin du Village," ii. 173.
Graziani, Sig., first joins the Royal Italian Opera company in 1854, i. 24.
 his excellent rendering of Count di Luna, in "Il Trovatore," i. 302.
Greek plays, their relation to operatic composition, i. 4.
Gretchen, Goethe's character, i. 181.
Grieg, the Norwegian, peculiarities of his music, ii. 208.
Grisi, Mdme., joins the Covent Garden company, ii. 20.
 contributes to success of "Les Huguenots," i. 253.
 as Desdemona in "Otello," ii. 23.
 imparts to Leonora a "heavy" soprana character, i. 297.
 gives her series of farewell performances, i. 23.
 returns in 1857 to give more farewell performances, i. 25.
Grisi, Mdlle. Carlotta, ii. 91, 92.
Grove, Dr. George, his "Dictionary of Music and Musicians," ii. 164, 200.
Gruneisen, Mr. C. L., announces the formation of the Royal Italian Opera, i. 18.
"Guillaume Tell," Rossini's, ii. 27.
 suggestion to divide into two performances, ii. 29.
"Gustave III.," Auber's, i. 311.
Gye, Mr. F., senior, wins a lottery ticket, i. 15.
 founds the London Genuine Tea Company, i. 16.
 retires to Brighton, i. 17.

# INDEX. 301

Gye, Mr. F., junior, his education and early occupations, i. 17.
joins the Royal Italian Opera, i. 17.
becomes manager of Royal Italian Opera in 1848, i. 18.
becomes lessee of Covent Garden Theatre, i. 19.
proposal to purchase his interest in Covent Garden Theatre, i. 28.
his services to the lyrical drama, i. 29.

## H.

HALÉVY, M., his "La Tempestà," ii. 60.
Halka, Polish opera, by Moniuszko, ii. 198.
"Hamlet," M. Ambroise Thomas's, ii. 50.
Handel, reaches England in 1710, i. 12.
firmly establishes the opera in England, i. 9.
his able management, i. 13.
his sacred music, ii. 9.
Hauk, Miss Minnie, her admirable impersonation of Carmen, ii. 70.
Haweis, Mr., his gross blunders in "Music and Morals," ii. 155, 156.
Haydn's "Seasons" and "Creation," ii. 9.
Hayes, Miss Catherine, as Bertha, i. 254.
Hayne, Gottlob, first musical instructor of Frederick the Great, ii. 208.
Heine, Heinrich, adapts "Faust" to the ballet, i. 172, 176.
his "Flying Dutchman" legend, i. 190.

Heine, Heinrich—*cont.*
his "Mephistophela," i. 178.
his opinion of Rossini's "Stabat Mater," ii. 11.
Hemans, Mrs., her "Hour of Prayer," ii. 10.
Her Majesty's Theatre, its history, i. 12.
English operas performed at, i. 14.
proposal to convert into public offices, i. 28.
rebuilding of, in 1870, i. 29.
Heroine, the ordinary operatic, i. 207.
Heroines, those of Herr Wagner, i. 208.
"Historical Dictionary of Musicians," by MM. Choron and Fayolle, ii. 185.
"Historico-Biographical Lexicon," by Gerber, ii. 185.
Hoffmann, Herr, his description of Mozart's "Don Giovanni," i. 119-127.
his analysis of the character of Donna Anna, i. 130.
his analysis of the character of Don Juan, i. 128.
Horse-riding, Dr. Johnson's opinion of, ii. 112.
Houssaye, M. Arsène, his managerial difficulties, ii. 100, 101.
proposes to re-assume the cares of management, ii. 97.
Hueffer, Dr., his account of the "Flying Dutchman" legend, i. 189.
Hugo, Victor, his three musically suggestive plays, i. 291.
his libretto for "Esmeralda," ii. 243.
Hungarian opera called "Hunniades," ii. 52.
Hungary, gipsy begging in, ii. 267.

## I.

"IL TROVATORE," by Verdi, produced at Covent Garden, i. 24.
  the first cast of, i. 302.
  description of, i. 295.
  the unreality of its incidents, i. 296.
  the established popularity of its melodies, i. 299.
Index-makers' misapprehensions, ii. 284.
"I Puritani," Bellini's, ii. 42.
Italian version of "Don Juan," i. 74.
Italy, as the nursery of music a hundred years ago, ii. 81.
  the earliest musical dramas of, i. 3.
  stage effects there, 150 years ago, ii. 130.

## J.

JANOWKA, M., his "Key to Musical Knowledge," ii. 183.
Jews, their rarity in operas, i. 301.
"Joconde," of La Fontaine, i. 95.
John of Leyden, in "Le Prophète," trying nature of the part, i. 255.
Johnson, Dr. S., his appreciation of horse-riding, ii. 112.
Jullien, Mons., gives promenade concerts at Covent Garden, i. 17.
Juno, the statue of, legendary account of the talking of, i. 54.

## K.

"KEY to Musical Knowledge," Janowka's, ii. 183.
King's Theatre, in the Haymarket, i. 9.
  burnt down in 1789, i. 14.
Knox, Col. Brownlow, joins Mr. Gye in supporting the Royal Italian Opera, i. 19.
Koch, his "Musical Lexicon," ii. 185.

## L.

LABLACHE, Sig., one of the striking figures in modern opera, ii. 88.
  as Brabantio in "Otello," ii. 23.
"La Dame aux Camélias," purified American version of, i. 307.
"La Duchesse de Guise," Flotow's, ii. 71.
"La Favorita," Donizetti's, ii. 33.
  based on notions of decorum, i. 303.
Lafférmas, Barthélemy, held to be the first musical agent, ii. 113.
"La Figlia del Reggimento," Donizetti's, ii. 37.
  almost the prettiest music which Donizetti ever wrote, ii. 38.
La Fontaine's "Joconde," i. 95.
"L'Africaine," produced at Paris, 1865, i. 253.
  produced at Covent Garden, i. 28.
  description of the opera, i. 262-273.

" L'Africaine "—*cont.*
  effects of inquisition scene due to operatic form, ii. 249.
Lamb, Charles, his lack of appreciation of music, ii. 157.
" L'Ame en Peine," Flotow's, ii. 72.
Larousse, M., his " Grand Dictionnaire Universel du 19me. Siècle," ii. 193.
" La Sonnambula," Bellini's, ii. 39.
  criticism of its airs criticized, ii. 40.
" La Tempestà," M. Halévy's, ii. 60.
" La Traviata," by Verdi, produced at the Lyceum, i. 25.
  contrasted with M. Dumas' " Dame aux Camélias," i. 305.
  reason for the outcry against, i. 302.
  gradually gains public esteem, i. 309.
Lauragais, Count de, abolishes stage-seats at the Paris opera, ii. 134.
Lawes, Henry, composes for Sir W. Davenant, i. 8.
" Leading motives " in opera, i. 213.
" Le Devin du Village," by J. J. Rousseau, ii. 172.
" Le Forestier," Flotow's, ii. 72.
Legrand D'Aussy, M., his version of the " Don Juan " legend, i. 50.
" Le Naufrage de la Méduse," Flotow's, ii. 72.
" Leoline," another name for Flotow's " L'Ame en Peine," ii. 72.
Leonora, in " La Favorita," the part written for Mdme. Stolz, ii. 33.
Leonora, of " Il Trovatore," the part made "heavy " soprano by Mdme. Grisi, i. 297.
  passion of prime donne for the part of, i. 295.
" Le Pardon de Ploermel," or " Dinorah," of Meyerbeer, i. 286.
" Le Prophète," plot of the opera, i. 257.
  first cast of singers at Covent Garden, i. 254.
" L'Esclave de Camoens," Flotow's, ii. 72.
" Les Huguenots " first opera with " light " and " dramatic " soprano parts, i. 250.
  one air in, composed for Mdme. Alboni, i. 254.
  its success in England in part due to the leading singers, i. 253.
  live horse first appears in, ii. 131.
" Le Sicilien," of Molière, ii. 21.
" Les Muses Galantes," by J. J. Rousseau, ii. 172.
" Les Operas " of St. Evremond, ii. 245.
" L'Étoile du Nord," by Meyerbeer, produced at Covent Garden, i. 24.
  based on an older opera, i. 274.
  description of the opera, i. 275.
  the duet of vivandières in, i. 283.
  its great length, i. 282.
" Libertine," the, of Shadwell, i. 109.
Libretti, ii. 116.
  appropriate themes for, i. 31 32.
  those suitable to the composer, ii. 120.
  English, their failings, ii. 146.

Libretto, Cardinal Riario, author of the first, i. 9.
Lichtenthal, Dr., his "Dizionario," ii. 186.
Lincoln's-Inn Theatre, temporary home of the opera, i. 18.
Lind, Jenny, her cadenzas, ii. 214.
   the part of the heroine in the "Camp of Silesia" written for her, i. 281.
Liszt, Abbé, on Hungarian gipsy music, i. 300.
   his visits to Pius IX., i. 9.
Literary maltreatment of music, ii. 144.
Locke, the philosopher, interests himself in a *danseuse*, ii. 109.
"Lohengrin" of Wagner, i. 228.
   description of the opera of, i. 229.
   the moral of, i. 234.
   beauties and defects of, i. 240.
   different editions of, i. 236.
   abridged by Sir Michael Costa, i. 237.
Loriquet, M. Le Père, his "History," ii. 280.
Lucca, Mdlle. Pauline, first appears at Covent Garden, i. 27.
   her reading of the part of Margaret, i. 186.
"Lucia di Lammermoor," Donizetti's, ii. 31.
Lucian's tale of the walking statue, i. 56.
Lully introduces the opera into France, i. 7.
Lumley, Mr., refuses to engage Mdme. Persiani, i. 17.
   organises his celebrated *pas de quatre*, ii. 95.

Lyceum Theatre, the Royal Italian Opera company temporarily transferred there, i. 19.

## M.

"Macbeth," Verdi's, ii. 59.
Macheath, Capt., his relation to Don Juan, i. 75.
Mailly, Abbé, composes the first French opera, i. 7.
Malibran, Mdme., as Desdemona in "Otello," ii. 23.
Mantua, Duke of, patronizes the opera, i. 6.
"Margaret," the name, in Germany, for Gounod's opera, i. 166.
   development of the character in the "Faust" legend, i. 163, 164.
Margherita, or Marguerite, i. 180.
   different representations of the character, i. 182.
   fatiguing nature of the part, i. 182.
   as rendered by Mdlle. Pauline Lucca, i. 186.
"Maritana," Wallace's, i. 299.
Mario, Signor, joins the Covent Garden company, i. 20.
   as Roderigo in "Otello," ii. 23.
   as John of Leyden, i. 254.
   contributes to success of "Les Huguenots," i. 253.
Mark Anthony compared with Don Juan, i. 107.
Marlbrook, history of the tune so called, ii. 216.
Marlowe's drama of "Faust," i. 44.

# INDEX. 305

Marryat, Capt., his "Flying Dutchman," i. 190.
"Martha," Flotow's last and greatest work, ii. 72.
  its amazing popularity, ii. 73.
  secret of the charm of, ii. 75.
"Martiri," by Donizetti, produced at Covent Garden, i. 22.
"Masaniello," effects of market scene due to operatic form, ii. 250.
Maurepas, M. de, Minister of State, negociates with Handel for his assistance at Paris, ii. 110.
Mazarin, Cardinal, introduces the Italian opera into France, i. 7; ii. 109.
Melancthon, his estimate of "Faustus, junior," i. 152.
Mellon, Mr. A., director of the ballet at Covent Garden, i. 20.
Melody, Verdi's use of, in Aïda, ii. 6.
Mendelssohn's "Midsummer Night's Dream," ii. 59.
Mephistopheles, changes in dress of the character, i. 183.
"Mercante di Venezia," Sig. Petrella's, ii. 60.
"Merchant of Venice," Mr. A. Sullivan's music for, ii. 60.
Mérimée, M. Prosper, his legend of the "Vénus d'Ille," i. 61.
"Merry Wives of Windsor," Balfe's, ii. 61.
  Nicolai's, ii. 62.
Meyerbeer's operatic scenery, i. 247.
  introduces live horses into the opera, ii. 131.
  his fondness for animals, i. 288.

Meyerbeer—*cont.*
  his operas, held to be antagonistic to Christianity, i. 256.
  his "Dinorah," i. 285.
  his "Étoile du Nord," produced at Covent Garden, i. 24.
  his ritornello in "L'Africaine," i. 271.
Molière's comedy of "Don Juan," i. 71.
  particular description of, i. 93-105.
  his "Sicilien," ii. 21.
Molina, Tirso de, author of the first drama of Don Juan, i. 69.
Monday Popular Concerts, ii. 230.
  character of music produced at, ii. 234.
Mongini, Sig., as John of Leyden, i. 255.
"M. de Camors," of Octave Feuillet, i. 102.
Montesquieu, M., interests himself in the affairs of operatic artistes, ii. 109.
Monteverde, the real founder of the modern opera, i. 7.
  his improvements establish the opera, i. 6.
  his "Orfeo," i. 6.
Moscow, the singing gipsies of, ii. 268.
Mozart's "Don Juan," i. 42, 45.
  symbolical character of "Don Juan," i. 117.
  his "Don Juan" described by Hoffmann, i. 119-127.
Middlesex, Earl of, succeeds Handel as operatic manager, i. 13.
"Midsummer Night's Dream," Mendelssohn's, ii. 59.
"Mignon," M. Ambroise Thomas's, ii. 44, 47.

Military discipline superior to operatic requirements, ii. 141.
Miracle-plays, their relation to operatic composition, i. 4.
Murska, Mdlle. de, her impersonation of Lucia, ii. 31.
Music superior to declamation in vast theatres, ii. 248.
  its power of characterization, ii. 51.
  called an "unknown language," i. 10.
  literary maltreatment of, ii. 144.
Musical agents, ii. 108.
  Barthélemy Lafférnas held to be the first, ii. 113.
Musical blunders of great writers, ii. 150-158.
Musical dictionaries, ii. 164.
"Musical Dictionary," Brossard's, ii. 183.
Musical feuds of London and Paris, ii. 83.
"Musical Lexicon," by Koch, ii. 185.
  by Wolf, ii. 185.
Musset, Alfred de, his "Don Juan," i. 132.
"Muzikaal Kunst Woordenbook," by Reynvaan, ii. 185.
"Mysteries," precursors of the opera, i. 3.

## N.

NAPOLEON BUONAPARTE, arrests disobedient singers, ii. 107.
Ney, Mdlle., appears at Covent Garden, i. 24.
Nicolai's "Die Lustige Weiber," ii. 62.
Nilsson, Mdme., her rendering of Leonora, i. 295.

Nilsson, Mdme.—*cont.*
  her impersonation of Lucia, ii. 31.
  her impersonation of Martha, ii. 73.
  her impersonation of Mignon, ii. 48.
  her impersonation of Ophelia, ii. 51.

## O.

"OLD men's chorus" in "Faust," its eccentricity, i. 185.
Opera, its origin, i. 3.
  Rousseau's definition of, ii. 178.
  its reasonableness, ii. 248.
  its wide sphere of intelligibility, i. 10.
  allows of simultaneous expression of conflicting sentiments, ii. 251.
  established by Monteverde's innovations, i. 6.
  partly supersedes drama, ii. 121.
  the machinery thereof, a hundred years ago, ii. 82.
  charges of admission to, a hundred years ago, ii. 84.
  introduced into England during the Commonwealth, i. 8.
  Oliver Cromwell's reason for permitting, i. 10.
  not firmly established in England till Handel's time, i. 9.
  its aristocratic origin and associations, i. 9, ii. 79.
Opera-books, their unpoetic character, i. 206.
Opera concerts at the Crystal Palace, i. 24.
Operas in five acts, ii. 28.
Operatic anomalies, ii. 140-143.

Operatic heroine, the ordinary, i. 207.
Operatic management, ii. 97.
an obdurate baritone, ii. 103.
"Orfeo," by Gluck, produced at Covent Garden, i. 26.
by Monteverde, A.D. 1608, i. 6.
by Poliziano, the first real opera, i. 5.
Orloff, Count, acquires literary fame without writing a line, ii. 281.
"Orphée aux Enfers," Offenbach's, ii. 74.
"Otello," Rossini's, ii. 22.
the first opera containing a leading part for baritone or bass, ii. 24.
Oulibicheff's remarks on Salieri's temporary triumph over Mozart, i. 144.
"Ovid," Sir A. Cokain's tragedy of, i. 109-114.

## P.

Paisiello's "Barber of Seville," ii. 21.
Paley's "Natural Theology," G. A. Sala exposes the source of, ii. 278.
Paris opera in Rousseau's time, absurd position of audience, ii. 133.
Paris theatre, live sheep introduced at a, ii. 132.
*Pas de quatre*, the, which killed the ballet, ii. 94.
Patti, Mdme. Adelina, her birth and education, ii. 224.
her dramatic genius, i. 278.
extensive range of her dramatic genius, ii. 16.
first appears at Covent Garden, i. 26.
Patti, Mdme.—*cont.*
her inapproachable impersonation of Rosina in the "Barber of Seville," ii. 14.
her intensely dramatic impersonation of Catarina, i. 282.
her impersonation of Dinorah, i. 287.
her impersonation of Leonora, i. 295.
her impersonation of Lucia, ii. 31.
as Desdemona in "Otello," ii. 24.
Pausanias's story of Theagenes, i. 53.
Pavlovsky regiment of Russia, traditions of, i. 277.
Pegasus, stage tricks for performing effects with, ii. 131.
Persiani, Mdme., Mr. Lumley refuses to engage her, i. 17.
joins the Covent Garden company, i. 20.
Persiani, Signor, starts the Royal Italian Opera in opposition to Her Majesty's, i. 18.
"Peter and Catherine," Flotow's, ii. 71.
Petrella, his "Mercante di Venezia," ii. 60.
Picinni, his rivalry with Gluck, ii. 226.
Pius IX., his method of inviting Abbé Liszt to play the piano, i. 9.
Plagiarism, M. Richesource on the art of, ii. 274.
Plutarch's Life of Anthony, i. 54.
Poets and composers, ii. 117.
Polish opera called "Halka," ii. 52.
Poliziano, produces the first opera, A.D. 1480, i. 5.

Ponte, Lorenzo da, his libretto of "Don Juan," i. 76.
Popes of Rome, their patronage of the opera, i. 9.
Popular Concerts, Monday, ii. 230.
Popular taste, the basis of, ii. 232.
Pougin, M. Arthur, his supplement to M. Fétis's "Biography," ii. 197.
Poushkin's dramatic compositions, i. 142-147.
Powell, Mr., calls his "dresser" from the tomb, ii. 140.
Pradon, joins in hissing his own tragedy, ii. 139.
"Preciosa," Weber's, i. 300.
Prima donna, importance now assigned to the, ii. 90.
Printers, their errors of omission and commission, ii. 286.
Programmes, the publication of singers' names on, ii. 135.
"Pygmalion," by J. J. Rousseau, ii. 172.

## Q.

QUEEN's Theatre, i. 12.

## R.

RAMEAU, directs the Académie Royale of Paris, i. 12.
Readers, printers', their qualifications and failings, ii. 286.
"Requiem for Manzoni," Verdi's latest work, ii. 1.
"Revue de la Musique Dramatique en France," by M. F. Crozet, ii. 194.

Reynvaan, his "Muzikaal Kunst Woordenbook," ii. 185.
Riario, Cardinal, author of the first operatic libretto, i. 9.
Richesource, M., on the art of plagiarism, ii. 274.
"Rigoletto," by Verdi, produced at Covent Garden, i. 22.
"Robert le Diable," the legend of, i. 35, 243.
 his human original, i. 244, 245.
 the opera of, i. 242.
 produced at Paris, 1831, i. 253.
 a masterpiece of operatic art, i. 248.
 a typical specimen of the "grand opera," i. 251.
 startling accidents connected with its first performance, i. 249.
"Robin Hood," by Macfarren, performed at Her Majesty's, i. 14.
Roger, M., as John of Leyden, i. 254.
Rome, the source of modern opera, i. 5.
"Romeo and Juliet" of Gounod, ii. 57.
 produced at Covent Garden, i. 28.
 five operas of, during this century, ii. 61.
Ronconi, Sig., joins the Covent Garden company, i. 20.
 as Iago in "Otello," ii. 23.
Rosati, Mdlle., the last of the *ballerine*, ii. 91.
Rosina, airs sung by the various impersonators of, in the "Barber of Seville," ii. 19.
Rossini, does not employ gipsy character, i. 301.
 his "Barber of Seville," ii. 14, 22.
 his "Count Ory" performed at Covent Garden, i. 22.

Rossini—*cont.*
  his "Guillaume Tell," ii. 27, 211.
  his "Otello," ii. 22.
  the first opera containing a leading part for baritone or base, ii. 24.
  his "Semiramide," ii. 25.
  his "Stabat Mater," ii. 8.
  Heine's opinion of, ii. 11.
Rousseau, J. J., his views on the object of opera, ii. 182.
  as to supernatural subjects for opera, ii. 181.
  his opinion of operatic melodies, ii. 180.
  his description of stage properties, ii. 127-129.
  charged with blundering in the "Encyclopédie," ii. 171.
  his "Devin du Village," ii. 172.
  his "Muses Galantes," ii. 172.
  his "Pygmalion," ii. 172.
  his "Dictionnaire de Musique," ii. 172.
Royal Italian Opera Company, circumstances of its formation, i. 17.
  formed by assistance of Sig. Persiani, Sig. Galetti, and by Cramer, Beale, & Co., i. 18.
  purposes for which formed, i. 19.
  Mr. Beale first manager of, i. 18.
  Mr. Gye becomes manager of, in 1848, i. 18.
  adopts the co-operative principle, i. 18.
  much indebted to Meyerbeer, i. 273.
Rubini, Sig., as Otello, ii. 23.
Russia, great encouragement given to music in, ii. 198.

Russian opera called "Life of the Czar," ii. 52.
Rutebœuf's miracle-play of Theophilus, i. 48, 173.

## S.

Sacred and secular music, ii. 8-11.
St. Evremond's "Les Operas," ii. 245.
St. George, miraculous image of, i. 56.
St. Leger, Mr., his indiscretion occasions the removal of stage seats for auditors, ii. 134.
St. Nicholas, legend of the statue of, i. 62.
Sainton, Mr., leads the Covent Garden orchestra, i. 20.
Sala, Mr. G. A., exposes the source of Paley's "Natural Theology," ii. 278.
Salieri, his temporary triumph over Mozart, i. 144.
Sallé, Mdlle., reforms stage costumes in France, ii. 138.
Salvi, Sig., joins the Covent Garden company, i. 20.
Sangalli, Mdlle., her lamentations over the decay of the ballet, ii. 91.
"Sappho," by Gounod, produced at Covent Garden, i. 22.
"Sardanapalus," of Byron, i. 140.
Scala Opera House, Milan, its hundredth anniversary, ii. 77.
Scheible's legend of "Faust," i. 162.
Schlegel, W. A., his preference for supernatural stories for libretti, i. 31; ii. 180.
Schumann, his opinion of Herr Wagner as a composer, i. 224.

Scribe, M., his treatment of history, i. 277.
  introduces live horses into opera, ii. 131.
  his version of "Robert le Diable," i. 36, 243.
Secular and sacred music, ii. 8-11.
"Semiramide," Rossini's, its rich melodies, ii. 25.
Servandoni, Sig., scene-painter at Paris, 150 years ago, ii. 130.
Sganarelle, his reflections on his master Don Juan, i. 98.
Shadwell's "Banquet of Don Pedro," i. 115.
  his "Don Juan, or the Atheist struck down," i. 45.
  his "Libertine," i. 109.
Shakespearian operas, ii. 57.
"Siege of Rhodes," produced during the Commonwealth, i. 8.
Simon Magus, his aerial flight before Nero, i. 170.
Singer, an obdurate, ii. 103.
"Song of Solomon," the first opera, i. 3.
Sopranos, "light" and "dramatic," i. 250.
Spanish version of "Don Juan," i. 73.
Spiess, author of the earliest version of the "Faust" story, i. 156, 160.
Spohr's "Faust" produced at Covent Garden, i. 22.
"Stabat Mater," Rossini's, ii. 8.
  Heine's opinions of, ii. 11.
Stainer and Barrett, Messrs., their "Dictionary of Musical Terms," ii. 195.
Stage costumes reformed in France by Mdlle. Sallé, ii. 138.
  reformed in London, ii. 138.
Stage properties, described by Rousseau, ii. 127-129.

Stage-seats, anecdotes of occupants of, ii. 137.
Statues, legends of walking and talking, i. 52-56.
Stolz, Mdme., the part of Leonora in "La Favorita" written for her, ii. 33.
"Stradella," Flotow's first thoroughly successful opera, ii. 72.
Sullivan, Mr. Arthur, his music for "The Merchant of Venice," ii. 60.
  his music for "The Tempest," ii. 59.
Sylvester, the legend of, i. 171.

T.

Taglioni, Mdlle., ii. 91, 92.
Tagliafico, Sig., as the Count of Oberthal, i. 254.
Tamberlik, Sig., appears at Covent Garden, i. 24.
  as John of Leyden, i. 254.
  as Otello, ii. 23.
Tamburini, Sig., joins the Covent Garden company, i. 20.
  as Iago in "Otello," ii. 23.
  the violent demonstration on his account, ii. 88.
"Tannhäuser," the legend of, i. 216.
  Herr Wagner's, i. 215.
Tatra Füred, its associations and surroundings, ii. 253.
  brigandage at, ii. 259.
  Hungarian cookery there, ii. 257.
  the violin-playing gipsies of, ii. 268.
"Tempest," by Mr. Arthur Sullivan, ii. 59.
Tenor, the decline and fall of the, ii. 86.

# INDEX. 311

Thackeray, Mr., confers a new composition on Beethoven, ii. 150.
Theagenes, Pausanias's story of, i. 53.
Theatre, Her Majesty's, its history, i. 12.
Theophilus of Syracuse, the legend of, i. 48, 157, 172.
Thespis; and operatic origins, i. 9.
Thistlethwayte, Mr., joins in supporting the Royal Italian Opera, i. 19.
Thomas, M. Ambroise, his orchestration, ii. 56.
  his "Hamlet," ii. 50.
  his mis-treatment of the ghost in "Hamlet," ii. 54.
  his "Mignon," ii. 44, 47.
Time in music, effects of changes in, ii. 215.
Titiens, Mdme., as Fidès, i. 255.
  contributes to success of "Les Huguenots," i. 253.
Torelli's version of "Don Juan," i. 76-87.
Tournefort's legend of the moving image of St. George, i. 56.
Translators, errors of, ii. 290.
Trebelli, Mdme., admirably renders Urbino in "Les Huguenots," i. 254.
  her impersonation of Nancy, ii. 76.
"Twardowski," the Polish version of "Faust," i. 45, 151, 169.

## U.

"Un Ballo in Maschera," one of Verdi's finest operas, i. 310.
"Undine," Hoffman's device for announcing entries and exits in, i. 6.
"Universal Biography of Musicians," by M. Fétis, ii. 185.
"Universal History of Music," by Forkel, ii. 185.
Urbino, in "Les Huguenots," admirably rendered by Mdme. Trebelli, i. 254.

## V.

Vauxhall Gardens, managed by Mr. F. Gye, sen., i. 16.
Venus, the moving statue of, i. 61.
Verdi, his fondness for melody, ii. 3.
  his anachronisms in dance-music, i. 314.
  his "Aïda," i. 311.
  composes "Aïda" for the Khedive of Egypt, ii. 1.
  his "Ballo in Maschera," i. 310.
  produced at Covent Garden, i. 26.
  his "Don Carlos," produced at Covent Garden, i. 28.
  his "Ernani," i. 290.
  his "Il Trovatore," i. 295.
  produced at Covent Garden, i. 24.
  his "La Traviata," produced at the Lyceum, i. 25.
  his "Macbeth," ii. 59.
  his "Requiem for Manzoni," ii. 1, 10.
  his "Rigoletto," produced at Covent Garden, i. 22.
Véron, Dr., his notice of the first production of "Robert the Devil," i. 247.
Viardot, Mdme., appears at Covent Garden, i. 24.
  as Fidès, i. 254.

Vienna, scenery there in Mozart's time, ii. 129.
Violetta, absorbing interest of the character in "La Traviata," i. 308.
different renderings of, i. 303.
Virgin, The, marrying the statue of, i. 59.

## W.

WAGNER, Herr, his preference for legendary subjects as themes for libretti, i. 32.
his orchestration, i. 233.
his passion for marches, i. 238.
his alleged poverty as an inventor of melodies, i. 224.
the strength and delicacy of his female characters, i. 208.
his treatment of the "Flying Dutchman," i. 193, 210.
his "Lohengrin," i. 228.
description of his "Tannhäuser," i. 218.
objects to an Italian rendering of "William Tell," i. 165, 285.
Wagner, Mdlle. Joanna, appears at Her Majesty's, i. 22.
Wallace's "Maritana," i. 299.
Walthern, Herr, his "Musical Lexicon," ii. 184.

"Wandering Jew," the legend of, i. 37.
the oldest legendary subject treated operatically, i. 33.
Ward, Mr., his opinion of the effect of opera on drama, ii. 122.
Warren, Mr. Powell's "dresser," rises from the tomb to obey his master, ii. 141.
Washburne, Mr., Secretary of the American Legation, Paris, advertizes a riding-circus, ii. 108.
Weber's "Preciosa," i. 300.
Widman, his legend of "Faust," i. 154, 161.
Wierms, or Weiher, his anecdote of "Faustus, junior," i. 153.
"Wilhelm Meister" of Goethe, ii. 44.
"William Tell," Rossini's, ii. 27, 211.
effect of gathering of the cantons due to operatic form, ii. 250.
Herr Wagner objects to an Italian rendering of the opera of, i. 165.
Wolf, Mr. G. F., his "Musical Lexicon," ii. 185.
Words, misuse of, by composers, ii. 145.
Wynkyn de Worde, publishes an English version of "Robert the Devil," i. 244.

---

London: Printed by W. H. Allen & Co., 13 Waterloo Place, S.W.

www.ingramcontent.com/pod-product-compliance
Lightning Source LLC
Chambersburg PA
CBHW022024240426
43667CB00042B/1119